THE GIANT BOOK OF USELESS INFORMATION

CONSTABLE

Constable & Robinson Ltd
55-56 Russell Square
London WC1B 4HP

www.constablerobinson.com

Originally published as The Giant Bathroom Book of Knowledge
This edition published in the UK in 2013 by Constable,
an imprint of Constable & Robinson Ltd

A copy of the British Library Cataloguing in Publication Data
is available from the British Library

ISBN 978-1-47211-608-6

Printed and bound by CPI Group (UK) Ltd, Croydon, CR0 4YY

10 9 8 7 6 5 4 3 2 1

Contents

The Barbados Coffins   1
Lesser-Known Massacres   3
The Bermuda Triangle   29
Hollywood Quotes   41
Bad King James   47
Cosmology   51
Was She A Werewolf   55
Moby Dick   57
The Flying Monk   59
The Piltdown Man   61
Atlantis   65
Out of Body Experiences   69
A Brief History of Automobiles   77
The Mayerling Affair   87
Macbeth   93
From the Deep   97
Maiden Voyage   99
The Drummer   105
Famous Music Name Changes   107
A Brief History of Air Travel   115
Queen Victoria and John Brown   125
True Life Miracles   143

The Naughty Poltergeist 149
The Serpent from the Sea 151
The King and Mrs Simpson 155
A Brief History of Radio and Television 183
Ghostblaster 193
The Living Dead 197
Pride and Prejudice 199
The Lunatic General 203
Back from the Dead 207
Music of Irving Berlin 209
A Brief History of Computers 211
The Mayor of Casterbridge 219
Modern Day Mammoths? 221
The Vampire 223
Knocking Shop 225
Loch Ness 227
Strange Tales 243
The Buckingham Palace Security Scandal 269
A Brief History of the Telephone 277
The Inscrutable Yeti? 285
Art Botch 287
Healthcare and Medical Technology 289
Hollywood Tales 297
The Wounded Vampire 301
Of Mice and Men 303
A Brief History of Spacecraft 307
King George III: The Fat Philanderer 317
Christopher Columbus 335
A Christmas Carol 339
Bigfoot in Canada 341
Spaced Out 343
A Brief History of Nuclear Technology 345
The Red Scratch Case 353
The Scandalous Princess 355
Creative World 391

Mysteries of the World

The Barbados Coffins

On the island of Barbados in the nineteenth century, there was a strange occurrence involving a burial vault. The burial vault belonged to the Chase family, who were slave owners on the island of Barbados, in the Caribbean. In the early nineteenth century, the head of the family was a harsh and ruthless man called the Honourable Thomas Chase, who seems to have been a tyrant both to his slaves and his family. His daughter, Dorcas Chase, is believed to have starved herself to death because of her father's brutality. In July 1812, her coffin joined those of two others already buried in the vault – a woman named Goddard and a baby.

On 9 August 1812, the coffin of the Honourable Thomas Chase himself was carried down the steps to the family vault in the graveyard of Christ Church. It was encased in lead, and took eight men to lift. As the heavy stone slab was moved aside, and the lamplight revealed the interior, it was obvious that some intruder had already been inside. The baby's coffin was found upside down in a corner, while Dorcas Chase's coffin lay on its side. Only the coffin of Mrs Goddard was undisturbed.

The odd thing was that there was no sign of a forced entrance. But because Thomas Chase was a much-hated man, his surviving family members assumed that the desecration was the work of rebellious black slaves. Therefore the coffins were simply replaced, and the vault closed up again, and the marble slab sealed in place with cement. Only the slaves who carried Thomas Chase's coffin seemed alarmed; they seemed to suspect black magic.

Yet when the next burial took place, four years later in 1816, the vault was again in confusion, with all the coffins in different positions. The same happened again, four weeks later, when a man murdered in a slave rebellion was buried there. Yet the cement round the marble slab was untouched. And the most careful examination of the vault revealed no other way of entering it. The frightened slaves who carried the coffins into the vault were convinced that the explanation lay in voodoo – or black magic – that "voodoo magicians" had deliberately sent spirits to throw the coffins around.

When the next burial took place three years later, in July 1819, there was widespread curiosity, for the strange events had caused much gossip. Even when the cement was chipped away, the slab proved very hard to move. And this was because the heavy lead coffin of Thomas Chase was jammed against it. All the other coffins were in disorder, except that of Mrs Goddard, which had been left leaning against the wall.

The governor of the island, Lord Combermere, was present, and he ordered that the floor should be scattered with sand, which would show the footprints of any intruders.

Eight months later, in April 1820, the guests at a dinner party at Lord Combermere's began to discuss the vault, and it was decided to re-open it. Yet again, all the coffins – except Mrs Goddard's – were scattered. And the sand on the floor was undisturbed. This time, Lord Combermere ordered that the coffins should be buried elsewhere. The tomb has remained empty ever since.

Lesser-Known Massacres

1. St. Bartholomew's Day massacre

Beginning on 24th August 1572 (the feast of Bartholomew the Apostle), the St. Bartholomew's Day massacre (*Massacre de la Saint-Barthélemy* in French) refers to a wave of Catholic mob violence against the Huguenots (French Calvinist Protestants), during the French Wars of Religion. It is believed by historians that the massacre was instigated by Catherine de Medici, the mother of King Charles IX. The killings took place six days after the wedding of the king's sister to the Protestant Henry of Navarre. This was an occasion for which many of the most wealthy and prominent Huguenots had gathered in largely Catholic Paris. The murders began two days after the attempted assassination of Admiral Gaspard de Coligny, a Huguenot military leader. Coligny was eventually murdered on 24 August, and the subsequent massacres spread throughout Paris, and later to other cities and the countryside, lasting for several months. The exact number of fatalities is not known, but it has been estimated that over 2,000 Huguenots were killed in Paris and over 3,000 in the French provinces.

 # Boobs and Misprints

The British Prime Minister, Mrs Thatcher, issued a statement from Downing Street saying: "The IRA are now indiscriminately killing men, women and children, and now they have killed two Australians."
Daily Mirror

As the war faded and peace loomed, Vera Lynn was able to advise her husband and business manager Harry Lewis that she was going to have a baby. It is a symbolic and logical clinax to five gruelling years as a "Forces Sweetheart."
Sydney Morning Herald

She said yesterday: "Julia was born profoundly dead and wears two hearing aids."
Evening Standard

"Heavyweight news on the Oxford Poetry Chair front: W.H. Auden and Cecil Day Lewis, the Poet Laureate, are expected to nominate Roy Fuller, the much respected poet (and solicitor), whose recent slimy volume *New Poems* has been received with something approaching rapture."
Sunday Telegraph

2. 1066 Granada massacre

A poem, written by Abu Ishaq in Al-Andalus, Granada in 1066, is considered to be the reason for this massacre. It contains the following lines:

> Do not consider it a breach of faith to kill them,
> the breach of faith would be to let them carry on.
> They have violated our covenant with them,
> so how can you be held guilty against the violators?
> How can they have any pact when we are obscure
> and they are prominent?
> Now we are humble, beside them,
> as if we were wrong and they were right!

In 1066, on 30th December, a Muslim mob stormed the royal palace in Al-Andalus, Granada. The mob assassinated Jewish vizier Joseph ibn Naghrela and murdered most of the Jewish population of the city. It is estimated that, more than 1,500 Jewish families, numbering 4,000 persons, fell in one day.

3. Batak massacre

In Batak in 1876, Ottoman troops massacred Bulgarian civilians at what was to be the beginning of the April Uprising. Reports of the number of victims varies from 3,000 to 5,000 according to different sources. On 30 April 1876, 8,000 Turkish soldiers, mainly Bashi-bazouk, led by Ahmet Aga Barun surrounded the city. A battle ensued after which the men from Batak decided to try to negotiate with Ahmet Aga. He promised them the withdrawal of his troops, under the condition of their disarmament. After the rebels had laid down their weapons, the Bashi-bazouk attacked the now defenseless population. Almost all of the victims were beheaded.

4. Massacre of Thessaloniki

In AD390 the inhabitants of the Greek city of Thessaloniki, rose up against Roman Emperor Theodosius I. The cause of the uprising was the order to arrest a popular wagon driver for trying to seduce and have sex with Butherich, a servant of the Emperor. The wagon driver was locked up in prison, but the citizens of Thessaloniki demanded his release. Things got out of hand and Butherich was murdered in the ensuing turmoil, so the Emperor intervened and ordered executions. The citizens of the city were furious and in the hippodrome in Thessaloniki angry Roman troops massacred around 7,000 people. This incident aroused the wrath of the Bishop of Milan, Ambrose, and the church urged the emperor to repentance.

5. Srebrenica massacre

In July 1995, an estimated 8,000 Bosniak men, including at least 500 children in the region of Srebrenica in Bosnia and Herzegovina were killed by units of the Army of Republika Srpska (VRS) under the command of General Ratko Mladic during the Bosnian War. This has become known as the Srebrenica Massacre (also known as Srebrenica Genocide). In addition to the VRS, a paramilitary unit from Serbia known as the Scorpions also participated in the massacre. So far, more than 5,600 victims of genocide have been identified through DNA analysis. Prior to the genocide, the United Nations had declared Srebrenica a UN protected "safe area," but that did not prevent the massacre, even though 400 armed Dutch peace-keepers were present at the time. After reviewing a comprehensive report, the Dutch government resigned over this matter in 2002.

6. Massacre of Elphinstone's Army

In January 1842, British and Indian troops led by William
Elphinstone were beaten in battle by Afghan forces led by
Akbar Khan, the son of Dost Mohammad Khan in what has
become known as the Massacre of Elphinstone's Army. After
the British and Indian troops captured Kabul in 1839, an Afghan
uprising forced the occupying garrison out of the city. The
British army, consisting of 4,500 troops and 12,000 working
personnel or camp followers, left Kabul on 6 January 1842.
They attempted to reach the British garrison at Jalalabad, 90
miles away, but were immediately surrounded by Afghan forces.
The last remnants were eventually annihilated near Gandamak
on January 13. Only one man, the assistant surgeon William
Brydon, survived and managed to reach Jalalabad.

7. Katyn massacre

On 5 March 1940, Soviet authorities ordered the mass execution of
Polish military officers, policemen, and civilian prisoners of war.
The victims were murdered in the Katyn forest in Russia, the
Kalinin (Tver) and Kharkiv prisons and elsewhere. About 8,000
were officers taken prisoner during the 1939 Soviet invasion of
Poland, the rest being Poles arrested for allegedly being "intelli-
gence agents, gendarmes, spies, saboteurs, landowners, factory
owners, lawyers, priests, and officials."

In what has become known as the Katyn massacre, also
known as the Katyn Forest massacre, the number of victims
was estimated at about 22,000, with the most commonly cited
number of 21,768. Since Poland's conscription system required
every non-exempted university graduate to become a reserve
officer, the Soviets were able to round up much of the Polish
intelligentsia, and the Jewish, Ukrainian, Georgian, and
Belarusian intelligentsia of Polish citizenship.

8. Babi Yar

Babi Yar is a ravine in Kiev, the capital of Ukraine. In the course of two days, 29 and 30 September, 1941, a special team of German Nazi SS supported by other German units, local collaborators, and Ukrainian police murdered 33,771 Jewish civilians. The Babi Yar massacre is considered to be the largest single massacre in the history of the Holocaust.

9. NKVD prisoner massacres

After the German invasion of the Soviet Union in 1941, the Soviet NKVD ordered a series of mass executions of prisoners in Poland, the Baltic states, and parts of the Soviet Union from which the Red Army was withdrawing. The overall death toll is estimated at around 100,000, including more than 10,000 in Western Ukraine.

10. Nanking Massacre

The Nanking Massacre, often termed the Rape of Nanking, was an infamous war crime committed by the Japanese military in Nanjing (Nanking), the then capital of the Republic of China, after it fell to the Imperial Japanese Army on 13 December 1937. The violence continued over the next six weeks, until early February 1938.

During this period of the occupation of Nanking, the Japanese army committed numerous atrocities, such as rape, looting, arson and the execution of prisoners of war and civilians. Although the executions began under the pretext of eliminating Chinese soldiers disguised as civilians, it is claimed that a large number of innocent men were intentionally misidentified as enemy combatants and executed as the massacre gathered momentum. A large number of women and children were also killed, as rape and murder became more widespread.

IT'S THE LAW

In Mesquite, Texas, it is deemed to be against regulations for youngsters to have haircuts that are "startling or unusual."

It is illegal to hunt camels in the state of Arizona.

In Athens, Greece, a driver's license can be confiscated if the driver is deemed either "poorly dressed" or "unbathed."

In Cleveland, Ohio, it's illegal to catch mice without a hunting license.

On the island of Jersey it is illegal for a man to knit during the fishing season.

In Alabama, USA. it is illegal to carry a comb in your pocket, because it may be used as a weapon.

In Michigan, USA. you cannot chain an alligator to a fire hydrant.

In Fairbanks, Alaska it is illegal for a moose to walk on the sidewalk. Apparently, this law dates back to the early days in the town settlement when the owner of the bar had a pet moose that he used to get drunk. The moose would then stumble around the town drunk. The only way the officials could prevent this from happening was to create this law so the moose could not cross the sidewalk and get into the bar.

Estimates by the International Military Tribunal for the Far East have put the victims of the Nanking massacre at over 200,000. These estimates are not exaggerated, burial societies and other organizations have counted more than 155,000 buried bodies in the area.

11. Kent State Shootings

On Monday, 4 May 1970 the Ohio National Guard shot and killed four students and wounded nine others one of whom suffered permanent paralysis, at Kent State University in the city of Kent, Ohio.

The students had been protesting against the American invasion of Cambodia, which President Richard Nixon had announced in a television address on 30 April. However, according to local reports, some students who were shot had simply been walking nearby or observing the protest from a distance. There was national outrage following the attack, hundreds of universities, colleges, and high schools closed throughout the United States due to a student strike of eight million students.

12. St Peter's Massacre

In March 1819, Joseph Johnson, John Knight, and James Wroe formed the Manchester Patriotic Union Society. The main objective of the organisation was to obtain parliamentary reform by joining together all the radicals in Manchester to speak as one voice. Johnson became secretary and Wroe was appointed treasurer. During the summer of 1819 it was decided to invite Major Cartwright, Henry "Orator" Hunt and Richard Carlile to speak at a public meeting in Manchester. The men were told that this was to be "a meeting of the county of Lancashire, rather than Manchester alone. I think by good management the largest

Joke of the Day
Did you hear about the millionaire who
had a bad accident? He fell off his
wallet.

assembly may be procured that was ever seen in this country."
Cartwright was unable to attend but Hunt and Carlile agreed and
the meeting was arranged to take place at St Peter's Field,
Manchester, on 16 August 1891.

The local magistrates were worried that such a large gathering
of reformers might give rise to violence. They decided therefore
to arrange for a large number of soldiers to be in Manchester on
the day of the meeting, supposedly to keep the peace. The
appointed military included four squadrons of Cavalry of the
15th Hussars (600 men), several hundred infantrymen, the
Cheshire Yeomanry Cavalry (400 men), a detachment of the
Royal Horse Artillery and two six-pounder guns and the
Manchester and Salford Yeomanry (120 men) and all
Manchester's special constables (400 men).

By 11:00 a.m. on 16th August, 1819 an estimated 50,000
people had gathered in St Peter's Field. The special constables
were told to clear a path through the crowd and the 400 special
constables accordingly formed two continuous lines. The main
speakers at the meeting arrived at 1:20 p.m. These included
Henry Hunt, Richard Carlile, John Knight, Joseph Johnson and
Mary Fildes. Several newspaper reporters, including John Tyas
of *The Times*, Edward Baines of the *Leeds Mercury*, John Smith
of the *Liverpool Mercury*, and John Saxton of the *Manchester
Observer*, joined the speakers on the podium.

Because of the large numbers of angry people involved, the

magistrates came to the conclusion that "the town was in great danger." Concerned that a riot would break out William Hulton, the leader of the magistrates decided to instruct Joseph Nadin, Deputy Constable of Manchester, to arrest Henry Hunt and other leaders of the demonstration. Nadin replied that this could not be done without the help of the military. Hulton immediately sent letters to Lieutenant Colonel L'Estrange, the commander of the military forces in Manchester and Major Thomas Trafford, the commander of the Manchester and Salford Yeomanry.

Major Trafford, who was positioned only a few yards away at Pickford's Yard, was the first to receive the order to arrest the men. Major Trafford chose Captain Hugh Birley, his second-in-command, to carry out the order. Local eyewitnesses claimed that most of the 60 men who Birley led into St Peter's Field were drunk. Birley later insisted that the troop's seemingly erratic behaviour was because the horses were afraid of the crowd. The Yeomanry entered St. Peter's Field along the path cleared by the special constables and members of the crowd began to link arms to stop them arresting Henry Hunt and the other leaders.

Captain Hugh Birley and his men eventually arrested Henry Hunt, John Knight, Joseph Johnson, George Swift, John Saxton, John Tyas, John Moorhouse, and Robert Wild. As well as the speakers and the organisers of the meeting, Birley also arrested the newspaper reporters. However, arriving as this scene was taking place, Lieutenant Colonel L'Estrange got the impression that the speakers were attacking the Yeomanry and gave orders for his troops to clear the field. In the process, 18 people were killed and about 500, including 100 women, were wounded.

Richard Carlile managed to avoid being arrested and after being hidden by local radicals, he took the first mail coach to

London. The following day, placards for *Sherwin's Political Register* began appearing in London with the words: "Horrid Massacres at Manchester." A full report of the meeting appeared in the next edition of the newspaper. Carlile was later imprisoned for publishing this story.

After the St Peter's Massacre, Viscount Sidmouth, the Home Secretary, sent a letter of congratulations to the Manchester magistrates for the action they had taken. Parliament also passed the Six Acts in an attempt to make sure reform meetings like the one at St Peter's Field did not happened again.

The trial of the organizers of the St Peter's Field meeting took place in York between 16 and 27 March 1820. The men were charged with "assembling with unlawful banners at an unlawful meeting for the purpose of exciting discontent." Henry Hunt was found guilty and was sent to Manchester Prison for two years and six months.

13. Crow Creek Massacre

The Crow Creek Massacre occurred in the early fourteenth century between opposing American Indian tribes. The Crow Creek site is located in central South Dakota and is now an archaeological site and a U.S. National Historic Landmark. At the time, the area was home to the Lakota Sioux people of the Initial Coalescent tradition.

It is thought that Middle Missou Indians moved into the area and the overcrowding grew to a point that both sides conducted raids on each other's camps and the ensuing deaths resulted in mass graves being dug. In 1978, an archaeologist, Robert Alex, was attending a meeting hosted by the South Dakota Archaeological Society when he toured the Crow Creek site and discovered human bones while exploring the fortifications at the site. It was revealed that one group of villagers numbering

Fascinating Facts

The term "skid row" was first used in the lumberjacking days in Seattle. The logs were sent from a hilltop down a long chute and into the sea. Around the lower end of this chute there was a slum area where drunks and down-and-outs often slept in the gutter.

Until the 1930s, no one knew why the sun shines. It was only then that it was understood that it is a vast nuclear furnace.

The camel has never been "domesticated," in the sense of being friendly to man. It remains a sullen and aggressive creature.

Benjamin Franklin suggested that clocks should be moved forward in spring to save daylight hours. His plan was not adopted in America and Europe until World War I, over a hundred years after his death, in order to save electricity.

George Asher of Joplin, Missouri, was obsessed by horses, who he felt to be superior to human beings. His hair was cut like a mane, his shoes shod with horseshoes, and he had a harness made with which he pulled a wagon. He even entered competitions against horses to prove he could pull heavier weights. He ate grass, beans, hay, bran and oats – although he also ate normal human food.

around 50 houses on top of a bluff, tried to build a ditch and new wall to give them security from attack. However, they were attacked before the fortifications were completed and archeological investigations show that the attacking group slaughtered the people on the bluff. Many of these remains had signs of torture and mutilation. These included tongues being cut out, scalping, teeth broken, heads cut off, and other forms of dismemberment. After receiving permission to excavate this site, skeletal remains of at least 486 Crow Creek villagers were found.

14. Massacre of Glencoe
In Glencoe, Scotland during the era of the Glorious Revolution and Jacobitism, 38 MacDonalds from the Clan MacDonald of Glencoe were killed early in the morning of 13 Feburuary 1692, by the guests who had accepted their hospitality. The killings were justified on the grounds that the MacDonalds had not been prompt in pledging allegiance to the new king, William of Orange. Another 40 women and children died of exposure after their homes were burned. The massacre began simultaneously in three settlements along the glen – Invercoe, Inverrigan, and Achacon – although the killing took place in a much broader area as fleeing MacDonalds were pursued and murdered.

15. Bloody Falls Massacre
On 17 July 1771, Samuel Hearne, led by Chipewyan Dene warriors was exploring the Coppermine River when his party discovered a group of local Copper Inuit camped by rapids around 15 kilometres upstream from the mouth of the Coppermine. The Chipewyan waited until just after midnight when they then set upon the Inuit camp and slaughtered around 20 men, women, and children. It was said that after witnessing

the massacre, Hearne was traumatised by his memories until he died. The site of the massacre is now located in Kugluk/Bloody Falls Territorial Park near Kugluktuk, Nunavut. It was designated a National Historic Site in 1978.

16. The September Massacres
In 1792 the Duke of Brunswick led the Prussian army through France. As the Prussians advanced on the capital, Paris, news of Brunswick's manifesto was being circulated through the city. Brunswick aimed:

> ". . . to put an end to the anarchy in the interior of France, to check the attacks upon the throne and the altar, to reestablish the legal power, to restore to the king the security and the liberty of which he is now deprived and to place him in a position to exercise once more the legitimate authority which belongs to him."

The Duke was also intent on reinstating the monarchy. Rumors spread around Paris that some people who secretly opposed the revolution would support Brunswick. In addition to this, Paris was low on food stocks and the general public were getting restless. The political mood was somber, no one could really claim to be in control of the city.

Over a 48 hour period beginning on 2 September 1792, as the French Legislative Assembly (successor to the National Constituent Assembly) dissolved into chaos, angry mobs massacred three bishops, including the Archbishop of Arles, and more than 200 priests. Religious figures featured prominently among the victims because at the time there was rising resentment against the Roman Catholic Church. This eventually led to the temporary abandonment of Christianity in France. The first

> **Classic One-Liners**
> W.S. Gilbert said of an acquaintance: "No one
> can have a higher opinion of him than I have, and
> I think he's a dirty little beast."

attack occurred on 24 non-juring priests being transported to the prison of the Abbey of Saint-Germain-des-Prés, which had become a national prison of the revolutionary government. An angry mob killed them all as they were trying to escape into the prison, then mutilated the bodies. Of 284 prisoners, 135 were killed, 27 were transferred, 86 were set free, and 36 had uncertain fates. On 3 September and 4 September, crowds broke into other Paris prisons, where they murdered the prisoners, it was feared that some of the prisoners were counter-revolutionaries who would aid the invading Prussians.

The crowds are then said to have raped, killed, and grotesquely mutilated the Princesse de Lamballe, friend of Marie Antoinette and sister-in-law to the Duc d'Orleans. It was said that her head was paraded on a pike under the captive Queen's windows at the Temple.

By the time the September Massacre had subsided, half the prison population of Paris had been executed: some 1,200 trapped prisoners, including many women and young boys. Sporadic violence, in particular against the Roman Catholic Church, would continue throughout France for nearly a decade to come.

17. Mountain Meadows Massacre

Harper's Weekly ran a cover story on 13 August 1859 about the slaughter in Mountain Meadows. The cover showed an illustration of the killing field as described by Brevet Major Carleton:

". . . one too horrible and sickening for language to describe. Human skeletons, disjointed bones, ghastly skulls, and the hair of women were scattered in frightful profusion over a distance of two miles. The remains were not buried at all until after they had been dismembered by the wolves and the flesh stripped from the bones, and then only such bones were buried as lay scattered along nearest the road."

In 1857, Mormons throughout the Utah Territory joined together to fight the United States Army, which they believed was intending to destroy them as a people. Rumors abounded that the arriving Francher-Baker train was linked to recent persecutions of Mormons. In fact, the Francher-Baker train was made up of Arkansas emigrants who were traveling to California. In September 1857, they had stopped to rest and regroup their approximately 800 head of cattle at Mountain Meadows, a valley within the Iron County Military District, a popular designation for the Mormon militia of the Utah Territory. The local Mormon militia set out to attack the convoy that they believed was guilty of malicious acts against them.

However, the emigrants fought back and the initial attack turned into a siege. Militiamen demanded that the emigrants surrender and give up their weapons. The emigrants surrendered on 11 September. After escorting them out of their fortification, the militiamen and their tribesmen auxiliaries killed approximately 120 men, women, and children. The lives of 17 younger children were spared.

 # Boobs and Misprints

"Mrs Harrison is friendly, likeable and easy to talk to. She has a fine, fair skin which, she admits ruefully, comes out in a mass of freckles at the first hint of sin. Her husband is away in London from Monday to Thursday most weeks."
Essex County Standard

"Mr Ivan Neill (Bailynafeigh) replied favourably to the first question, and on the second said he would use his influence to ensure the preservation of the Lord's Dad."
Belfast Telegraph

"The store detective revealed: 'We arrested one woman with a whole salami in her knickers. When asked why, she said she was missing her Italian boyfriend."
Manchester Evening News

"Pinker, a man whose bedside manner is legendary in royal circles, also delivered Prince William and seven other royal babies. They included Londoner Christina Harte, who arrived with a pair of baby shoes tied to green balloons."
Sydney Daily Telegraph

18. The Novocherkassk riots

On 1st June 1962, Nikita Khrushchev, President of the
Soviet Union, raised the price of meat and butter. For workers
at the Budenny Electric Locomotive Factory in the city
of Novocherkassk this was the last straw. Managers in
Novocherkassk had raised production norms, thereby effectively
reducing pay rates. On 2 June 1962, laborers from the foundry
and forge shops stopped work after factory management refused
to hear their complaints. The workers were concerned about
shortages of food and provisions as well as the poor working
conditions in the factory. By noon the strike and attendant
discussions had spread throughout the whole factory.

The striking workers began a march on the town hall and police
headquarters. Police arrested 30 workers and in doing so caused the
strike to spread as workers from other factories began their own
strike action in support. As hundreds began to gather in the town
hall square, police and the Red Army were called to keep peace and
order. Accounts of their exact actions on that day vary but all agree
that the Red Army began firing shots into the demonstrators.
According to one source 87, protesters were killed and many more
wounded. Three of the wounded died later.

After the initial demonstrations, a curfew was implemented in
the town but the following morning, a large group of several
hundred demonstrators again gathered in the square. This time,
116 were arrested, of which 14 were tried by show trials, and
7 of those received a death sentence. The others were sentenced
to prison terms of 10 to 15 years or exiled to Siberia with their
families.

19. The Tlatelolco Massacre

After months of political unrest in the Mexican capital, Mexico
City, students demonstrated for better human rights. Echoing

21

student demonstrations around the world in 1968, Mexican students wanted attention focused on Mexico City for the 1968 Summer Olympics. The students demanded:

- A repeal of the Penal Code that deemed that gatherings of three or more people threatened public order (and was an imprisonable offense).
- Freedom of political prisoners.
- The sacking of the Chief of Police and his Deputy.
- That officials responsible for the recent bloodshed be identified and put in trial.

President Gustavo Díaz Ordaz was determined to stop the demonstrations and, in September 1968, he ordered the army to occupy the campus of the National Autonomous University of Mexico, the country's largest university. Students were beaten and arrested indiscriminately. Student demonstrators were not deterred. The demonstrations grew in size, until, on 2 October, after student strikes lasting nine weeks, 15,000 students from various universities marched through the streets of Mexico City, carrying red carnations to protest the army's occupation of the university campus. By nightfall, 5,000 students and workers, many of them with spouses and children, had congregated outside an apartment complex in the Plaza de las Tres Culturas in Tlatelolco for what was supposed to be a peaceful rally.

The massacre began at sunset when police and military forces equipped with armored cars and tanks surrounded the square and began firing live rounds into the crowd, hitting not only the protestors, but also other people who were present for reasons unrelated to the demonstration. Many passersby including children were hit with bullets, and mounds of bodies soon lay on

Joke of the Day
Teacher: "That's an excellent essay for someone your age." Girl: "How about for someone my Mom's age?"

the ground. The killing continued through the night, with soldiers operating on a house-to-house basis in the apartment buildings adjacent to the square. Witnesses to the event claim that the bodies were later removed in garbage trucks.

The official government explanation of the incident was that armed provocateurs among the demonstrators, stationed in buildings overlooking the crowd, had begun the firefight. Suddenly finding themselves sniper targets, the security forces had simply returned the shooting in self-defense.

In October 1997, the Congress of Mexico established a committee to investigate the Tlatelolco massacre. Former president Luis Echeverría Álvarez who was Odaz's misiter of the interior at the time admitted that the students had been unarmed, and also suggested that the military action was planned in advance, as a means to destroy the student movement.

20. The École Polytechnique Massacre

The École Polytechnique Massacre, also known as the Montreal Massacre, occurred on 6 December, 1989 at the École Polytechnique in Montreal, Quebec, Canada. Twenty-five year-old misogynist, Marc Lépine, shot twenty-eight people, killing fourteen (all of them women) and injuring the other fourteen before killing himself. Armed with a legally obtained semi-

> **Classic One-Liners**
> Abraham Lincoln remarked of a congressman: 'He can compress the most words into the fewest ideas of anyone I've ever known.'

automatic rifle and a hunting knife he began his attack by entering a classroom at the university, where he separated the male and female students. After claiming that he was "fighting feminism," he shot all nine women in the room, killing six. He then moved through corridors, the cafeteria, and another class-room, specifically targeting women to shoot. He killed fourteen women and injured four men and ten women in less than twenty minutes before turning the gun on himself.

21. The Haximu Massacre

The Haximu Massacre, also known as the Yanomami Massacre, was an armed conflict in Brazil in 1993. The conflict occurred just outside of Haximu, Brazil, near the Venezuela border, during the summer of 1993. This massacre was initiated by the tensions surrounding the gold rush in Brazil between Brazilian miners and the Yanomami people. A group of garimpeiros (gold miners who were mining the land illegally) killed four or five young men of the Yanomami Haximu-teri. In response, the Yanomami natives formed two raids against the miners, killing at least two of them and wounding two more. Following this attack, the garimpeiros attacked again, killing about 12 Yanomami (almost all of them were sunarmed elderly, youths or infants) and burned down the Haximu village.

The Yanomami tribe had remained alone until sometime

between 1973 and 1976 when Brazilians built the Perimetral Norte through the southern area of the natives' territory. This road initiated the arrival of gold miners, which includes those that came during a gold rush beginning in 1987.

Science: How it Works

Capillary Action

Even though we usually think of water as running with the pull of gravity, it can also flow against it using a process called capillary action. This explains how water goes from the soil upwards into the stem of plants. Plants contain many vein-like tubes that carry water from the plant's roots upward to the plant's highest leafs via capillary action. The narrower the tube, the more pronounced the capillary effect will be.

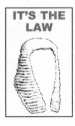

IT'S THE LAW

It is against the law to whale hunt in Oklahoma.

It is illegal to sell an ET doll in France as it is against the law to sell a doll that does not have a human face.

A local ordinance in Atwoodville, Connecticut prohibits people from playing Scrabble while waiting for a politician to speak.

A Virginia law requires all bathtubs to be kept out in the yards, not inside the houses.

It is illegal to ride a streetcar on Sunday if you have been eating garlic in Toronto, Canada.

In the country of Turkey, in the sixteenth and seventeenth centuries, anyone caught drinking coffee was put to death.

Before the enactment of the 1978 law that made it mandatory for dog owners in New York City to clean up after their pets, approximately 40 million pounds of dog excrement were deposited on the streets every year.

In Harrisburg, Pennsylvania it is illegal to have sex with a truck driver inside a tollbooth.

In Kentucky anyone who has been drinking is deemed "sober" until he or she "cannot hold onto the ground."

Beasts and Monsters

The Amazing Ape-man

In 1920 the Polish medium Franek Klusky had a series of
sittings with the International Metaphysical Institute, among
whose prominent members were the French investigators
Professor Charles Richet and Gustave Geley. The seance circle
sat with hands linked, and the expert researchers kept the
medium under careful observation. Unlike many mediums,
Klusky did not go into trance during a seance. He worked in a
state of full consciousness, but with deep concentration.

Klusky was noted for a remarkable ability to materialize both
humans and animals. His most electrifying seances were those in
which strange forms loomed out of the darkness – on one
occasion a great hulking creature halfway between human and
ape. It was about the stature of a man, but had a similar face,
long arms, and hair all over. It smelled, sitters said, like a wet
dog. Once the big hairy head leaned heavily on a sitter's
shoulder. Another sitter put out a hand, which the creature
licked with a large soft tongue.

The scientifically minded sitters called Klusky's materialized
apeman Pithecanthropus. Geley believed totally in the medium's
psychic powers. On the other hand, British psychic researcher
Harry Price doubted his abilities.

ANIMAL SCIENCE

The first bird domesticated by man was the goose.

There are more chickens in the world than people.

Chickens absorb vitamin D through their combs from sunshine.

The average hen will lay 227 eggs a year.

Roosters can't crow if they can't fully extend their necks.

A group of geese on the ground is gaggle, a group of geese in the air is skein.

A duck's quack doesn't echo, and no one knows why.

Chickens that lay brown eggs have red ear lobes. There is a genetic link between the two.

The female pig is the fastest breeder. A pig gestates in three months, three weeks, and three days.

The underside of a horse's hoof is called a frog. The frog peels off several times a year with new growth.

A pig is a hog – hog is a generic name for all swine – but a hog is not a pig. In the terminology of hog raising, a pig is a baby hog less than ten weeks old.

Mysteries of the World

The Bermuda Triangle
On the afternoon of 5 December 1945, five Avenger torpedo-bombers took off from Fort Lauderdale, Florida, for a routine two-hour patrol over the Atlantic. Flight 19 was commanded by Flight Leader Charles Taylor; the other four pilots were trainees, flying what is known as a "milk run" that is, a flight whose purpose is simply to increase their number of hours in the air without instructors. By 2:15 p.m. the planes were well over the Atlantic, and following their usual patrol route. The weather was warm and clear.

At 3:45 p.m. the control tower received a message from Taylor:

"This is an emergency. We seem to be off course. We cannot see land . . . repeat . . . we cannot see land."

"What is your position?"

"We're not sure of our position. We can't be sure where we are. We seem to be lost."

"Head due west," replied the tower.

"We don't know which way is west. Everything is wrong . . . strange. We can't be sure of any direction. Even the ocean doesn't look as it should."

The tower was perplexed; even if some kind of magnetic interference caused all five compasses to malfunction, the pilot should still be able to see the sun low in the western sky. Radio contact was now getting worse, restricting any messages to short sentences. At one point the tower picked up one pilot speaking to another, saying that all the instruments in his plane were "going crazy". At 4 p.m. the flight leader decided to hand over to someone else. At 4:25 p.m. the new leader told the tower:

"We're not certain where we are."

Unless the planes could find their way back over land during the next four hours, they would run out of fuel and be forced to land in the sea. At 6:27 p.m. a rescue mission was launched. A giant Martin Mariner flying-boat, with a crew of thirteen, took off toward the last reported position of the flight. Twenty-three minutes later, the sky to the east was lit briefly by a bright orange flash. Neither the Martin Mariner nor the five Avengers ever returned. They vanished completely, as other planes and ships have vanished in the area that has become known as "the Devil's Triangle" and "the Bermuda Triangle."

What finally happened to the missing aircraft is certainly no mystery. The weather became worse during the course of that afternoon; ships reported "high winds and tremendous seas." Flight 19 and its would-be rescuer must have run out of fuel and landed in the sea. The mystery is *why* they became so completely lost and confused. Even if the navigation instruments had ceased to function, and visibility had become restricted to a

---

Joke of the Day
Beautician: "Did that mud pack I gave you for your wife improve her appearance?" Man: "It did for a while – then it fell off."

few yards, it should have been possible to fly up above the clouds to regain their bearings. What seems stranger still is that this tragedy should have failed to alert the authorities that there was something frightening and dangerous about the stretch of ocean between Florida and the Bahamas – a chain of islands that begins a mere fifty miles off the coast of Florida. But then the authorities no doubt took the view of many more recent sceptics, that the disappearance was a rather complex accident, due to a number of chance factors: bad weather, electrical interference with the compasses, the inexperience of some of the pilots and the fact that the flight leader, Charles Taylor, had only recently been posted to Fort Lauderdale and was unfamiliar with the area.

Similar explanations were adopted to explain a number of similar tragedies during the next two decades: the disappearance of a Superfortress in 1947, of a four-engined Tudor IV in January 1948, of a DC3 in December 1948, of another Tudor IV in 1949, of a Globemaster in 1950, of a British York transport plane in 1952, of a Navy Super Constellation in 1954, of another Martin seaplane in 1956, of an Air Force tanker in 1962, of two Stratotankers in 1963, of a flying boxcar in 1965, of a civilian cargo plane in 1966, another cargo plane in 1967, and yet another in 1973 . . . The total number of lives lost in all these disappearances was well in excess of 200.

During the 1930s, the United Fruit Company cleared vast areas of Costa Rican jungle in order to create banana planta-tions. When the workers came to burn and hack the vegetation of the Diquìs Delta they were surprised to discover vast numbers of granite spheres, entirely buried in the foliage. They ranged from the small, about the size of a cricket ball and weighing a few pounds, to the enormous, eight feet in diameter and weighing sixteen tons. Many were rounded with astonishing

 # Boobs and Misprints

"Bill Davidson's two children, Kim and Tania, were overjoyed when he came home with a scruffy black and white mongrel from the RSPCA. The newcomer had a touch of whippet, so they called it Streaker.

A few days later, Bill Davidson, of St Saviour's Hill, felt less happy about the new acquisition when Streaker came into the kitchen with a dead rabbit in his mouth. The creature was plump and well-groomed, and was obviously a domestic pet. Tania identified it as the property of her friend Sita Chatterji, who lived next door but one.

Fortunately, the Chatterji family was away on holiday in Doncaster. So after dark that evening, Bill Davidson sneaked into their garden and replaced the rabbit in the empty hutch. There were no marks on it, and he hoped they would assume it had died of natural causes.

A week later Bill Davidson saw his friend Varun Chatterji in the local pub and asked after the health of his family. 'They are well. But my daughter Sita is very upset. Her pet rabbit died just before we went on holiday, and some sick bastard has gone and put a dead rabbit in its cage.'"
Leicester Chronicle

"Wife beaters form group to help others."
The Press (Christchurch)

accuracy, appearing to the eye to be perfectly spherical, yet their surfaces showed no sign of mechanical grinding. They were clearly man-made, not least because the granite from which they were cut did not occur naturally where they were found. Locals broke some open, believing them to contain treasure.

They remain entirely mysterious. Some were found over graves, others arranged in lines, curves and triangles. Pottery found underneath them dates from many centuries, the latest being the sixteenth. That they had some religious significance seems to be the only certain conclusion, for it is difficult to imagine a practical use for such an array of objects. The more impressive of the balls now adorn the gardens of wealthy locals.

Oddly enough, the first person to realize that all this amounted to a frightening mystery was a journalist called Vincent Gaddis; it was in February 1964 that his article "The Deadly Bermuda Triangle" appeared in the American *Argosy* magazine, and bestowed the now familiar name on that mysterious stretch of ocean. A year later, in a book about sea mysteries called *Invisible Horizons*, Gaddis included his article in a chapter called "The Triangle of Death." His chapter also contained a long list of ships that had vanished in the area, beginning with the *Rosalie*, which vanished in 1840, and ending with the yacht *Connemara IV* in 1956. In the final chapter, Gaddis entered the realm of science fiction, and speculated on "space-time continua [that] may exist around us on the earth, interpenetrating our known world," implying that perhaps some of the missing planes and ships had vanished down a kind of fourth-dimensional plughole.

Soon after the publication of his book Gaddis received a letter from a man called Gerald Hawkes, who told of his own experience in the Bermuda Triangle in April 1952.

On a flight from Idlewild Airport (now Kennedy) to Bermuda,

> **Classic One-Liners**
> Abraham Lincoln: "If this is coffee, please bring me some tea; if this is tea, please bring me some coffee."

Hawkes's plane suddenly dropped about two hundred feet. This was not a nose-dive, but felt as if he had suddenly fallen down a lift-shaft in the air; then the plane shot back up again. "It was as if a giant hand was holding the plane and jerking it up and down," and the wings seemed to flap like the wings of a bird. The captain then told them that he was unable to find Bermuda, and that the operator was unable to make radio contact with either the USA or Bermuda. An hour or so later the plane made contact with a radio ship, and was able to get its bearings and fly to Bermuda. As they climbed out of the plane they observed that it was a clear and starry night, with no wind. The writer concluded that he was still wondering whether he was caught in an area "where time and space seem to disappear."

Ivan Sanderson, a friend of Gaddis's began taking a map of the world, and marking on it a number of areas where strange disappearances had occurred. There was, for example, another "Devil's Triangle" south of the Japanese island of Honshu where ships and planes had vanished. A correspondent told Sanderson about a strange experience on a flight to Guam, in the western Pacific, when his ancient propeller-driven plane covered 340 miles in one hour, although there was no wind – about 200 miles more than it should have covered; checks showed that many planes had vanished in this area.

Fascinating Facts

Mary Shelley's novel *Frankenstein*, written in 1816, was based on a real scientist, Andrew Crosse, whose lectures on electricity were attended by the poet Shelley and his wife in 1814. But many years after the novel was written, Crosse achieved notoriety when he announced that he had actually created life in his laboratory. In 1837, he tried make crystals of natural glass; he made glass out of ground flint and potassium carbonate, and dissolved it in sulphuric acid. He then allowed the mixture to drip porous iron oxide which was "electrified." He believed that this process created tiny buglike creatures. A paper on his "discovery," read to the London Electrical Society, caused him to be denounced by as a blasphemer. The mystery of the "bugs" has never been solved.

The most literate people in the world are Icelanders, who read more books per capita than any other nation.

The first piece of science fiction was Kepler's story *Somnium*, published after his death in 1630. Cyrano de Bergerac's *Voyage to the Moon* (published 1657), often cited as the first work of science fiction, is not only later, but it is also political satire rather than science fiction.

Marking these areas on the map, Sanderson observed that they were shaped like lozenges, and that these lozenges seemed to ring the globe in a neat symmetry, running in two rings, each between 30 degrees and 40 degrees north and south of the equator. There were ten of these "funny places," about 72 degrees apart. An earthquake specialist named George Rouse had argued that earthquakes originated in a certain layer below the earth's surface, and had speculated that there was a kind of trough running round the central core of the earth, which determined the direction of seismic activities. Rouse's map of these seismic disturbance areas corresponded closely with Sanderson's "lozenges." So Sanderson was inclined to believe that if "whirlpools" really caused the disappearance of ships and planes, then they were perfectly normal physical whirlpools, caused, so to speak, by the earth's tendency to "burp."

Now, all pilots know about air pockets, where a sudden change in pressure causes the plane to lurch and fall, and about air turbulence which causes the wings of a plane to "flap." What seems odd about this case is the total radio blackout.

Is there, then, an alternative which combines common sense with the boldness necessary to recognize that all the disappearances cannot be conveniently explained away? There is, and it rests on the evidence of some of those who have escaped the Bermuda Triangle. In November 1964 a charter pilot named Chuck Wakely was returning from Nassau to Miami, Florida, and had climbed up to 8,000 feet. He noticed a faint glow around the wings of his plane, which he put down to some optical illusion caused by cockpit lights. But the glow increased steadily, and all his electronic equipment began to go wrong. He was forced to operate the craft manually. The glow became so blinding that he was dazzled; then slowly it faded, and his instruments began to function normally again.

In 1966 Captain Don Henry was steering his tug from Puerto Rico to Fort Lauderdale on a clear afternoon. He heard shouting, and hurried to the bridge. There he saw that the compass was spinning clockwise. A strange darkness came down, and the horizon disappeared. "The water seemed to be coming from all directions." And although the electric generators were still running, all electric power faded away. An auxiliary generator refused to start. The boat seemed to be surrounded by a kind of fog. Fortunately the engines were still working, and suddenly the boat emerged from the fog. To Henry's amazement, the fog seemed to be concentrated into a single solid bank, and within this area the sea was turbulent; outside it was calm. Henry remarked that the compass behaved as it did on the St Lawrence river at Kingson, where some large deposit of iron or a meteorite affects the needle.

Our earth is, of course, a gigantic magnet (no one quite knows why), and the magnetic lines of force run around its surface in strange patterns. Birds and animals use these lines of force for "homing," and water-diviners seem able to respond to them with their "dowsing rods." But there are areas of the earth's surface where birds lose their way because the lines somehow cancel one another out, forming a magnetic anomaly or vortex. The *Marine Observer* for 1930 warns sailors about a magnetic disturbance in the neighbourhood of the Tambora volcano, near Sumbawa, which deflected a ship's compass by six points,

Joke of the Day
"Waiter, why is my apple pie all mashed up?' 'You did ask me to step on it, sir."

leading it off course. In 1932 Captain Scutt of the *Australia* observed a magnetic disturbance near Fremantle that deflected the compass 12 degrees either side of the ship's course. Dozens of similar anomalies have been collected and documented by an American investigator, William Corliss, in books with titles like *Unknown Earth* and *Strange Planet*. It was Corliss, who pointed out to me the investigations of Dr John de Laurier of Ottawa, who in 1974 went to camp on the ice-floes of northern Canada in search of an enormous magnetic anomaly 43 miles long, which he believes to originate about 18 miles below the surface of the earth. De Laurier's theory is that such anomalies are due to the earth's tectonic plates rubbing together – an occurrence that also causes earthquakes.

The central point to emerge from all this is that our earth is not like an ordinary bar magnet, whose field is symmetrical and precise; it is full of magnetic "pitfalls" and anomalies. Scientists are not sure why the earth has a magnetic field, but one theory suggests that it is due to movements in its molten iron core. Such movements would in fact produce shifting patterns in the earth's field, and bursts of magnetic activity, which might be compared to the bursts of solar energy known as sunspots. If they *are* related to earth-tensions and therefore to earthquakes then we would expect them to occur in certain definite zones, just as earthquakes do.

What effects would a sudden "earthquake" of magnetic activity produce? One would be to cause compasses to spin, for it would be rather as if a huge magnetic meteor was roaring up from the center of the earth. On the sea it would produce an effect of violent turbulence, for it would affect the water in the same way the moon affects the tides, but in an irregular pattern, so that the water would appear to be coming "from all directions." Clouds and mist would be sucked into the vortex, forming a "bank" in its immediate area. And electronic gadgetry would probably be put out of action . . .

Most often people take the "common sense route to an explanation. The Naval authorities in 1945 assumed that the disappearances were all due to natural causes, particularly to freak storms. In many cases it is difficult not to agree that this is indeed the most plausible explanation. But when we look at the long list of disappearances in the area, most of them never even yielding a body or a trace of wreckage, the explanation begins to sound thin.

Many people have come to believe that to simplify any answer to the Bermuda Triangle mystery discourages the investigation of what could be one of the most interesting scientific enigmas of our time. With satellites circling the earth at a height of 150 miles, it should be possible to observe bursts of magnetic activity with the same accuracy that earth tremors are recorded on seismographs. We should be able to observe their frequency and intensity precisely enough to plot them in advance. The result could not only be the solution of the mystery, but the prevention of future tragedies like that of Flight 19.

Classic One-Liners
Jack Benny on his reputation for prudence: "It's absolutely true. I don't want to tell you how much insurance I carry with the Prudential, but all I can say is – when I go, they go."

40

In Kentucky, it is illegal to transport an ice-cream cone in your pocket.

In Louisana, it is illegal to rob a bank and then shoot at the bank teller with a water pistol.

In Louisana, biting someone with your natural teeth is "simple assault," while biting someone with your false teeth is "aggravated assault."

In Massachusetts, mourners at a wake may not eat more than three sandwiches.

In Massachusetts, snoring is prohibited unless all bedroom windows are closed and securely locked.

In Florida, men may not be seen publicly in any kind of strapless gown.

In Massachusetts, an old ordinance declares goatees illegal unless you first pay a special license fee for the privilege of wearing one in public.

In Willowdale, Oregon, no man may curse while having sex with his wife.

In Texas, 16-year-old divorced girls are prohibited from talking about sex during high school extracurricular activities.

Hollywood Quotes

Dorothy Parker: "If all the people attending the Yale Prom were laid end to end, I wouldn't be at all surprised."

Dorothy Parker, when told that socialite Claire Booth Luce was always kind to her inferiors, asked: "Wherever does she find them?"

Groucho Marx: "I've been around so long I knew Doris Day before she was a virgin."

Groucho Marx to his hostess as he left a party: "I've had a lovely evening. But this wasn't it."

Groucho Marx: "A man is only as old as the woman he feels."

Groucho Marx: "Anyone who says he can see through women is missing a lot."

W.C. Fields: "If at first you don't succeed, try, try again. Then give up. No use being a damn fool about it."

Film star Ava Gardner: "Deep down I'm pretty superficial."

Woody Allen: "If my film makes even one more person miserable, I feel I've done my job."

Woody Allen: "It's not that I'm afraid to die. I just don't want to be there when it happens."

Joe Frisco on Hollywood Smog: "This is the only town where you can wake up and hear the birds coughing in the trees."

Novelist and screen writer Scott Fitzgerald: "You always knew where you stood with Sam Goldwyn – nowhere . . ."

Sid Grauman said: "I saw this empty taxicab drive up, and out stepped Sam Goldwyn."

Sam Goldwyn: Anyone who goes to a psychiatrist should have his head examined.

Goldwyn explained the crowds at Louis B. Mayer's funeral: "The only reason so many people showed up was to make sure he was dead."

Film producer Harry Cohn: "Give me two years and I'll make her an overnight star."

Harry Cohn, after sacking a director: "Never let that bastard back in here – unless we need him."

Fascinating Facts

The first best-selling novel was Samuel Richardson's *Pamela*, or *Virtue Rewarded* (1740), which went into edition after edition, and was translated into most European languages. Rousseau's *La Nouvelle Heloise* (1760) was even more popular, so much so that lending libraries would lend it out by the hour. The first American best-seller was *Charlotte Temple* (1791) by an Englishwoman, Susanna Haswell Rowson, a rather melodramatic book that went through 200 editions.

The word "gat" – American slang for a gun – was derived from the Gatling gun, the world's first machine-gun, which was invented during the American Civil War by Richard Jordan Gatling.

The practice of tapping a patient's chest was invented by an Austrian doctor, Leopold Auenbrugger, who used to watch his father – a wine manufactrer – tapping wine barrels to find out how full they were.

In the early days of World War I, French airmen carried bags of bricks in their planes. Machine-guns were not in use, since the problem of firing through the propeller had not yet been solved. The French tried to bring down German planes by throwing bricks into their propellers, with only limited success – only two planes were ever brought down by this method.

Comedian Red Skelton, on the crowds at Harry Cohn's funeral: "It proves what they always say: give the public what they want and they'll come out for it."

Orson Welles on pop singer Donny Osmond: "He has Van Gogh's ear for music."

Hollywood writer Gene Fowler on an editor: "He should have a pimp for a brother so he'd have somebody to look up to."

Hollywood writer Wilson Mizner on Jack Warner: "He has oilcloth pockets so he can steal soup."

Columnist Walter Winchell on Hollywood: "The place where they shoot too many pictures and not enough actors."

Herrnan Manciewicz on Louis B. Mayer: "There but for the grace of God goes God."

Comedian Will Rogers on Congress: "Every time they make a joke it's a law, and every time they make a law, it's a joke."

Much-married film star Mickey Rooney: "I'm the only man who has a marriage licence made out To Whom It May Concern."

Actor Beerbohm Tree, to a man in the street who was staggering under the weight of a grandfather clock: "My poor fellow, why not carry a watch?"

Bette Davis on a starlet: "There goes the good time that was had by all."

Actress Tallulah Bankhead: "I'm as pure as the driven slush."

Science: How it Works

How We Hear Sounds

Sound is actually nothing more than moving air and the way we perceive that moving air with our ears. Your eardrums pick up the vibrations and send them to your brain where they are translated into what the brain perceives as sound.

People in History

Strange Historical Stories

Bad King James

One afternoon King James VI of Scotland, later to become King
James I of England, was out hunting near Perth, when his friend
Alexander Ruthven, a beautiful boy and the brother of the
much-loved Earl of Gowrie, rode up to him and asked him
over for supper in Gowrie's castle nearby. After some
hemming and hawing, the King, who liked the company of
beautiful boys, agreed and Alexander rode off home to make
preparations.

The King duly arrived at Gowrie's castle with a small
company of men and was given a modest supper – due to the
lack of time for preparation. According to some reports the Earl
of Gowrie behaved rather strangely at supper and didn't spend
as much time talking to the King as he ought to have. The King,
at least, was keen to tell everyone that the Earl had behaved
strangely.

Just as the meal was ending, young Alexander and the King
went off together to an upper room in the castle where according
to the King – Ruthven promised to introduce the King to a Jesuit
spy he had caught that afternoon. About half an hour into the

48

enquiry, which, for reasons best known to the King, involved him and Ruthven being locked by themselves in a room containing nothing but a bed, a number of people in the street below the bedroom window heard a loud hullabaloo emanating from the chamber in which they knew the King was conducting a special, private investigation. Worried for their monarch's safety, they quickly alerted the King's soldiers who rushed up to the room and found James and Alexander on their own, apparently wrestling. Alexander was immediately killed by the guards.

The Earl of Gowrie ran to the bedroom to discover his brother dead on the floor. King James immediately claimed that the two men had plotted to kill him and that he had somehow miraculously escaped the effects of treason – well, what else could he say? – and Gowrie too was instantaneously executed.

A huge number of influential people all over Europe didn't believe the King, who immediately started ferreting around for evidence to incriminate the Earl and his brother. Not a single person could be found to give evidence against the young nobles, and there was a storm of protest. According to the brutal custom of the time, the corpses of the brothers were taken to Edinburgh and subjected to the pantomime of a trial. In October (when they had already been dead for ten weeks in mid-

---

Classic One-Liners
Lincoln on General Burnside: "Only he could snatch a spectacular defeat out of the jaws of victory."

49

summer) the rotting bodies were hanged, drawn, and quartered and their heads were stuck on poles above Cowgate in Edinburgh.

None of this prevented James succeeding to the English throne just three years later.

Cosmology

Light takes approximately 8 minutes and 18 seconds to reach the earth from the sun.

The distance between the Earth and the Moon varies from about 360,000 to 405,000 kilometers, depending on the position in the Moon's orbit.

The Sun is roughly 1.4 million kilometres (900,000 miles) across compared to the Earth's 13,000 kilometres (8,000 miles) across.

Mercury is the closest planet to the sun.

The most recently discovered planet is Quaoar.

The Sun is made up of about 70 per cent hydrogen and 28 per cent helium by mass.

The sun is powered by fusion, the same as a hydrogen bomb.

The sun is about 5 billion years old.

The earth is about 4.5 billion years old.

IT'S THE LAW

In Florida, it is illegal to sing in a public place while attired in a swimsuit.

In Florida, a special law prohibits unmarried women from parachuting on Sunday or she shall risk arrest, fine, and/or jailing.

In Florida, if an elephant is left tied to a parking meter, the parking fee has to be paid just as it would for a vehicle.

Hotel owners in Hastings, Nebraska are required by law to provide a clean, white cotton nightshirt to each guest. According to the law, no couple may have sex unless they are wearing the nightshirts.

In Illinois, it is illegal for anyone to give lighted cigars to dogs, cats, and other domesticated animal kept as pets.

In Indiana, bathing is prohibited during the winter.

In Indiana citizens are not allowed to attend a movie house or theater nor ride in a public streetcar within at least four hours after eating garlic.

In Massachusetts, taxi drivers are prohibited from having sex in the front seat of their taxi during their shifts.

In Bozeman, Montana, you can't perform any sexual acts in the front yard of any home, after sundown, or if you are nude.

The Universe is at least 15 billion years old, but probably no more than 20 billion years old.

Jupiter is the fastest-spinning planet in our solar system, rotating on average once every 10 hours.

Venus is the slowest-spinning planet in the solar system. It rotates only once every 243 Earth days.

A Martian year is 686.9726 days, matching the orbital period.

The movements of the sunspots indicate that the Sun rotates once every 27 days at the equator, but only once in 31 days at the poles.

The Milky Way is huge, its mass is probably between 750 billion and one trillion solar masses, and its diameter is about 100,000 light years.

The Milky Way is a spiral galaxy.

The star closest to the sun is Proxima Centauri, the nearest member of the Alpha Centauri triple star system.

Joke of the Day
How does a pig go to hospital? In an hambulance.

Fascinating Facts

There were more opium addicts in America – per head of population – in 1865 than there are today. During the Civil War, opium was used as an anaesthetic during operations, and created 100,000 addicts in a population of 40 million. Today, with a population of 200 million, there are about 300,000 addicts.

The invention of transparent sticky tape was delayed by unsuccessful attempts to find a way of preventing the rubber-based gum from sticking to the back of the tape when wound into a roll. Finally, it was discovered that the experiments had been unnecessary: the gum has a natural tendency to remain only on one side of the tape.

Some clams in Australia's coral reef are ten feet long and weigh more than a ton.

The world hiccup record is held by Vera Strong of Tennessee, who hiccupped for fifty-eight days without a break.

Mother Goose was a real person – the authoress of songs and jingles published in 1716. Her name was Elizabeth Foster. She was born in 1665, married Isaac Goose at the age of twenty-eight, and died in Boston, where her nursery rhymes were published, at the age of ninety-two.

Beasts and Monsters

Was She A Werewolf?

By the admission of William Seabrook who tells the story, it was perfectly true that Nastatia Filipovna was not ordinary. A Russian aristocrat who had fled the revolution, she seemed slightly larger than life. She was tall and powerful with challenging tawny eyes. She had a fearful temper, but also charm when she chose to use it. She didn't like reality – it bored her – but although she fell into a self-induced trance easily, she didn't like that world either.

Then she decided to try the I Ching, the ancient Chinese method of opening the mind to future possibilities. For Nastatia Filipovna it seemed to open a door. "But it's opening into the outdoors!" she murmured. "Everything is white – everywhere snow. I am lying in the snow . . . I am lying naked in my fur coat . . . and I am warm."

Joke of the Day
Why did the python go to the army?
He was coiled up.

She moved restlessly and muttered: "I'm running lightly like the wind . . . how good the snow smells!" She began to make unhuman sounds, like a wolf baying. Alarmed, her friends tried to rouse her. Her face changed. Her tawny eyes wide open. the wolf-woman sprang straight for a friend's throat. She fell short. Her companions snared her in blankets and held ammonia under her nose. She came out of it.

But Nastasia Filipovna remembered. And she liked it.

The One Minute Novel

Moby Dick – H. Melville (1851)

Moby Dick was a ferocious and feared whale that had caused many disasters. On one such occasion it had bitten off the leg of Captain Ahab. Captain Ahab was understandably a little unhappy about this and set about getting his revenge.

He set off in a ship called *Pequod*. Onboard with him were lots of weird and wonderful (if a little strange) people. However, Captain Ahab was weirder than all of them because of his monomaniac need to get this particular whale whom he believed was his own personal enemy.

They searched three-quarters of the globe until they eventually found Moby Dick and had a nasty fight with the whale that lasted three days. At the end of the story Moby breaks Ahab's neck then crunches and sinks all the boats before finally sinking the *Pequod* herself which sinks with all hands except for one survivor left to tell the tale.

Classic One-Liners
Mark Twain: "I have overcome my will-power and taken up smoking again."

ANIMAL SCIENCE

When a female horse and male donkey mate, the offspring is called a mule, but when a male horse and female donkey mate, the offspring is called a hinny.

A donkey will sink in quicksand but a mule won't.

Pigs, walruses, and light-colored horses can be sunburned.

Today's cattle are descended from two species: wild aurochs – fierce and agile herd animals that populated Asia, North Africa, and Europe – and eotragus – an antelope-like, Asian forest creature.

Horses cannot vomit.

Goat's eyes have rectangular pupils.

A 1,200-pound horse eats about seven times its own weight each year.

A capon is a castrated rooster.

A Cornish game hen is really a young chicken, usually 5 to 6 weeks of age, that weighs no more than 2 pounds.

A cow gives nearly 200,000 glasses of milk in her lifetime.

A Holstein's spots are like a fingerprint or snowflake. No two cows have exactly the same pattern of spots.

Real Ghost Stories

The Flying Monk

St Joseph of Copertino became known as the "flying monk" because of the way he levitated during ecstatic states. Born Giuseppe Desa in 1603, he was a strange and sickly child. As a teenager with strong religious tendencies – and later as a monk – he tortured himself for penance. But in moments of rapturous joy, usually inspired by religious feeling, Joseph rose in the air with loud shouts and, sometimes, wild movements.

At the age of 22, Joseph became a Franciscan monk in the district of Copertino in southern Italy. He became known to the neighboring people for his kindness and holiness, even though his noisy levitations disturbed his fellow friars. In fact, he was not allowed to join the rest of his brothers in the choir. One day he went away from the others into an obscure corner of the chapel to pray by himself. Suddenly he cried out with special intensity, rose straight up into the air and – to the astonishment of all present – flew to the altar. With another cry, he flew back to his corner in a kneeling position, and then began to whirl around in song and dance. Joseph was investigated by the Church, but was acquitted of the charge of practicing deception by false miracles.

People in History

Strange Historical Stories

The Piltdown Man

In 1913 Charles Dawson, a solicitor and amateur anthropologist, was digging about in a gravel pit in Sussex when he came across the skull fragments and bones of a creature which looked remarkably human. He published his findings in the Quarterly Journal of the Geological Society of London claiming that, at last, here was the incontrovertible evidence for Charles Darwin's theory of evolution – he had discovered the remains of the missing link in the evolutionary chain between ape and man. It was remarkably fortunate for believers in the Empire that the earliest man just happened to be British. The reconstructed skull was named Eoanthropus Dawsoni as a tribute to the man who found it and the whole scientific world was abuzz with the news.

Meanwhile back in Piltdown, the closest village to the site of the gravel pit in which the bones were found, all sorts of things were happening. The town had become a tourist attraction and coachloads of eminent scientists were to be seen wandering around the area and checking out the site. Further evidence was found to support the original claim and the bones were given to

 # Boobs and Misprints

Early in his career as a senator, John F. Kennedy began a speech at a Democratic convention: "I was almost late here today, but I had a very good taxi driver who brought me through the traffic jam. I was going to give him a very large tip and tell him to vote Democrat, and then I remembered some advice Senator Green had given me. So I gave him no tip at all, and told him to vote Republican." Associated Press ran the story, and Kennedy received dozens of angry letters from cab drivers – as a result of which he had to persuade Associated Press to print another story explaining it was supposed to be a joke.
Theodore Sorenson

The MP for west England and Berkeley reckons that a thousand or more Conservatives abstained from voting specifically because of the homosexuality issue. "I reckoned I was endangering my seat."
The Times

"Did you watch the Olympics last night? If you did, chances are you're not reading this, but taking a well-earned snooze instead."
The News (Southampton)

the British Museum who were just thrilled at their own importance and sent copies of the bones to musems all over the world. Piltdown Man had a place in history.

Years later, when dating techniques had improved beyond recognition, the bones were reexammed and discovered to be not 500,000 years old, as Charles Dawson had believed, but a mere 50,000. Piltdown Man's teeth were twentieth-century and, rather more drastically, not actually human at all but those of an orang-utan.

Mysteries of the World

Atlantis
Atlantis, the fabled lost continent, is first mentioned in Plato's
dialogues between *Timaeus* and *Critias* written around 350 BC.
There it is described as an enormous island "beyond the Pillars
of Hercules" (the Straits of Gibraltar). On this island, civilization flourished long before Athens was founded in 9600 BC.
The inhabitants were great engineers and aggressive warriors,
harassing early European and Asian civilization until the
Athenians finally conquered them on their own territory. At that
point great floods overwhelmed the island, and both the
Athenian army and the Atlantean civilization disappeared
beneath the ocean in a day and a night.

Plato describes their culture and territory in detail. The city
was eleven miles in diameter, formed from concentric rings of
land and water. The Atlanteans were fed by crops grown on a
large plain 230 by 340 miles located behind the city. Plato
describes their buildings and their habits, setting the pattern for
all future Utopian literature; indeed that is all that his writings
on Atlantis were considered to be for roughly 2,000 years. Then
in 1882, Ignatius Donnelly, American senator and well-read
theorist published a book suggesting that Plato's "fable" was
based upon a real civilization. He pointed out that scientists
were now relatively certain that continents do appear and

ANIMAL SCIENCE

A normal cow's stomach has four compartments: the rumen, the recticulum (storage area), the omasum (where water is absorbed), and the abomasum (the only compartment with digestive juices).

A quarter of the horses in the USA died of a vast virus epidemic in 1872.

It is physically impossible for pigs to look up into the sky.

Brown eggs come from hens with red feathers and red ear lobes; white eggs come from hens with white feathers and white ear lobes. Shell color is determined by the breed of hen and has no effect on its quality, nutrients, or flavor.

Cats in Halifax, Nova Scotia, have a very high probability of having six toes.

A cat's jaw can not move sideways.

Armadillos can be house broken.

Armadillos have four babies at a time, always all the same sex. They are perfect quadruplets, the fertilized cell split into quarters, resulting in four identical armadillos.

Armadillos get an average of 18.5 hours of sleep per day.

disappear beneath the waves, and that earthquakes and volcanic activity are capable of terrible damage. Much of the minutiae of Donnelly's argument proves to be inaccurate on close examination, but the idea that there was an entirely lost civilization beneath the waves proved too romantic to be stifled.

Atlantis has been associated with Lyoness, the sunken area of land between Land's End in Cornwall and the Isles of Scilly. Regular patterns of stones and carvings found on the sea bed near Bimini in the Bahamas have been identified as Atlantean. More plausible in some ways is Professor Angelos Galanopoulos's theory that Santorini in the Mediterranean was the source of Plato's story.

Santorini is a volcanic island whose last major explosion was in 1,500 BC. The eruption ripped the island apart and sent a tidal wave out that devastated many surrounding islands. Only two problems exist with this explanation. Firstly Santorini is a great deal too small to be Plato's Atlantis. Galanopoulos explains this by positing an error in transcription that multiplied all the figures Plato gives by a factor of ten. Indeed if one does remove a nought from all of Plato's measurements a fair approximation of Santorini's size does appear. The second problem is more difficult to resolve: Santorini is on the wrong side of the Pillars of Hercules. Galanopoulos's arguments on this score are more difficult to credit, as they place the Pillars of Hercules at the southernmost promontories of Greece. The area of Atlantean subjugation according to Plato does not marry well with this revision; Santorini is only marginally more likely as a sight for Atlantis than Cornwall.

The story of Atlantis still fascinates, but without more positive evidence it must be regarded as more a cautionary tale than a historical treatise.

Out of Body Experiences

The Diver's Suit

"I neither drink nor take drugs, and all I brought to my bed was a considerable nervous exhaustion which sleep was required to restore." So begins William Gerhardie's description of his out-of-the-body experience in his semi-autobiographical novel *Resurrection*.

When he became conscious in his astral body he was suspended in mid-air, light as a feather. Once on his feet he felt as if he were defying gravity. In appearance he seemed identical to his physical body on the bed, to which he was attached by a luminous cable. When he tried to open the door, he found he could not turn the handle. Then he discovered that he could pass right through the door, and he moved around the apartment, making observations, lit by his own cord.

His new body responded to his thoughts and floated this way and that according to his whims. Part of him wished to fly to distant places, but part was afraid this might sever the link with the sleeping body.

When he awoke, he found that his earlier ideas of life after death had been shattered. It seemed to him that. we already have a body stored away, rather like a diver's suit, in our own everyday bodies, "always at hand in case of death or for special use."

IT'S THE LAW

In Ames, Iowa, a husband may not take more than three gulps of beer while lying in bed with his wife.

A law in Oblong, Illinois makes it a crime to have sex while fishing or hunting on your wedding day.

If a police officer in Coeur d'Alene, Idaho, suspects a couple is having sex inside a vehicle they must honk their horn three times, and wait two minutes before being allowed to approach the scene.

In Ventura County, California, cats and dogs are not allowed to have sex without a permit.

A law in Fairbanks, Alaska, does not allow moose to have sex on city streets.

A Helena, Montana, law states that a woman cannot dance on a saloon table unless her clothing weighs more than three pounds, two ounces.

In Connorsville, Wisconsin, it is forbidden for a man to shoot a gun while his female partner is having a sexual orgasm.

Hotels in Sioux Falls, South Dakota, are required by law to furnish their rooms with twin beds only. There should be a minimum of two feet between the beds, and it is illegal for a couple to make love on the floor between the beds.

Joke of the Day
Model: 'That painting you did of me doesn't do me justice.' Artist: 'It's not justice you want, it's mercy!'

The Safari Crash

The biologist and author Lyall Watson was driving with a safari party through the bush of Kenya when suddenly the little bus skidded in the dust and overturned. It rolled over twice and then balanced on the edge of a gully.

A moment later, Watson found himself standing outside the bus looking at it. And yet he could see his own physical body slumped unconscious in the front seat of the bus. A more alarming sight was the head and shoulders, of a young boy who had been pushed through the canvas top of the vehicle when it had come to a stop. If the bus fell into the gully – which seemed likely – the boy would be crushed.

The thought scarcely crossed his mind when Watson found himself regaining consciousness in the front of the bus. He rubbed the red dust from his eyes. The memory of what he had just seen was extraordinarily vivid. At once he climbed through the window of the bus and freed the boy, moments before the vehicle rolled over.

Telling the story in his book *The Romeo Error*, published in 1974, Watson said "there is no doubt in my own mind that my vantage point at that moment was detached from my body," but he was unable to provide a scientific explanation for his experience.

The Glorious Sky

The records of the Society for Psychical Research include the following account: "One grey windy day in 1929 a man named Robert went for a swim in the ocean with a friend named Mildred. He had an extraordinary experience, which he related some years later.

The sea was rough that day and the current extremely strong. He was about to head for shore when he heard a faint cry from a frightened youngster clinging desperately to a board. Robert managed to reach him and hoist him onto the board just before he himself was overcome by a mountainous wave. He felt himself sinking. Suddenly, he found himself high above the water and looking down upon it. The sky, which had been grey and menacing, glowed with a glorious light. Waves of color and music vibrated around him, and he felt an indescribable peace.

Then below him he saw his friend Mildred in a rowboat with two men. Floating near them was a limp and ungainly object that he recognized as his own body. He felt a great sense of relief that he no longer needed it. The men pulled the body out of the water and lifted it into the boat. The next thing he knew, he was lying on the beach, cold and aching. He later learned that it had taken two hours to revive him. His help had saved the boy from drowning."

Classic One-Liners
Humourist Don Marquis on an acquaintance: "He is so unlucky that he runs into accidents that started out to happen to somebody else."

Predictions of Catastrophe

"Having found, Sir, that the City of London should be sadly afflicted with a great plague, and not long after with an exorbitant fire; I framed these two hieroglyphics . . . which in effect have proved very true." So spoke William Lilly, a seventeenth-century astrologer, suspected of intrigue in the Great Fire of London by a government inquiry committee in 1666. One of the astrologer's "hieroglyphics" of prophecy is a drawing of Gemini, the sign of the City of London, falling into flames, and it was done fifteen years before the fire that destroyed most of London. According to Lilly's report about the Parliamentary committee, he was released with "great civility".

Out-of-Body Experience

Few people have had the strange experience of seeing their own body from outside it. One man who did is a British Army colonel. It happened when he was desperately ill with pneumonia. Through the haze of his illness he heard his doctor say there was nothing more that could be done. The colonel, however, promised himself, "You shall get better." He then felt his body getting heavier and heavier, and suddenly discovered he was sitting on top of the cupboard in the corner of the room. He was watching a nurse tending his own unshaven, apparently unconscious body. The colonel was aware of all the small details of the room. He saw the mirror on the dressing table, the frame of the bed, and his inert body under the bedclothes.

The next thing he remembers he was back in his body, and the nurse was holding his hand and murmuring, "The crisis has passed."

During his convalescence he told the nurse what had happened to him, describing the exact motions she had made

 # Boobs and Misprints

"It is quite amazing how much damage and destruction these mindless vandals can cause when they put their minds to it," said a bitter Mr Rattray last night.
Courier and Advertiser

"Fortunately for me, at the time when sex was beginning to loom in my life as an enormous and insoluble problem, I began to take an interest in keeping animals."
Armand Denise, News of The World

"Mr Wielden was taken to Warwick Hospital for treatment but escaped serious injury."
Leamington Spa Morning News

"Miss Morrison, a sociologist and police management researcher at Southclyde University near Glasgow, said she decided to go to Philadelphia because there were sixty-five rapes a month there."
The Star (South Africa)

"NO WATER – SO FIREMEN IMPROVIZED"
Liverpool Daily Post

and the details of the room that had been so clear to him. She suggested that perhaps he had been delirious.

The colonel had a different answer. "I was dead for that time," he said.

Astral Projection?

Among the cases in the records of the Society for Psychical Research is the story of a distinguished Italian engineer. He wrote that one June, studying hard for his examinations, he had fallen into a very deep sleep during which he apparently knocked over his kerosene lamp. Instead of going out, it gave off a dense smoke that filled the room. He gradually became aware that the thinking part of him had become entirely separate from his sleeping physical body. His independent mind recognized that to save his life he should pick up the fallen lamp and open the window. But he could not make his physical body wake up and respond in any way.

Then he thought of his mother, asleep in the next room, and he saw her clearly through the wall. He saw her hurriedly get up, go to the window, and throw it open as if carrying out the thought in his mind. He also saw her leave her room and come into his. She came to his body and touched it, and at her touch he was able to rejoin his physical body. He woke up with dry throat, throbbing temples, and a choking feeling.

Later his mother verified that she had opened the window before coming in to him – exactly as he had seen it through a solid wall.

Amazing Engineering Facts

A Brief History of Automobiles

In 1895, Thomas Edison predicted the future importance of the automobile in a newspaper, guessing correctly that it would only be a matter of time before cities and towns were full of the motorized "horseless carriage." Henry Ford later took the automobile into mass production with the "Tin Lizzie." Here are the important dates in a century of car production.

1901 – The Telescopic Shock Absorber
The "telescopic" shock absorber was designed in 1901 by C.L. Horock. A metal sleeve housed a pistol with a one-way valve and a cylinder. For a journey that wasn't as bumpy as earlier automobiles, air or oil moved from the valve into the cylinder, allowing the piston to move freely in one direction but be blocked in the opposite direction by the flowing air or oil coming through the one-way valve. In fact, we still use this design for shock absorption today.

1901 – The Olds Automobile Factory
In Detroit in 1901, Ransom E. Olds helped to originate the way we build cars today by contracting to outside companies for car parts, kicking off the mass production of automobiles. The big

Fascinating Facts

The most extraoridnary contest in the history of wrestling
was the one that was held between William Muldoon, the
"Solid Man," and Clarence Whistler, the "Kansas Demon,"
in 1880 in New York. They battled for nine hours
and thirty-eight minutes, until each collapsed from
exhaustion.

A ton of gold would be worth less at the Equator than at
the Poles. At the Equator, the centrifugal force of the
Earth's spin counteracts the force of gravity, and causes the
gold to weigh fractionally less.

All the gold in the world could be placed in a pile beneath
the curved base of the Eiffel Tower.

Ladak in Kashmir in the Himalayas has the greatest
temperature ranges in the world. The temperature can
drop from 160 degrees in the daytime to 45 degrees at
night.

All thoroughbred race horses in the world are descended
from three Eastern horses imported into England in the
early eighteenth century: they were known as the Byerly
Turk, the Darley Arabian, and the Godolphin Barb.
Although 174 sires are mentioned in the first General Stud
Book, these are the only three whose descent remained
intact.

success of the company was the Oldsmobile. Selling for
$650,425 were made in the factory's first year of production.
By 1905, 5,000 Oldsmobiles were being sold each year.

1902 – Invention of the Standard Drum Brakes
Louis Renault invented a brake that worked by using a cam to
separate two hinged shoes. These brakes are the standard for
rear wheels today.

1908 – General Motors
General Motors was formed in 1908 by William Durant. Making
car parts and automobiles his company became the largest and
best-known automobile company around the globe.

1908 – Henry Ford and the Model T
Ford sold 10,660 cars in its first year of production. Mass
production was now the way forward.

1911 – The Electric Starter
The electric starter was first used by Charles Kettering. This
ground-breaking method abolished the need for hand cranking.
In 1912 the electric starter was being used for the first time in
cadillacs.

1913 – The First Assembly Line at Ford
In 1913 the rolling assembly line was introduced. With this
method, workers could stay in one place, rather than having to walk
around the factory, and the car parts would be brought to them
using machines. Car workers now worked on single tasks rather
than developing the ability to assemble a whole car themselves.
300,000 cars were built by Ford in Michigan in 1914 resulting in
Ford lowering the price of its Model T and allowing ordinary

Joke of the Day
"Dad, can I have another glass of water please?" "But that's the tenth one I've given you tonight!" "Yes, but the baby's room is still on fire."

people to begin buying their own cars. Over the next 14 years, Ford continued to drop the price of the Model T.

1914 – Cars Made from Steel
Budd Company made the first car entirely built from steel, the Dodge, in Detroit.

1919 – Single Foot Pedal Brakes
A French luxury car, the Hispano-Suiza H6B was made with a single foot brake to operate four wheels. Prior to this drivers used both a hand brake and foot brake simultaneously.

1922 – Hydraulic Four Wheel Brakes
Hydraulic brakes operated by using a master cylinder in a hydraulic system to ensure that pressure was even on each car wheel when the driver pressed on the brake pedal with his foot. The first American car to use this system was the Duesenberg, made in Indianapolis.

1926 – Power Steering
Francis Wright Davis created the first power-steering system by integrating the steering linkage with a hydraulics system.

ANIMAL SCIENCE

Cats have over 100 vocal sounds, while dogs only have about ten.

Mice, whales, elephants, giraffes, and man all have seven neck vertebrae.

Murphy's Oil Soap is the chemical most commonly used to clean elephants.

Many hamsters only blink one eye at a time.

Hamsters love to eat crickets.

In the last 4,000 years, no new animals have been domesticated.

There are only two animals with blue tongues, the Black Bear and the Chow dog.

A 1,200-pound horse eats about seven times its own weight each year.

A chimpanzee can learn to recognize itself in a mirror, but a monkey can't.

1931 – The Modern Independent Front Suspension System
Mercedez-Benz made each front wheel more or less independent
of the other wheel even though they were attached to the same
axle. This prevented the transfer of road shock from one wheel
to the other and made it easier to handle the car.

1934 – Four-Wheel-Drive Car is Mass Produced
The French first succeeded in producing the four-wheel drive.
The Citroen Traction Avant was an all-steel frame car.

1935 – Left and Right Turn Signals Introduced.
A thermal interrupter switch created the prototype of modern
indicator signals. Electricity was used to create a circuit switch
that reached a light bulb when the switch was turned on.
Thermal interrupters were phased out in the 1960's when
transistor circuits were introduced.

1939 – Air Conditioning
The Nash Motor Company introduced an air conditioning
system to cars

1940 – The Jeep
Known as the workhorse of World War 2, the jeep was designed
by Karl Pabst. More than 360,000 were made for the Allied
armed forces. At the same time Oldsmobile developed the first
fully automatic massed-produced car.

1950 – Cruise Control
Interestingly, a blind man called Ralph Teeter who could sense,
using just his ears that cars travel at uneven speeds, developed
cruise control. In the 1940s he began to develop a mechanism to
hold the car at a steady speed. At first unpopular, more than per
cent of today's cars have cruise control.

1960s – Environmental Issues

By the end of the twentieth century, hydrocarbon emissions were reduced by 95 per cent. In the 1960s car manufacturers began to try to reduce harmful emissions. PCV valves (positive crankcase ventilation), directed gases back to cylinders to be combusted further. Catalytic converters were eventually introduced in the 1970s.

1966 – Electronic Fuel Injection

In order to keep a car's engine operating at its most efficient, an electronic fuel injection system was developed in the UK. This system delivers fuel and air in a much more controlled way than before.

1970s – Airbags

Airbags were first introduced in some cars in the 1970s on the driver's side. Today they have become standard in most cars and appear on the passenger side too. Also, in the 1970s as fuel prices rose, there was great demand for a fuel-efficient car. The Japanese car industry became globally dominant as demand increased for its smaller cars.

1980's – "Just in time" Delivery Developed in Japan

The Japanese method of delivery, "just in time", was applied to auto-parts to factories reducing demand for warehouse space and so reducing costs.

1985 – ABS (Antilock Braking System)

Teves of Germany made the first ABS braking system and the Lincoln became the first American car to offer the ABS system. The ABS system reduced skidding on emergency braking by allowing wheels to continue to move through a digital sensing of wheel movement and hydraulic pressure on each wheel and adjusted pressure accordingly, preventing the wheels from "locking up."

1992 – Energy Policy Act 1992
Experiments were conducted to find more environmentally friendly fuels for vehicles. Alcohols, gasolines, and battery power were all investigated.

1997 – Automatic Stability Control
Cadillac introduced automatic stability control which increased safety in emergency situations.

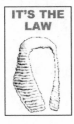

IT'S THE LAW

Belgium is the only country in the world never to have imposed censorship for adult films.

Chewing gum is outlawed in Singapore because it is a means of "tainting an environment free of dirt."

In Texas it's legal for a chicken to have sex with you, but it's illegal to reciprocate.

In Winnipeg, it is against the law to go naked in your own home if you leave the blinds up.

Dueling is legal in Paraguay as long as both parties are registered blood donors.

Impotence is grounds for divorce in 24 states in the United States.

Florida attempts to curb prostitution by giving prostitutes spending money, a five-year banishment, and a bus ticket out of town.

In Alaska it is illegal to look at a moose from the window of an airplane or any other flying vehicle.

In 1838, the city of Los Angeles passed an ordinance requiring that a man obtain a license before serenading a woman.

Royal Scandal

The Mayerling Affair

The suicide of Archduke Rudolf of Habsburg after killing his
18-year-old mistress has been described as the greatest royal
scandal of modern times.

If Rudolf had lived, he would have presided over a collapsing
empire. The dynasty of the Habsburgs had dominated Europe for
700 years. But by the end of the nineteenth century, it had
spread itself too far; it had too many ill-assorted subjects and
great social changes were ripping apart the old fabric. Subject
nations wanted their independence. The 1848 revolution had
made the Rudolph's father, Emperor Franz Joseph determined to
resist all change but it was like trying to hold on the lid of a
pressure cooker by manual force.

Franz Joseph was a rigid disciplinarian, who rose at 4 a.m. to
work on state papers; his life was one of exact routine. His
empress, Elisabeth, was beautiful and sensitive and she found
the atmosphere of her husband's court – dominated by her
mother-in-law – impossible to stomach; she spent most of her
time traveling over Europe, permanently dissatisfied.

Her eldest son Rudolf had his father's obstinacy and his
mother's sensitiveness. Born in August 1858, he became an
army officer and took pride in the number of his sexual

 # Boobs and Misprints

"Dead-eye Stewart Fraser, who got three against the league of Ireland recently, attempted a shit from twenty yards, but was so wide of the target that he actually found Carlyle with his attempt. The outside-right was so surprised at the 'pass' that he made a mess of his shot at the goal."
Jewish Chronicle

"ABATTOIR BULL ESCAPES – ATTACKS VEGETARIAN"
Cape Times (South Africa)

"There was less weather than usual; last month."
Bristol Evening News

"Christian Democrat Senator Giovanni Leone was named as premiere-designate Wednesday night and given the task of forming a new government crisis."
Bangkok World

"Of the 16 lets bought in 1964, 42 have crashed. 'That's not a bad attrition record', Public Relations Officer Wing Commander Hancox said."
Midweek Territorian (NT)

89

> **Classic One-Liners**
> Critic James Agate: "The English instinctively admire a man who has no talent and is modest about it."

conquests, entering their names in a ledger – red for aristocrats, black for commoners. He grew bored with seduction and flirted with left-wing ideas. Later, he wrote newspaper articles that revealed he had considerable literary talent. He was indeed highly intelligent.

It seems conceivable that at some point he contracted venereal disease. What is certain is that he contracted the rich dilettante's disease of boredom and a sense of meaninglessness. "He seemed to doubt the validity of everything he did," says one commentator. His father declined to allow him any taste of responsibility. At 23 he was married to the 17-year-old Princess Stephanie of Belgium, a silly, selfish, empty-headed girl, who bore him a daughter. Rudolf became increasingly depressed and listless, and began to take morphine. When the German emperor inspected Franz Joseph's army in 1888, he protested that the infantry ought not to be in the charge of an incompetent like Rudolf; he was removed causing one more blow to his self-esteem.

Meanwhile, Maria Vetsera was an attractive teenager of Greek extraction, whose mother had married into the minor Austrian nobility. She caught a few glimpses of Rudolf in society and decided she was passionately in love with him. Through her friend, Countess Marie Larisch, who was Rudolf's cousin, she succeeded in being presented to him in the Prater in Vienna. Rudolf was not one to turn down the opportunity to accept a girl's virginity when it was offered; the two became lovers in 1888. By this time he was already brooding on suicide.

On 28 January 1889, Rudolf received a telegram from Budapest. As he threw it aside he was heard to mutter, "It has to be. There is no other way." He spent the day writing farewell letters, then set out for his hunting lodge at Mayerling. He had arranged to meet Maria on the way; that morning, she slipped away from her mother and made off in a carriage sent by Rudolf. It seems likely that she had already agreed to the suicide pact. They met at an inn.

Rudolf had arranged a hunting party at his lodge and various friends were also there. But on 29 January 1889, he protested that he had a cold and stayed indoors. That evening, he dined with Count Hoyos, while Maria stayed upstairs. When Hoyos left, Rudolf's valet, Loschek, entertained them by singing for them. They both wrote farewell letters – Maria told her sister: "We are both going blissfully into the uncertain beyond . . ." They then discussed whether they preferred to die by poison or a bullet and decided on the revolver. Maria noted this decision on an ashtray. They went up to the bedroom where Rudolf shot Maria immediately. He himself waited until six in the morning, when he went downstairs and told Loschek to prepare breakfast. He returned to his room, drank a glass of brandy, and shot

Joke of the Day
Time flies like an arrow, but fruit flies like a banana.

himself in the head. The bodies were discovered a few hours later.

It is still not clear why Rudolf killed himself and why he, a Catholic, chose to die with the murder of Maria Vetsera on his conscience. The answer to the latter question may be that he was a physical coward and wanted someone else to die with him. He was probably not in love with Maria for he had spent the night before leaving Vienna with a prostitute named Mitzi Caspar. It seems conceivable that she was as anxious to die with the man she adored as he was to have someone to die with him. He may even have felt he was conferring a favour on her by involving her in the suicide pact – after all, he was heir to the throne and she was a nobody.

In 1983, ex-Empress Zita, the last survivor of the Habsburg monarchy, caused a sensation when she announced that the double-suicide was really a political murder. She claimed that she had received this information from her husband, Emperor Karl, and from Prince Rudolf's sisters, Archduchess Gisela and Archduchess Marie-Valerie and her aunts Archduchess Maria Theresia and the Duchess Marie-José. "I have recorded precisely everything that was told to me under the seal of deepest secrecy. I intend to publish these documents which are among my personal papers when the time is right." According to the ex-empress, Prince Rudolf was assassinated because of his republican sympathies and because he had made many political enemies. In a cloister built out of part of the hunting lodge, Carmelite nuns in a silent order still pray day and night for the "three dead" of Mayerling. Why three, rather than two, remains another mystery; according to some, Maria Vetsera was expecting Rudolf's child.

The empress points out that an enormous amount of documentation has disappeared from the state archives,

including a 2,000-word telegram, which the emperor sent to
Pope Leo XIII arguing that in spite of the official suicide
explanation, his son had a right to a Christian burial. This
telegram has also disappeared from the Vatican archives.

In September 1898, the Empress Elisabeth was stepping into a
boat at Geneva when she was stabbed to death by a young
anarchist named Luigi Lucheni. There were those who felt her
death was a release. Since Rudolf's suicide she had been
wandering all over Europe like an unhappy shade. Rudolf was
succeeded as heir to the throne by his cousin, Archduke Franz
Ferdinand. It was the assassination of the archduke and his wife
at Sarajevo on 28 June 1914 that precipitated World War I, and
brought about the final destruction of the Austrian Empire.

The One Minute Novel

Macbeth – **William Shakespeare (1623)**

Macbeth and his friend Banquo were Scottish generals serving Duncan, King of Scotland. Contented after a successful bit of battle, the two buddies encountered three witches huddled around a cauldron speaking mysterious curses and nonsense. They told Macbeth that he would be appointed thane of Cawdor and then King and told Banquo that he would be the father of Kings though never King himself. Macbeth was made Thane of Cawdor by King Duncan soon after and together with his wife Lady Macbeth, excited by the prophecy of the witches, decided to kill the King of Scotland whilst he was staying at their castle. They succeeded in killing the King but Duncan's two sons, Malcolm and Donalbain escaped. Macbeth assumed the role of King of Scotland.

Macbeth and his wife, their megalomaniac aspirations showing no bounds by this time, decided to kill Banquo to prevent the

---

Classic One-Liners
Comedian Fred Allen: "What's on your mind? – if you'll forgive the overstatement."

Joke of the Day
"Doctor, I keep dreaming of bats,
creepy-crawlies, demons, ghosts,
monsters, vampires, werewolves, and
yetis." Doctor: "How interesting. Do you
always dream in alphabetical order?"

witches' second prophecy from coming true. They murdered
Macbeth's poor friend but Banquo's son escaped leaving the new
King and Queen to revel in the power of their reign.

Things after this though went downhill very rapidly.
Banquo's ghost, who seemed to show up at every opportunity,
haunted them, especially when they were having tasty banquets
with their new social hanger-on friends. Macbeth soon got fed
up with this and decided to go back to see the witches in an
attempt to put a stop to Banquo spoiling their fun as King
and Queen. The three witches told him to watch out for
Macduff, thane of Fife and assured him that he was safe as
long as Birnam Wood didn't come to Dunsinane, his Scottish
castle.

Some time later Macbeth heard the news that Duncan's son
Malcolm was gathering an army in England. Worried by this
news he marched on the castle of Macduff and killed
Macduff's wife and children. By this time, Macbeth and
his wife Lady Macbeth had killed so many people in their
paranoid quest to keep power that Lady Macbeth was in a
serious nervous breakdown state. She ranted and raved
around their castle shouting about ghosts and blood and
then died.

The army of Malcolm and Macduff attacked Macbeth by hiding in Birnam Woods and then advancing covering themselves in branches for camouflage. Macduff, no doubt furious at him for killing his family and insisting he was King, killed Macbeth.

Such revenge for Macduff was sweet and he became King of Scotland.

Beasts and Monsters

From the Deep

Late in the eighteenth century, a sailing ship off the coast of
West Africa found itself becalmed in a placid ocean. The wind
had dropped, and Jean-Magnus Dens, the Danish captain,
ordered his crew to lower planks off the side from which they
could scrape and clean the ship. Three men climbed onto the
planks and began their work. They were scraping energetically
when suddenly, out of the quiet sea around them, rose an
immense octopus or squid. It seized two of the men and pulled
them under the water. The third man leaped desperately into the
rigging, but a gigantic arm pursued him, getting caught up in the
shrouds. The sailor fainted from shock, and his horrified
shipmates frantically hacked at the great tentacle, finally
chopping it off. Meanwhile, five harpoons were being driven
into the body of the beast in the forlorn hope of saving the two
who had disappeared. The frightful struggle went on until, one
by one, four of the lines broke. The men had to give up the
attempt at killing the monster, which sank out of view.

The unconscious. sailor, hanging limply in the shrouds, was
gently taken down and placed in his bunk. He revived a little,
but died in raving madness that night.

Joke of the Day
At the surgery:
Mrs Smith: I've been getting out of breath lately.
Doctor Jones: No wonder, it's because you're so fat.
Mrs Smith: That's a terrible thing to say, I want a second opinion.
Doctor Jones: OK, you're ugly too.

People in History

Strange Historical Stories

Maiden Voyage

On 28 November 1720, a court in London was called to pass
sentence on a large number of pirates who had all been captured
in Jamaica. A certain Lieutenant Barret testified that he had
caught the whole bend of brigands by boarding their boat off the
north coast of the island and they had all been so unprofession-
ally drunk that they had all, except two, offered no resistance.

The whole crew were thus hauled to London in chains, the
two who had put up a fight being most securely manacled. One
of the two had even fired a shot at members of his own crew,
enraged at their lack of masculinity in the face of adversity. All
the other sailors had conceded defeat meekly, most being
incapable of coherent speech.

The death sentence was declared on every single member of
the crew and the court went through the ritual of asking if
anyone knew of a good reason why this should not be carried
out. Normally this question was met with stony silence. On this
occasion, however, the two boisterous young lads who had been
the only ones to offer resistance called out the age-old
expression "Milord, we plead our bellies." This was greeted by

---

Classic One-Liners
Poisoner William Palmer on the scaffold: "Are you sure this damn thing's safe?"

---

hoots of derisory laughter since it was the phrase used by young ladies to indicate that they were pregnant and thus could not be hanged. Everyone in the tribunal naturally considered that this was part of the general ribald exchange for which pirates were notorious and carried on laughing but the sailors would not give up. Eventually a court physician was called in to examine the two young men. He came back to the court to announce to a stunned audience and even more stunned crew that the two young men were, in fact, two young women and both were pregnant. The two women, whose stories are now well-known, were called Ann Bonny and Mary Read and both had succeeded in being mistaken for men over an admirably long period of time.

Ann Bonny was apparently the daughter of a serving maid and a married solicitor, born in the Irish town of Kinsale. The affair between her parents caused such a scandal that the two fled Ireland, her father leaving behind him a wife, two children and a hitherto highly respectable practice.

They set up home in Carolina and within a few years Ann's father had become a wealthy man. Ann's mother died and Ann became a potentially very wealthy and therefore much wooed inheritress. She appears to have been unusually independent for someone of her times. On one occasion an ardent fan received nothing for his flirtatious pains save a good, sound thrashing.

 # Boobs and Misprints

"Dr Olafson said that while the problem of teenage pregnancy was as acute in Jamaica, in Africa the causes were somewhat different."
Daily Gleaner

"Mr Ross George, chairman of a Wellington advertising company involved in producing television commercials, said advertisements may not reflect society exactly but they certainly mirror it."
Auckland Star

"No casualties were reported, but communication or the 135 mile railway – the only link between Addis Ababa and Djibouti – have been disrupted."
Evening Standard (London)

"Yesterday it was announced that Cram would run against his Olympic conqueror and former world 1500 metres record-holder Sebastian Cow this weekend, but Cram said: 'I am going to have to wait to see what sort of reaction I get with my calf."
Press and Journal (Aberdeen)

Very shortly after this Ann eloped with an apparently
unemployed sailor called James Bonny and the two of them
went to live on the romantically outlawed colony of New
Providence in the Bahamas, which had been set up by the
legendary Captain Woodes Rogers.

James Bonny turned out to be such a total waste of space that
he was not only a good-for-nothing sailor but an even worse
outlaw. He betrayed every pirate he came across to the
authorities and thus sustained the intense dislike of everyone
on the island, but particlarly that of his wife.

A proper pirate turned up on the island and immediately
captured the romantic imagination of Ann Bonny and she
decided to marry him instead. To be fair to the couple, and to
Ann's genteel upbringing, they did try to get what was known as
a divorce by sale from her first husband. This was a process
where, by mutual consent, a wife could be transferred by bill of
sale from one man to another. Bonny, true to form, betrayed
both of them to the governor of the islands and thus forced the
couple to effect a daring escape and head for the open seas. Ann
dressed up in seaman's clothes and, together, the pair overpow-
ered the night-watchman at the harbour, stole his boat and set
off to sea to join the most notorious boat on the waves, *Haman's
Sloop*. Extraordinarily, Rackam was the only man on board
who knew that Ann was a woman, even when she, apparently,
had to be set ashore in Cuba in order to give birth to their first
child.

Ann was clearly a woman of spirit. A little while after the
birth of her first child a new sailor appeared on board and Ann
was seriously attracted to him. She had to be very careful about
revealing her secret but, eventually, no longer being able to
control her lovelorn passion, she took the young man aside and
declared her undying love. Much to her astonishment, the young

man took off his hat to reveal his luscious long tresses – he was a she and she was called Mary Read. Rackam, who had been watching his wife with jealous intensity, leapt out from behind the mainsail in an insane fury and accosted the two women. They therefore had no choice but to share their secret with him. Mary Read's story appears to have been even more complicated than Ann's but she also appeared to have a husband on board who was even more spineless than Ann's. Mary had apparently already saved her husband from death by fighting a duel on his behalf and winning.

These bizarre anecdotes saved the two women from the gallows and instead they were no doubt thrilled to be sentenced to life. Mary Read died in childbirth in prison but Ann Bonny survived and, apparently, several of her father's former friends turned up to bail her out and took her back to Jamaica where she lived for many years in peaceful retirement.

Classic One-Liners
Mark Twain: "The holy passion of friendship is of so sweet and steady and loyal and enduring a nature that it will last through a whole lifetime, if not asked to lend money."

Real Ghost Stories

The Drummer

The magistrate of Tedworth in Wiltshire, England, could not have imagined the consequences when he confiscated the drum belonging to William Drury – an itinerant musician caught in some shady dealings – and told him to leave the district.

That was in March 1662. Hardly had the culprit left Tedworth when the drum began to produce drumming noises itself. It also flew around Magistrate Mompesson's house, seen by several people besides the magistrate.

After several sleepless nights, he had the drum broken into pieces. Still the drumming continued. Nor was that all. Shoes flew through the air, and chamber pots were emptied onto beds. Children were levitated. A horse's rear leg was forced into its mouth.

The possibility that the exiled drummer had sneaked back and was causing the trouble was fairly well ruled out when it was discovered that he had been arrested for theft in the city of Gloucester and sent to the colonies. The Reverend Joseph Glanville, chaplain to King Charles II, came to Tedworth to investigate the phenomena. He heard the drumming himself, and collected eyewitness reports from the residents. No natural cause was found for the effects, which stopped exactly one year after they had started.

The manager and staff of the Co-operative Stores in the English village of Long Wittenham, Berkshire, were not amused in late 1962 when jam jars, cereal boxes, and other normally stationary objects began flying off the shelves and circling overhead. In fact, one sales assistant fainted. To add to the confusion, the invisible prankster switched the lights on and off. For some mysterious reason, the poltergeist concentrated on the bicarbonate of soda, transferring boxes of the substance from the shelf to the window ledge.

After a week of chaos, the local vicar offered his services and exorcized the shop. The ritual proved effective, and groceries stayed put at last. The exhausted manager and staff set about restoring the stock to order. Despite the apparent success of the exorcizing ceremony, however, they decided to take precautions with the bicarbonate of soda. They put it under lock and key.

This case is one of many in which possible natural causes, such as earth tremors or an underground river, fail to provide a satisfactory explanation for flying objects. If such natural vibrations were responsible, for example, the bicarbonate of soda would hardly have been given such special attention.

Joke of the Day
What do you get if you pour boiling water down a rabbit hole?
Hot Cross Bunnies

Famous Music Name Changes

Adam Ant was born Stuart Leslie Goddard in 1954.

Syd Barrett was born Roger Keith Barrett, 1946.

Captain Beefheart was born Don Van Vliet, 1941.

Frank Black aka Black Francis was born Charles Michael
Kittridge Thompson IV.

Boy George was born George Alan O'Dowd, 1961 (in Kent,
England).

Cher was born Cherilyn Sarkisian LaPierre, 1946.

Alice Cooper was born Vincent Furnier, 1948.
There are various tales as to how this name change happened.
Some say that it was spelled out during a Ouija board session, or
was picked simply as an innocent-sounding All-American name.
Cooper himself apparently once said of his name, "a Baby-
Jane/Lizzie-Borden-sweet-and-innocent-with-a-hatchet-behind-
the-back kind of rhythm to it."

Fascinating Facts

It is possible to sail 200 miles into the Atlantic and still remain in fresh water, by sailing out from the mouth of the Amazon, which disgorges over 1,000,000 cubic feet of water a second into the sea. Ships far out at sea used to stock up with fresh water from this current – even though they were 200 miles from land.

On 13 February 1746, a Frenchman named Jean Marie Dunbarry was hanged for murdering his father. Precisely a century later, on 13 February 1846, another Jean Marie Dunbarry, great-grandson of the other, was also hanged for murdering his father.

Big hailstones fall continually on the active volcano of Colima, in Mexico. The tremendous updraft from the boiling lava carries a column of air upward to cold regions were moisture turns to hail. Local peasants gather the ice, wrap it in straw, and sell it in the villages.

The coldest place on earth is not the North nor the South Pole, but Verkovank in Siberia, where a temperature of –100 degrees has been registered.

Waves do not actually travel, in spite of appearances. The water only moves up and down; it is the force that travels. The simplest way to demonstrate this is to throw a stone into a pond with a paper boat in it. Although the waves appear to travel outwards, the boat merely bobs up and down.

Elvis Costello was born Declan Patrick McManus, 1954 (in London, England).
The name is a combination of Elvis Presley's first name and his mother's maiden name. He had also gone under the aliases "Little Hands of Concrete," "Eamonn Singer," and "Napoleon Dynamite," in earlier bands.

Glenn Danzig was born Glenn Anzalone, 1955.
Said he named himself after the city in Poland, also known as Gdansk.

Bob Dylan was born Robert Zimmerman, 1941.
The rumors are that he named himself after either the character Matt Dillon from the TV western *Gunsmoke* or the poet Dylan Thomas, or a combination of both. He has also recorded under the names Blind Boy Grunt and Lucky Wilbury.

The Edge was born David Evans, 1961 (in Essex, England).
So named because of either his sharp chin or his sharp mind, depending on which story you read or believe.

Eminem was born Marshall Mathers, 1972.
This stage name originates from the sound of the rapper's initials.

Flea was born Michael Peter Balzary, 1962 (in Melbourne, Australia).

Howlin' Wolf was born Chester Arthur Burnett, 1910.
Wolf said he was given the nickname "Howlin' Wolf" in childhood by his grandfather. He has also been known as Bull Cow and Big Foot Chester.

Engelbert Humperdinck was born Arnold George Dorsey, 1936.
Humperdink apparently named himself after the German composer of the same name (1854–1921), most famous for his opera *Hansel und Gretel*.

Billy Idol was born William Michael Albert Broad, 1955 (in Middlesex, England).
The idea for his new name is supposed to have come to him after a schoolteacher called him "idle." Billy took the name for himself, but changed the spelling to match his pop ambitions.

Elton John was born Reginald Kenneth Dwight, 1947.
Elton John took his name by combining the first names of Bluesology's vocalist Elton Dean and saxophonist "Long" John Baldry. Allegedly also sported the nickname "Hercules" at one point.

LL Cool J was born James Todd Smith, 1968.
This name supposedly stands for "Ladies Love Cool James." Oh yeah??

Leadbelly aka **Lead Belly** was born Huddie Ledbetter, 1885 or possibly 1888.
The nickname was supposedly given to him in reference to his toughness, either chopping cotton or in prison (he did time for murder).

Courtney Love was born Love Michelle Harrison.

Marilyn Manson was born Brian Warner, 1969.
Manson named himself after two opposing icons of a bygone
era: silver-screen sex symbol Marilyn Monroe and killing spree
mastermind Charles Manson.

Roger McGuinn was born James Joseph McGuinn III, 1942.
Roger is said to have changed his name in 1967 on the advice of
an Indonesian guru.

Freddy Mercury was born Farouk Pluto Bulsara (the spelling
varies), 1946 (in Zanzibar).

Ozzy Osbourne was born John Michael Osbourne, 1948 (in
Birmingham, England).

Poe was born Ann Danielewski, 1968.
Supposedly received her nickname after wearing an Edgar Allen
Poe costume to a Halloween party when a child.

Joey Ramone was born Jeffrey Hyman, 1951.

Johnny Ramone was born John Cummings.

Dee Dee Ramone was born Douglas Colvin.
The last name "Ramone" is a tribute to Paul McCartney's early
stage name "Ramon."

Trent Reznor was born Michael Trent Reznor, 1965.
Reznor is said to have originally gone by his middle name to
avoid confusion with his father Michael but preferred the name
"Trent."

 # Boobs and Misprints

"Street crime has taken on a new meaning in South Tyneside where thieves are stripping paths of hundreds of paving stones and gully covers throughout the borough. According to council chiefs, 'The situation has got so bad that some weeks ago we had a whole cul-de-sac stolen from us overnight.'"
The Journal (Newcastle)

"Mushrooms Provençale stuffed with the chef's special recipe and friend in garlic butter."
Blackburn Citizen (UK)

"The service was attended by Woking mayor John Jewson and the town's MP Cranley Onslow who read the lesson. The Salvation Army band led the procession to the war memorial. Then, as the congregation stood with heads bowed, a lone burglar from the Welsh Guards played the Last Post."
Woking Informer (UK)

"Princess Anne attended the opening in a stunningly bright peach-coloured kimono-like gown that fittingly suited the evening's Japanese tenor."
Leader Post (Canada)

Axl Rose was born William Bailey OR William Bruce Rose, 1962
Differing accounts of Axl's original name exist. One story says he was born William Bailey, and changed his name to William Rose after discovering that his biological father's surname was Rose. A conflicting story says that he was born William Rose and that he may have dropped the Rose for a time as a way of distancing himself from his abusive and absent biological father.

Johnny Rotten was born John Lydon, 1956 (in London, England).
Supposedly named for his poor dental hygiene.

Gene Simmons was born Chaim Witz, 1947 (in Haifa, Israel).

Nikki Sixx was born Frank Carlton Serafino Ferrana, 1958.

Slash was born Saul Hudson, 1965 (in London, England).
He has said that he was given the nickname by a family friend when just a boy because he was always in a hurry, nipping from one thing to another.

Ringo Starr was born Richard Starkey, 1940.
Given the first name because of his habit for wearing rings, and he decided to shorten his last name to Starr so he could bill his drum act as "Starr time."

The Streets front man was born Michael Skinner (in Birmingham, England).

Cat Stevens was born Steve Demetre Georgiou, 1948 (in London, England).

He is now known as Yusuf Islam after converting to the Islamic faith.

Joe Strummer was born John Graham Mellor, 1952 (in Ankara, Turkey).
He also went under the name Woody Mellor briefly, apparently an homage to Woody Guthrie.

Nigel Tufnel was born Christopher Guest.

Sid Vicious was born John Simon Richie, 1957 (in London, England).
The stage name was supposedly inspired by band-mate Johnny Rotten's pet hamster.

Bono Vox was born Paul David Hewson, 1960 (in Dublin, Ireland).
Meaning "perfect voice" in Latin, this nickname was apparently given to him by people in the youth group that he was in as a schoolchild. A different story insists it was the name of a hearing aid store in Dublin.

Muddy Waters was born McKinley Morganfield, 1915.

Amazing Engineering Facts

A Brief History of Air Travel

In less than a century, air travel has become a common method of transport for millions of people. After an initial 12-second piloted flight at the beginning of the twentieth-century, passenger aircraft now routinely fly for up to 15 hours and carry hundreds of people around the world.

1901 – A Prototype Internal Combustion Engine Flies a Model Airplane
Samuel Pierpont Langley built a gasoline powered flying model plane in 1901. He had been experimenting with air flight since 1896.

1903 – The Wright Brothers
Wilbur and Orville Wright from Dayton, Ohio, undertake four flights with a controlled aircraft at Kill Devil Hills, North Carolina. Wilbur traveled 852 feet across the field in 59 seconds.

1904 – Beginnings of Aerodynamics
Ludvig Prandtl presented an important paper on air on the surface of the wing of an aircraft. It was to become the beginning of theoretical aerodynamics.

IT'S THE LAW

During the time of Peter the Great, any Russian man who wore a beard was required to pay a special tax.

Every citizen of Kentucky is required by law to take a bath once a year.

Federal law forbids recycling used eyeglasses in the United States.

The only legal sexual position in Washington DC is the missionary position – all other sexual positions are forbidden.

In Atlanta, Georgia, it is illegal to tie a giraffe to a telephone pole or street lamp.

In Canada, if a debt is higher than 25 cents, it is illegal to pay it with pennies.

In Idaho, it is illegal to give someone a box of candy that weighs more than 50 pounds.

In New Jersey, it is illegal to slurp soup.

In Eureka, Nevada, men who wear moustaches are forbidden from kissing women.

In Somalia, Africa, it is illegal to carry old chewing gum stuck on the tip of your nose.

1910 – Aircraft Takes Off from Ships Deck

Eugine Ely took off from the deck of a cruiser, anchored offshore in Virginia, and landed his aircraft on land. In 1911, he made the same move from a ship anchored further off shore in California.

1914 – Automatic Pilot

Lawrence Sperry tested an automatic gyrostabilizer at Lake Keuka, Hammondsport, New York. It used sensors to keep the aircraft level and travelling in a straight line without being controlled by a pilot.

1914–1918 – Improved Control and Propulsion

In World War I, demand was for faster, higher and better maneuverability. Over these four years groundbreaking improvements to flight were made.

1917 – The Junkers J4

The Junkers J4 was an all-metal airplane introduced by Hugo Junkers a German mechanics professor. It was created from duralumin, a lightweight aluminum alloy.

1918 – The Beginnings of Airmail

By 1918, airmail began to be offered by the US Postal Service from Polo Grounds in Washington, DC. By 1920, airmail could

---

Joke of the Day
What's the difference between a Peeping Tom and someone who's just got out of the bath? One is rude and nosey, the other is nude and rosey.

travel from San Fransisco to New York in 33 hours and 20 minutes, 3 days faster than delivery by train.

1919 – Flying Across the Atlantic
The first flight to cross the Atlantic Ocean was made by US Navy aviators in Curtiss NC-4 flying boats. The journey took them from Newfoundland to London, making stops in the Azores and Lisbon.

1919 – Passengers Fly Across the English Channel
In 1919, the British and the French introduced a passenger service from Paris to London and back

1923–1926 – The Introduction of Lightweight Air-Cooled Engines
These new engines made it possible to build bigger, faster planes.

1927 – Non-Stop Solo Flight Across the Atlantic
In 1927, Charles Lindbergh flew across the Atlantic in a monoplane called *Spirit of St. Louis*. The journey length was 3,600 miles.

1928 – First Flight Simulator
Edwin A. Link introduced the first electromechanical flight simulator, called the Link Trainer, that allowed the cock to roll, simulating real flight. The flight simulator was used for virtually all US pilot training during WWII.

1933 – The 12-Passenger Twin-Engine DC-1
Introduced by Douglas and designed by aeronautical engineer Arthur Raymond for a contract with TWA, the DC-1 could take off fully loaded if one engine failed. Later that year, TWA

introduced the DC-2 then the DC-3 two years later. The DC-3 was the first profit-making passenger plane and had a range of nearly 1500 miles.

1933 – First Modern Commercial Airliner
Boeing introduced the 247 in 1933, a twin-engine 10-passenger monoplane that was the first modern commercial airliner. The landing gear was retractable to reduce drag during flight.

1935 – First Radar
The first radar system for meteorological applications was patented by British scientist Sir Robert Watson-Watt. During World War II it was successfully used in Great Britain to detect incoming aircraft and provide information to intercept enemy bombers.

1935 – The First Trans-Pacific Airmail
Pan American began the first airmail service between San Fransisco and Manila. They also flew the first passenger service across the same route four years later. In 1939, Pan American and Britain's Imperial Airways began a scheduled transatlantic passenger service.

1937 – Design of the Jet Engine
Jet engines designed independently by Britain's Frank Whittle and Germany's Hans von Ohain made their first test runs in 1937.

1939 – The First Helicopter
The VS-300 single rotor helicopter was developed by Russian émigré Igor Sikorsky.

 ### ANIMAL SCIENCE

Armadillos are the only animal besides humans that can get leprosy.

Police dogs are trained to react to commands in a foreign language; commonly German but more recently Hungarian or some other Slavic tongue.

A cat has 32 muscles in each ear.

Reindeer like to eat bananas.

The Pug dog is thought to have gotten it's name from looking like the pug monkey.

The newest dog breed is the Bull Boxer, first bred in the United states in 1990–1.

The only domestic animal not mentioned in the Bible is the cat.

A cat has four rows of whiskers.

When angered, the ears of Tazmanian devils turn a pinkish-red.

Porcupines float in water.

Giraffes have no vocal cords.

Camel's milk does not curdle.

1939–1945 – World War II
Fortunately, the British developed airplane-detecting radar just in time for the Battle of Britain. Some have claimed that it was only radar that prevented a German victory in that battle. At the same time the Germans developed radio wave navigation techniques. Both had developed airborne radar, useful for attacking aircraft at night. The twin engine German ME 262 could fly at 540 miles an hour and Boeing modified its B-17 into the high altitude B-29 Superfortress. In Britain the Instrument Landing System (ILS) for landing in bad weather was put into use in 1944.

1947 – Breaking the Sound Barrior
US Air Force pilot Captain Charles "Chuck" Yeager piloted the Bell X-1 faster than the speed of sound over the town of Victorville, California.

1949 – Jet-Powered Commercial Aircraft
The prototype De Havilland Comet made its first flight on 27 July 1949. Three years later the Comet started regular passenger service as the first jet-powered commercial aircraft. It flew between London and South Africa.

1950 – The B-52 Bomber
The B-52 had eight turbojet engines, intercontinental range, and a weight capacity of 500,000 pounds.

1952 – The "Area Rule" of Aircraft Design
Richard Whitcomb, an engineer at Langley Memorial Aeronautical Laboratory, discovered the aircraft design concept known as the area rule. This involved designing aircraft wings to reduce drag and increase speed without additional power.

1963 – Mass Production of Small Jet Aircraft
The prototype Learjet 23, powered by two GE CJ610 turbojet engines, was 43 feet long, with a wingspan of 35.5 feet, and could carry seven passengers (including two pilots) in a fully pressurized cabin. More than 100 were sold by the end of 1965.

1969 – Boeing 747
One of the most successful airplanes ever produced is the 747, a wide-body, turbofan-powered commercial aircraft first flown by Boeing in 1969.

1976 – Concorde SST
Introduced by British Airways and Air France, Concorde could carry a hundred passengers at 55,000 feet flying at twice the speed of sound. The aircraft could fly to New York from London in 3.5 hours, half the usual flight time. Due to prohibitive costs to passengers the flights remained the privilege of the wealthy. In July 2000 an Air France Concorde crashed on take-off killing everyone on board. By 2003 Concorde was no longer flying.

1986 – Voyager

Aircraft designer Burt Rutan created Voyager using a carbon-composite material. Voyager could fly around the world non-stop on one load of fuel, circumnavigating the globe (26,000 miles) nonstop in 9 days. Voyager had two centerline engines, one fore and one aft, and weighed less than 2,000 pounds (fuel for the flight added another 5,000 pounds).

1990s – The B-2 Bomber

Developed by Northrop Grumman, the B-52 bomber cannot be detected by radar because it is made of composite materials instead of metal. Around the same time, Lockheed designed the F-117 stealth fighter, also unable to be detected by radar.

1995 – Computer-Aided Design (CAD) and Engineering

Boeing unveiled the twin-engine 777 in 1995. It is the biggest two-engine aircraft ever to fly and the first to be designed using computers. Apparently, only the nose was actually built before the first aircraft was fully assembled and this was only 0.03mm out of alignment on one wing.

Classic One-Liners

Sydney Smith, of an irritating acquaintance: "He deserves to be preached to death by wild curates."

Boobs and Misprints

"A parachutist gets tangled in the ropes as he disrupts the fight between Bowe and Holyfield, 1993."

"Lost donkey, answers to the name of Harold. Very attractive, dearly beloved by owner. Last seen in a nun's ouffit."
The Bulletin (Belgium)

"President Nixon set off today on a tour of six Asian nations to explain his intentions and assure the countries that he is-abandoning them to their enemies."
Daily Mail

"Retired doctor Aubrey Westlake is fed up with people asking if his caravan site and holiday centre is a nudist colony. For 79-year old Dr Westlake and his 71-year old wife cannot understand what makes people think their Sandy Balls holiday centre is for nudists."
The Sun

"Sales experience is desirable but not essential as comprehensive training is given. Starting income negotiable. Male or female preferred."
Crosby Herald

Royal Scandal

Queen Victoria and John Brown

Scandal involving the widowed Queen Victoria and her favorite, ghillie John Brown, reached such proportions in the 1860s that there were genuine fears for the future of the monarchy in Britain. Republicanism had already swept Europe in 1848, the year of the communist manifesto of Marx and Engels. Now it was on the rise in Britain, feeding off poverty and the struggle for electoral reform. Disenchantment with the monarchy stemmed from the Queen's virtual disappearance from public life following the death of the Prince Consort in 1861. Now rumors of her "affair" with John Brown, the one-time stable lad who had been appointed Victoria's Personal Highland Servant – with explicit instructions to take orders from no one but herself – fell on doubly fertile ground, both within the Establishment and with the mob.

That Queen Victoria and John Brown loved each other is a matter of record. After Brown's death in 1883, she wrote to his brother Hugh: "So often I told him that no one loved him more than I did or had a better friend than me . . . and he answered, 'Nor you than me. No one loves you more.'" What has always remained the subject for speculation, and scandal, is if that love was strictly platonic. When rumor was at its height, the press

Joke of the Day
First mouse: 'I've trained that crazy science teacher at last.' Second mouse: 'How have you done that?' First mouse: 'I don't know how, but every time I run through that maze and ring the bell, he gives me a piece of cheese.'

sailed as close to the wind as it dared, pillorying Brown personally and the Queen by inference, in savagely slanted reports and cartoons. One Swiss newspaper, the Gazette de Lausanne, "reported" their secret marriage, adding for good measure that Victoria was pregnant by Brown. An American diarist visiting Britain in 1868 wrote in *Tinsley's Magazine*: "Soon after my arrival in London at a table where all the company were gentlemen by rank or position, there were constant references to and jokes about 'Mrs Brown' . . . I lost the point of all the witty sayings and should have remained in blissful ignorance throughout the dinner, had not my host kindly informed me that 'Mrs Brown' was an English synonym for the Queen . . ." And if, after all that and much more, there were those left who still harboured any doubts about the relationship between the Queen and John Brown, their doubts must surely have been dispelled after her death in 1901, when her eldest son, now King Edward VII, ordered all his mother's treasured photographs of John Brown to be burned, his busts destroyed, and – pettiest of all – the ghillie's apartment at Windsor Castle, undisturbed since his death, to be turned into a billiards room.

John Brown, second of a family of 11 children, was born at

Crathienaird, opposite Balmoral on the north bank of the Dee, on 8 December 1826. His father was the local schoolmaster, his mother a blacksmith's daughter. He started his working life as ostler's boy at a coaching inn, joined the staff on Balmoral estate (then rented by a Scottish knight) as a 13 shillings-a-week stable hand and was retained as an under-groom when it passed into royal ownership in 1848. His rise in royal favor was swift. By 1858 "Johnny Brown" had been specially appointed to attend on the Queen, doubling as "keeper" to Prince Albert. When the Queen and her husband began their "Great Expeditions" in the Highlands in 1860, traveling incognito from Balmoral to stay at country inns and shooting lodges, Brown accompanied them as Victoria's valet. She wrote gushingly of him to her uncle, King Leopold I of the Belgians: "He takes wonderful care of me, combining Queen Victoria, the British queen whose name is synonymous with staid sexual attitudes and exaggerated propriety, may have been illegitimate. The theory is put forward in the book *Queen Victoria's Gene* by D.M. Potts and W.T.W. Potts.

Their theory rests upon the fact that some of Queen Victoria's offspring carried the gene for hemophilia, an inherited disease that prevents the blood from clotting. The disorder only affects male offspring; female children with the gene pass it on to their children without being affected.

It is known from the meticulous records of European royal houses that Edward, Duke of Kent, Victoria's supposed father, was not a sufferer.

Records relating to Princess Victoire, Victoria's mother, do not exist. However, by the time that she married the Duke of Kent, Victoire had already married once, and produced two children. If she were a carrier, one would expect haemophilia to show up in these two children, or in their descendants. Records

Fascinating Facts

Mules – the offspring of a horse and a donkey – are
generally thought to be sterile. In 1930 a mule owned by
the Texas Agricultural and Mechanical College called
Old Beck proved this idea wrong when she gave birth
to two offspring, one sired by a donkey, one by a
horse.

Albert E. Herpin of Trenton, New Jersey never slept
at all during his lifetime. Born with a disorder that
prevented him from falling asleep, Herpin worked as a
gardener; at night, he liked to read newspapers while others
slept, often as many as seven a night. He lived to an old
age.

On 5 December 1664, a man named Hugh Williams was
the only survivor of a boat that sank crossing the Menai
Strait – between Anglesey and Carnarvonshire in Wales.
On 5 December 1785, the sole survivor of another such
accident was also called Hugh Williams; 60 other
passengers were drowned.

show that branch of the royal family tree was free from the disease. It is therefore very unlikely that Victoria had inherited the disease.

So where did the gene come from? It could have been a fresh mutation in Victoria or her mother. In other words, the disease could have started spontaneously in either of the two women. As only 1 in 100,000 people per generation develop the hemophilia mutation, this is unlikely. This leaves the possibility that the Duke of Kent was not Victoria's father.

The authors of *Queen Victoria's Gene* suggest that Victoire could have chosen a lover to father her child because her husband Edward was infertile. Evidence for this, they say, can be found in the fact that Edward's mistress, with whom he slept for many years, never got pregnant. This was very uncommon in the early nineteenth century. William IV's mistress, for example, had ten children over the course of their affair.

But why would Victoire cuckold her husband? At the time of Victoria's birth, no child of George Ill had managed to have a legitimate, living child. George IV himself had no heirs. His brother William, who succeeded him, was beginning to look too old to produce a successor. And so it proved.

Victoria's mother, the Duchess of Kent, died in March 1861 and her husband, Albert, of typhoid fever in December the same year. At 42 she found herself in that unique, gilded-cage

Classic One-Liners
Arthur Beer, to a thin friend: "How much would you charge to haunt a house?"

isolation known only to monarchy, as mother of nine children as well as Queen of the world's greatest power. Perhaps not surprisingly she became so overwhelmed by grief and responsibility that many considered her behavior unbalanced, even a little mad. Henceforth a photograph of her dead spouse was to hang a foot above every bed she slept in, with a plaster cast of his hand on the dressing table nearby. The royal servants laid out a clean nightshirt each night for his ghost and as solemnly brought in hot shaving water every morning. Albert's rooms at Buckingham Palace, Windsor, Osborne, and Balmoral were sealed and their contents photographed, so that after cleaning each article could be restored to the exact spot it occupied at the moment of his death. So overwrought did she become that she blamed her son Bertie, the Prince of Wales (and a notorious rake) for hastening his father's death by his affairs. Tearful and brooding, she went into a purdah of mourning for several years, wilfully neglecting her royal duties to the point of forfeiting public sympathy and even loyalty.

It was into this unreal world of permanent mourning and near madness that John Brown was summoned in December 1864. He arrived at Osborne, the Queen's home on the Isle of Wight, in kilt and bonnet and leading her favorite pony through the snow, harnessed to her own carriage brought from Balmoral. As medicine, it worked from the start. According to author E.E.P. Tisdall: "it was said that the smile which lit the Queen's face was the first which had been seen since that dreadful night." Unfortunately while Brown's presence signaled the start of the Queen's return to normality, it also gave rise to gossip. She was still only forty-five and a passionate woman. Brown was thirty-eight, a handsome, red-headed giant of a man, already devoted to her. If it was only natural that she should rely more and more on this one man who was never far from her side, it was perhaps also inevitable that tongues should soon start to wag; especially as Brown had a positive genius for upsetting all but Her Majesty with his gruff, no-nonsense manner.

Within two months of his arrival at Osborne he had been appointed the Queen's "Personal Highland Servant," at a salary of £120 a year, with instructions to attend her both indoors and out and to take his orders "from none but herself." This he interpreted literally and while his respect for his royal mistress was sincere, no one could ever accuse him of kow-towing to her. He addressed her as an equal, calling her "wumman," openly scolding her for taking insufficient care with her appearance. ("What are ye daein' wi' that auld dress on ye agen?") No one else in Britain would have dared to speak to her in such a way and when extended to senior members of the Household it caused the deepest resentment. General Sir Charles Grey, her Personal Secretary, bristled at Brown's offhand manner when bearing royal messages. A clash with equerry General Sir John M'Neil brought a fiery retort from Brown, "Dinna be abrupt wi' me, I'm nae one of ye're private sodgers" and, within hours, an implied rebuke from the Queen, offering the General a remote command in India should he choose to accept it. Ministers-in-waiting knew better than to offend this former ghillie who wielded such immense influence with the Queen but few loved him for that.

The Queen's first, reluctant efforts to regain goodwill by appearing in public served only to worsen the situation. In February 1866, she opened Parliament for the first time since Albert's death in 1861 but disappointed the crowds by eschewing all pomp and pageantry, even entering the Palace of Westminster by a side door. The following month she reviewed a parade of troops at Aldershot, likewise for the first time in years; but instead of sitting on her own horse to take the salute,

IT'S THE LAW

In Milan, Italy there is a law that requires a smile on the face of all citizens at all times. Exemptions include time spent visiting patients in hospitals or attending funerals. Otherwise the fine is $100 if they are seen in public without a smile on their face.

In New York State it is still illegal to shoot a rabbit from a moving trolley car.

In Pennsylvania, ministers are forbidden from performing marriages when either the bride or groom is drunk.

In San Salvador drunk drivers can be punished by death before a firing squad.

In seventeenth-century Japan, no citizen was allowed to leave the country on penalty of death. Anyone caught coming or going without permission was executed on the spot.

In Hazelton, Pennsylvania, there is a law that prohibits a person from sipping a carbonated drink while lecturing students in a school auditorium.

In Omaha, Nebraska, if a child burps during a church service his/her parents may be arrested.

Joke of the Day
"My dog is a nuisance. He chases everyone on a bicycle. What can I do?"
"Take his bike away."

as of yore, she remained in her carriage – leaving John Brown in full view, on the box above.

Rumors of the "association" were already rife; now they multiplied, with Brown the target for attack. In June, rumor said, "Brown was to blame" for the Queen's failure to return immediately to London from Balmoral, following the defeat of Lord John Russell's government. In July, their mutual fondness for whisky ("Begg's Best," distilled on the Balmoral estate, was a favourite tipple) was used as a weapon by the reporters keeping watch on the royal holiday there. According to rumor, John Brown had been mortally offended by a mock Court Circular in Punch which debunked him, so much so that he tendered his resignation in drunken fury when the Queen dared to laugh at the article. Soon the John O' Groats Journal published a letter from its London correspondent:

"I suppose all my readers have heard of the great Court favourite John Brown. His dismissal some weeks ago was generally talked about at the time, and I observe that the fact has now found its way into print, coupled with the suggestion of John Brown's probable restoration to power before long. The reason assigned for his dismissal is an inordinate indulgence in the national taste for whisky, and the restraining of that appetite is mentioned as a likely condition of his

readmission to favour. Far be it from me to question Mr
Brown's powers of suction. They may rival those of Dickens'
character, the elder Weller, I think, who would have made an
uncommon good oyster if he'd been born in that sphere of life
. . . But Brown's fall has been more commonly ascribed to Mr
Punch than to any shortcomings of his own . . ."

In September 1866 an anonymous "Special Correspondent" of
the Gazette de Lausanne said in print what the rumormongers in
London society were saying at their dinner tables – that the
Queen had secretly married Brown in a morganatic ceremony,
and was avoiding public appearances to try to hide the fact that
she was pregnant again. "They say that with Brown and by him
she consoles herself for Prince Albert, and they go even further.
They add that she is in an interesting condition, and that if she
was not present for the Volunteers Review, and at the inaugura-
tion of the monument to Prince Albert, it was only in order to
hide her pregnancy. I hasten to add that the Queen has been
morganatically married to her attendant for a long time, which
diminishes the gravity of the thing . . ."

In his book *Queen Victoria's Private Life* author E.E.P.
Tisdall (who discounted the notion that the affair was platonic)
says that a pamphlet entitled Mrs John Brown was privately
printed in Britain ". . . to circulate very widely in stately homes
and servants' halls . . . The pamphlet declared that the Queen
had married John Brown at a secret ceremony. It was never
discovered who had paid for the printing and organized the
distribution of the pamphlet, but a suggestion was made that the
money came from the funds of the Republican party, which was
active and growing, as might be expected with such a queer state
of affairs existing around the Throne . . "

To boost circulation, the satirical magazine *Tomahawk* lost no

Fascinating Facts

Oswaldus Norhingerus, who lived in the time of Shakespeare, specialized in carving miniature objects out of ivory. He once carved 16,000 table utensils so small that they could be accommodated in a cup the size of a coffee bean. Each dish was almost invisible to the naked eye, yet perfect in every detail. They could only be viewed through powerful magnifying glasses.

Both ice and steam are dry; ice is only wet when it melts, steam is only wet when it condenses. Uncondensed steam is also invisible.

Edgar Allan Poe received only $10 for his most famous poem, *The Raven*. The original manuscript was later sold for $200,000.

As well as Alexandria, Alexander the Great, also built a city called Bucephala, named after his horse Bucephalus, which was killed in battle in 326 BC.

The largest statue of the Buddha in the world is in Pegu, Burma – it is 180 feet long and is in a reclining position. The statue was lost for 400 years: all records of it vanish around the middle of the fifteenth century, and it was not found again until 1881, when a railway was being built. The statue was covered with earth and vegetation.

time in joining the anti-royalist pack. In its first issue of May 1867, the caption to a caricature of Landseer's painting of Victoria on horseback at Osborne, attended by John Brown, read slyly: "All is black that is not Brown." In his painting, the artist had over-emphasized the Queen in mourning; not only did he show her in full widow's weeds, mounted on a black charger, he even put Brown into a black kilt. The public, who flocked to the Royal Academy's Spring Exhibition – and had heard all the rumors – first giggled and finally laughed out loud on seeing the painting. Press comment was brutal. Said the *Saturday Review:* "We respect the privacy of Her Majesty but when Sir Edwin Landseer puts the Queen and her black favourites into what are, during the season, the most public rooms in England, he does more harm to her popularity than he imagines."

Tomahawk's June edition carried a more spiteful cartoon. This time it portrayed an empty throne, with the royal robes flung across it and alongside, an equally neglected crown – under a glass dust-cover. The caption asked bluntly: "Where is Britannia?" The magazine's August cartoon was downright vicious. Captioned "A Brown Study," it showed kilted John Brown leaning indolently on the vacant throne, with a clay pipe in his hand, wearing a bonnet and hobnailed ghillie's boots, staring down unconcernedly at an angry British Lion. Tisdall called it ". . . the most daring and ferocious anti-royalist cartoon ever seen in Britain, or possibly

---

Classic One-Liners
Margaret Halsey: 'The English never smash in a face. They merely refrain from asking it to dinner.'

anywhere, in a public journal . . . If such an insult to the Sovereign appeared today in the Press, questions in Parliament and assurances from the Prime Minister would doubtless be followed by a sensational prosecution. But nothing followed the publication of "A Brown Study" . . . except an uproar of bitter laughter . . . Nobody called attention to it in the House; Ministers of the Crown kept their silence. They suspected that *Tomahawk* with its "Brown Study" was more or less telling the truth."

By July 1867, government fears of a hostile demonstration against the Queen were such that an excuse was invented to cancel a military review in Hyde Park rather than risk her attendance there in the company of John Brown. Although she had agreed, reluctantly, to the Prime Minister's suggestion to leave Brown at home to avoid possible incidents "of an unpleasant nature," the Cabinet feared she might defy ministerial advice and take Brown anyway. So, the assassination in far-off Mexico of the Emperor Maximilian (a distant relative, by marriage, of the Queen) was used as a pretext to put the court back into mourning and cancel the review altogether.

The year 1871 saw the Republican movement reach its zenith in Britain and not only because of her supposed dalliance with Brown. In an age when 15 shillings a week was a factory hand's wage, a request that Parliament should approve a dowry of £30,000, plus an annuity, on the Queen's daughter, Princess Louise's marriage to the Marquis of Lorne, dismayed even the most ardent royalist supporters. The Queen herself was even accused in a pamphlet of misappropriating public funds. Signed by a critic styling himself "Solomon Temple," and headed "What Does She Do With It?", the pamphlet complained that cash saved from Civil List funds was diverted to her own account.

Neglect of royal duties was still the main weapon in the

 # Boobs and Misprints

"Mr Gumo said, however, that the introduction of speed trains would not be an immediate undertaking. 'With speed trains one would arrive at one's destination too early. At the present time you get to your destination just at the right time.'"
The Nation (Kenya)

"Audrey Hepburn, aged thirty-nine, is to marry Rome psychiatrist Andrea Dotti."
Sunday Times

"Sagittarius: So far as your love life is concerned, this is a time for discretion. Try to create jealousy and bad feeling by thoughtless actions."
The Standard (Kenya)

"The court was told that, after the attack, Payne told a VicRail employee that he was God. The employee had then asked for some identification."
Melbourne Sun

"The resealing work on Leawood Aqueduct is now complete but unfortunately the Aqueduct is still leaking."
Newark Post

Republican army, however. *The Times* labeled Queen Victoria "The Great Absentee," while to the *Pall Mall Gazette* she had become "The Invisible Monarch." When she fell ill in the autumn of that year no medical bulletins were issued, so that the country remained unaware of her condition even though, at one stage, she was apparently not expected to live another twenty-four hours. In contrast, when the Prince of Wales (himself no stranger to scandal) went down that winter with typhoid fever – the same illness which had killed his father ten years earlier – the whole nation prayed for his recovery. This time bulletins were issued and as the Prince's condition reached crisis point, so the public attitude to the royal family changed to one of compassion and sympathy. ("An epidemic . . . of typhoid loyalty," sneered the anti-royalist *Reynold's News*.) So complete was the turn around, however, that by mid-December 1871, when the royal recovery was assured, republicanism in Britain was a spent force.

Now it was Brown's turn to benefit from the wind of change. On 27 February 1872, a Thanksgiving Service for the Prince's recovery was held at St Paul's Cathedral. Two days later the Queen drove through Regent's Park in an open carriage, accompanied by her sons Alfred and Leopold, to thank her subjects for their demonstration of loyalty. Brown was on the box, as always. As the carriage re-entered Buckingham Palace a young man scaled the railings, ran up and pointed a pistol at the Queen's face. In the split-second of confusion that followed, the two Princes hesitated, as did the mounted equerries nearby. Brown alone proved equal to the occasion. As the Queen screamed, "Save me!" and flung herself against her lady-in-waiting, Lady Jane Churchill, he leapt down and shouldered the gunman aside, then pursued him as he made for the other side of the carriage. He described what happened next to Bow Street

Joke of the Day
"We had roast boar for dinner last night." "Was it a wild boar?" "Well, it wasn't very pleased."

magistrates, "I took hold o' him wi one o' my hauns, and I grippit him wi' the other by the scruff o' the neck . . . till half a dizzen had a grip o' him, grooms, equerries, I kenna' how mony there was . . ."

The pistol was later found to be defective, the intruder mentally unstable, but none of that detracted from John Brown's courage or presence of mind. In the eyes of the public, at least, he was transformed at a stroke from villain to hero. The Queen presented him with a new award, the Devoted Service Medal, which carried with it an annuity of £25 (but lapsed with his death; John Brown was the sole recipient). She later made him "John Brown, Esquire" and he was listed in Whitaker's Almanack as a member of the Household, at a salary of £400 a year.

After his death (from erysipelas) in 1883, aged only 56, he lay in state for six days, in the Clarence Tower at Windsor. His Court Circular obituary occupied 25 lines, compared with Disraeli's five lines, two years earlier. The Queen attended his funeral service at Windsor, although most of her family found excuses to be elsewhere. Her card on his coffin read: "A tribute of loving, grateful, and everlasting friendship and affection from his truest, best, and most faithful friend, Victoria. R & I." Five hundred mourners attended his burial at Crathie, on 5 April 1883. His opponents within the Establishment were to have the last word, however. Encouraged by the success of her previous book, *More Leaves from the Journal of a Life in the Highlands*, which she had dedicated to Brown, the Queen now declared her intention of writing *The Life of Brown*. Her Household was appalled, knowing it could only revive the scandal, but lacked the courage to say so. It was left to the Dean of Windsor (the Reverend Randall Davidson, later Archbishop of Canterbury) to urge her, after reading the rough draft, not to publish. When she persisted, he offered to resign – and the Queen gave in.

After his mother's death in 1901, Edward VII inflicted the final indignities on Brown's memory, as mentioned above, by ordering her photographs of him to be burned, and his quarters at Windsor turned into a games room. Author Tom Cullen wrote a fitting epitaph for the best-loved and most hated of all British royal servants in his book *The Empress Brown*: "Although John Brown has been dead for eighty-six years, his bones still rattle in the Royal closet at Windsor, where, as a subject for scandal he is regarded as second to the Abdication . . ."

Joke of the Day
Two men went duck-hunting with their dogs but without success. "I know what we're doing wrong," said the first one. "What's that then?" said the second. "We're not throwing the dogs high enough!"

142

In Montana, it is a felony for a wife to open her husband's mail.

In Waterville, Maine, it is illegal to blow one's nose in public.

In Gary, Indiana, it is illegal to attend the theater within four hours of eating garlic.

In Los Angeles courts it is illegal to cry on the witness stand.

In Arkansas, a man can legally beat his wife, but not more than once a month.

In Chicago, Illinois, it is illegal to fish in pajamas.

In Chicago, people who are diseased, maimed, mutilated, or "otherwise an unsightly or disgusting object" are banned from going out in public.

In Chicago it is also illegal to take a French poodle to the opera, and for women over 200 pounds (90 kilos) to ride horses in shorts.

In Miami, Florida, it is illegal for a man to wear any kind of strapless gown.

In Sarasota, Florida, it is illegal to sing while wearing a bathing suit.

True Life Miracles

A Miracle at Lourdes

Josephine Hoare, a healthy girl of 21, had been married for only six months when she developed chronic nephritis, a serious inflammation of the kidneys. Her family was told that she had no more than two years to live. At her mother's suggestion, she was taken to Lourdes.

At the famous French shrine, Josephine braved the icy waters of the spring. Although she felt peaceful, she was not conscious of any change. When she went home, however, her doctor said in amazement that the disorder seemed to have cleared. Her swollen legs returned to normal size, her blood pressure became normal, and her energy increased. But she was warned that pregnancy would certainly cause a relapse.

Several years passed. Then Josephine and her husband had the opportunity to revisit Lourdes, and Josephine lit a candle of thanksgiving. Soon after they got home, she felt a sharp pain in her back. Fearful that nephritis was recurring, she went to her doctor. His diagnosis was simply that she was six months pregnant – and she had had no relapse. Josephine Hoare had her baby, a son, and remained in good health. For her and her family, the spring of Lourdes had produced a double miracle.

Fascinating Facts

There was one queen of England who never even saw her realm. She was the wife of Richard the Lionheart, Queen Berengaria, daughter of Sancho VI of Navarre. They were married in Cyprus in May 1191. The King's travels meant that she saw him only twice more; she lived in France and Italy and died in Le Mans, about 1230.

Francis Bacon can be said to be the father of the modern computer: in 1605 he developed a cipher using only a and b in five letter combinations, each representing a letter of the alphabet, demonstrating that only two signs are required to transmit information. Toward the end of the century, Leibniz developed the principle into the binary system which is the basis of modern computers. Any number can be expressed by using a combination of the digits 0 and 1.

Francis Bacon died as a result of his passion for science. He wanted to test the refrigeration of meat, so he left his carriage to gather snow to stuff a chicken, and caught pneumonia as a result.

A gravestone in Sarajevo, Bosnia, has been almost entirely digested by human beings. It was believed that the pulverized stone, drunk in milk, would ensure pregnancy, so over the centuries most of the gravestone was chipped away. Finally, it was protected by a fence. The gravestone bears a medieval coat of arms, but the name of the owner has long since been eaten.

Kidnapped by a Giant Bird

In 1933 a six-year-old boy vanished from his home in Miège in the Swiss Alps. After an unsuccessful search for the boy, the town's mayor wrote to Abbé Mermet, who had often assisted police in locating missing people. The Abbé needed an article used by the missing, person, a description of the last place he or she was seen, and a map of the surrounding area to do his work. He used a pendulum and a form of dowsing to find the missing person.

After the Abbé applied his pendulum to the problem of the missing boy, he reported that the child had been carried away into the mountains by a large bird of prey, probably an eagle. He also said that the bird – although enormous – had dropped its load twice to rest and regain its strength.

There was no trace of the boy at the first place the Abbé indicated. A recent heavy snowfall prevented a thorough search at the second place, but the conclusion was that Abbé Mermet had made a mistake.

When the snow melted two weeks later, however, a gang of woodcutters found the torn and mangled body of a small boy. It was the missing child. The bird had apparently been prevented from completely savaging the child's body by the sudden heavy storm that had also hidden the forlorn evidence.

Scientific investigation established that the boy's shoes and clothes had not come into contact with the ground where the body was found. He could only have reached the remote spot by air – the pitiful victim of the bird of prey. Later the boy's father apologized to the Abbé for having doubted him.

Miracle Underground

It was November 1971 in London on a day like any other. In one of the city's underground stations, a train was approaching the platform. Suddenly a young man hurled himself directly into the path of the moving train. The horrified driver slammed on the brakes, certain that there was no way to stop the train before the man was crushed under the wheels. But miraculously the train did stop. The first carriage had to be jacked up to remove the badly injured man, but the wheels had not passed over him and he survived.

The young man turned out to be a gifted architect who was recovering from a nervous breakdown. His amazing rescue from death was based on coincidence. For the investigation of the accident revealed that the train had not stopped because of the driver's hasty braking. Seconds before, acting on an impulse and completely unaware of the man about to throw himself on the tracks, a passenger had pulled down the emergency handle, which automatically applies the brakes of the train. The passenger had no particular reason for doing so. In fact, the Transport Authority considered prosecuting him on the grounds that he had had no reasonable cause for using the emergency system!

The Magical Chamber
Eliphas Lévi, the nineteenth-century writer on theories of magic, seldom practiced what he wrote about. But when he was offered a complete magical chamber, he decided to try to evoke Apollonius of Tyana.

Classic One-Liners
James Barrie: 'There are few more impressive sights in the world than a Scotsman on the make.'

Lévi made his circle, kindled the ritual fires, and began reading the evocations of the ritual.

A ghostly figure appeared before the altar. Lévi found himself seized with a great chill. He placed his hand on the pentagram, the five-pointed symbol used to protect magicians against harm. He also pointed his sword at the figure, commanding it mentally to obey and not to alarm him. Something touched the hand holding the sword, and his arm became numb from the elbow down. Lévi realized that the figure objected to the sword, and he lowered it to the ground. At this, a great weakness came over him, and he fainted without having asked his questions.

After his swoon, however, he seemed to have the answers to his unasked questions. He had meant to ask one about the possibility of forgiveness and reconciliation between "two persons who occupied my thought." The answer was, "Dead."

It was his marriage that was dead. His wife, who had recently left him, never returned.

 # Boobs and Misprints

"Architect with modernized Herefordshire farmhouse and beautiful Hereford cow, seeks similar companion, preferably with a sense of humour."
Youth Hostelling News

"Toronto lawyer, David Himelfarb, who represented Reynolds, wouldn't comment on this agreement. 'One of the terms of the settlement was that we not release any of the terms of the settlement,' he said."
Toronto Sun

"The thieves broke into the centre on Sunday and took 50 dog choker chains and 12 studded leather collars, valued at $366. Police said they were following several leads."
The Dominion (New Zealand)

"Among the other semitropical guest workers is *Paratrechina* longicornis, also known as the crazy ant. A colony of crazy ants was recently found inside a psychiatric hospital."
New Scientist

"Once agam the Maurician Party has raised a storm in a teacup."
Advance (Mauritius)

Real Ghost Stories

The Naughty Poltergeist

Father Karl Pazelt, a Jesuit priest, came to the aid of a California couple in 1974 when they were troubled by a poltergeist. The couple, who reported their story to the *San Francisco Examiner* anonymously, believed that it was a devil.

The poltergeist pulled the standard prank of throwing shoes, but also plagued them by setting fires. At one point a plastic wastebasket caught fire and melted. Frightened for the safety of their 20-year-old son as well as for themselves, they asked Father Pazelt to exorcize the malevolent force. In his opinion this was a case of "demonic obsession" – that is, the "devil is not in the people, but around the people." According to the couple, the devilish spirit made its presence strongly felt during the exorcism rite "by knocking both of us down."

Joke of the Day
"Why did you leave your last job?"
"Something the boss said." "Was he
abusive?" "Not exactly." "What did he
say, then?" "You're fired!"

Beasts and Monsters

The Serpent from the Sea

From the 1660 report of Captain William Taylor, Master, British Banner:

"On the 25th of April, in lat. 12 deg. 7 min. 8 sec., and long. 93 deg. 52 min. E., with the sun over the main-yard, felt a strong sensation as if the ship was trembling. Sent the second mate aloft to see what was up. The latter called out to me to go up the fore rigging and look over the bows. I did so, and saw an enormous serpent shaking the bowsprit with his mouth. It must have been at least about 300 feet long; was about the circumference of a very wide crinoline petticoat, with black back, shaggy mane, horn on the forehead, and large glaring eyes placed rather near the nose, and jaws about eight feet long. He did not observe me, and continued shaking the bowsprit and throwing the sea alongside into a foam until the former came clear away of the ship. The serpent was powerful enough, although the ship was carrying all sail, and going at about ten knots at the time he attacked us, to stop her way completely. When the bowsprit, with the jibboom, sails, and rigging, went by the board, the monster swallowed the fore-topmast, staysail jib, and flying-jib, with the greatest apparent ease. He shoved off a little after this, and returned apparently to scratch himself against the side of the

ANIMAL SCIENCE

A Holstein's spots are like a fingerprint or snowflake. No two cows have exactly the same pattern of spots.

A polecat is not a cat. It is a nocturnal European weasel.

A zebra is white with black stripes.

All pet hamsters are descended from a single female wild golden hamster found with a litter of 12 young in Syria in 1930.

An adult lion's roar can be heard up to five miles away, and warns off intruders or reunites scattered members of the pride.

Beaver teeth are so sharp that Native Americans once used them as knife blades.

Camels have three eyelids to protect themselves from blowing sand.

Catnip can affect lions and tigers as well as house cats. It excites them because it contains a chemical that resembles an excretion of the dominant female's urine.

Cheetahs make a chirping sound that is much like a bird's chirp or a dog's yelp. The sound is so an intense, it can be heard a mile away.

ship, making a most extraordinary noise, resembling that on board a steamer when the boilers are blowing off. The serpent darted off like a flash of lightning, striking the vessel with its tail, and striving in all the starboard quarter gallery with its tail. Saw no more of it."

Science: How it Works

Momentum

When a totally motionless object gets in the way of a moving one, the motionless one usually ends up moving and the one that's been moving ends up slowing to a stop. The momentum of the moving object transfers to the other one, stopping the first and setting the second in motion.

Momentum can pass through one motionless object to another if the other one is in direct contact with it, something seen often on pool tables.

A rolling ball on a smooth, level surface may seem like it would roll forever if nothing stops it. In fact, friction and air pushing against the moving ball will eventually bring it to a stop.

Classic One-Liners
Maurice Chevalier: 'Old age isn't so bad when you consider the alternative.'

Royal Scandal

The King and Mrs Simpson

No single incident in all that fateful year of 1936, which saw
Hitler's troops march into the Rhineland, Mussolini's forces
conquer Abyssinia, and the outbreak of civil war in Spain,
caused a bigger sensation in the Old World or the New than a
love affair between a middle-aged couple, and its aftermath; the
love of King Edward VIII for American divorcee Mrs Wallis
Simpson. It developed into the greatest of all British royal
scandals, since it was seen as a possible threat to the monarchy
and thus to the Constitution itself, and it ended in the King's
abdication and exile.

The King's love for twice-married Mrs Simpson, which began
when he was still Prince of Wales, was an open secret for years
within the royal family, the Establishment, and café society
circles in London, New York, and the capitals of Europe. Yet
incredibly, even when it had progressed to the stage where
American newspapers were openly predicting "King to marry
'Wally'" – and naming the date – all mention of the royal
romance was deliberately withheld from the ordinary people of
Great Britain until the constitutional crisis it had engendered
reached flashpoint; a cover-up without precedent in the nation's
history. Then, unable to have the woman of his choice

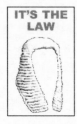

IT'S THE LAW

In Utah, the husband is responsible for every criminal act committed by his wife while she is in his presence.

In Vermont, women must obtain written permission from their husbands to wear false teeth.

In Wisconsin, it is illegal to cut a woman's hair or to kiss on a train.

In Mesquite, Texas it is illegal for kids to have unusual haircuts.

In Oklahoma, people who make "ugly faces" at dogs may be fined and jailed.

In Cleveland, Ohio, women are forbidden from wearing patent leather shoes, lest men see reflections of their underwear.

Hornytown, North Carolina has banned all massage parlors.

An old Virginia law was titled, "An Act to Prevent Corrupt Practices or Bribery by Any Person Other Than a Candidate."

In Alabama it is illegal for a driver to be blindfolded while operating a vehicle.

proclaimed Queen at his forthcoming coronation, denied the
alternative of a morganatic marriage, and presented by his
ministers with the stark choice of renouncing either the woman
he loved or the crown, the King chose to abdicate in favor of his
brother Albert, Duke of York (later George VI). The former
King sailed into exile on the night of 11 December 1936, aboard
a British destroyer, after addressing the nation by radio. He
married Mrs Simpson in France at the Château de Candé, near
Tours, in June 1937. No member of the British royal family
attended the wedding and most of his former friends stayed
away. The service was conducted by an unknown, volunteer
Anglican priest from Darlington.

On his wedding eve, the ex-King was officially informed that
while he would henceforth be styled His Royal Highness the
Duke of Windsor, the magic initials HRH were to be denied his
wife, the Duchess – "a damnable wedding present," he called it.
For the rest of their lives together (the Duke died of cancer in
May 1972) the Windsors remained objects of curiosity – and
gossip – wherever they went.

Prince Edward was born to be king on 23 June 1894, the
eldest son of George V and Queen Mary; at White Lodge,
Richmond Park. He was christened Edward Albert Christian
George Andrew Patrick David (but known to his family simply
as "David"). Mrs Simpson was born on 19 June 1896 at Blue

Classic One-Liners
John Buchan: "An atheist is a man who has no
invisible means of support."

Ridge Summit, Pennsylvania, USA, and christened Bessie
Wallis (Warfield) – she was known throughout her childhood as
"Bessiewallis." Both her parents came from good stock contrary
to scurrilous rumor, once her name became linked with the
King's. Her mother was a Montague from Baltimore, of
Virginian ancestry and her father Teackle Wallis Warfield from
Maryland. Both were of British descent.

"David" became the most popular Prince of Wales in history,
idolized not only in Britain but throughout the Dominions and
Empire. He travelled extensively as heir to the throne, winning
instant acclaim with his good looks and boyish charm from the
crowds who welcomed him everywhere. Bessie Wallis
Warfield's father died at 27, leaving very little money. Mother
and daughter moved to Baltimore, where relatives paid Bessie's
board-school fees. The widowed Mrs Warfield remarried in
1905, and, following the death of her second husband, for a third
time in 1926.

In 1916 Bessie Wallis Warfield met and married her first
husband, US Navy pilot Lieutenant Earl Winfield Spencer,
Jr. They separated five years later and she was granted a
divorce in 1927. That petition was already pending when she
met the man who was to become her second husband and
accompany her into the pages of history – Ernest Aldrich
Simpson. His mother was American, his father an
Englishman who headed a prosperous firm of shipbrokers
with offices in New York and London. During World War I
young Ernest Simpson sailed for London to enlist in the
British forces; in June 1918 he was commissioned in the
Coldstream Guards (but did not serve in France). His own
first marriage, to divorcee Mrs Dorothy Parsons Dechert,
also ended in divorce; that suit, too, was pending when he
met Mrs Wallis Warfield Spencer in 1926. Both went

159

Joke of the Day
Mom and dad are in the iron and steel business. She does the ironing and he does the stealing.

separately to Europe in 1928, when they met in London and were married at the Chelsea registrar's office on 21 July.

The Simpsons' flat in Bryanston Court became a rendezvous for businessmen, diplomats and influential journalists, and for the first years their marriage was a happy one. Husband and wife were introduced to the Prince of Wales in the winter of 1930, at a cocktail party given by Thelma, Lady Furness, at her home in Grosvenor Square.

The Prince of Wales fell in love three times before he was 40, on each occasion with someone else's wife. The first was Mrs Freda Dudley Ward, wife of Liberal Whip, William Dudley Ward, MP. She was caught in an air raid in 1918 as she was being escorted through Belgrave Square, in London, and sought refuge in a house there. Among those in the cellar which served as makeshift air raid shelter was the young Prince of Wales, on leave from France (where he served as staff officer). It was the beginning of a romance which lasted 16 years and – by astonishing coincidence – the hostess who introduced them was the then-unknown Ernest Simpson's married sister. Mrs Dudley Ward took an entirely practical view of her own affair with the Prince and wrote later: "I never met either the King or the Queen. They regarded me as a scarlet woman. They were always after David to leave me and marry within his rank – some Princess or other . . . Heavens, it wasn't as if I were trying to marry David! Or even wanted to. He asked me often enough,

Fascinating Facts

The nearest relative of the elephant is almost certainly the rock rabbit – this can be demonstrated by observing the similarity of their skeletons. The rock rabbit mows its own hay and lets it dry in the sun, turning it regularly, then storing it for the winter.

The misplacing of a comma once cost the United States treasury over a million dollars. In the Tariff Act of 1872, 'fruit plants, tropical and semi-tropical' were exempted from tax. A clerk miscopied it: 'fruit, plants tropical and semi-tropical.' Importers contended that this meant that tropical and semitropical fruits should be exempted. The treasury disagreed and collected the tax, but finally gave way and refunded over a million dollars. The wording was then changed.

In Montana, snowflakes 15 inches across and 8 inches thick fell during the record snowstorm in the winter of 1887.

Little Jack Horner of the nursery rhyme was a real person. When Henry VIII was preparing to pillage the monasteries, the abbot of Glastonbury sent the title deeds of the abbey to the king hidden in a pie, and carried by Jack Horner. Horner extracted the 'plum' deed of the manor of Mells, which remained in the family for many years.

ardently too. But just as often I said no . . . the whole idea was ridiculous. I was already married, of course, so there'd have to be a divorce, and his parents and friends and the Church would never have allowed it . . ."

The Prince's second love was Thelma, Lady Furness. She was an American who had eloped at 16, divorced her first husband, and married again at 21 to the widowed Marmaduke, Viscount Furness, the shipping magnate. (They, too, were divorced in 1933.) She had known the Prince of Wales for more than two years when he gave the Simpsons a lift home, from a party at the Furness house, early in 1931. Soon the Prince was a regular visitor to Bryanston Court and in January 1932 he invited the Simpsons to join him as his guests at Fort Belvedere, his residence on the outskirts of Windsor Great Park.

In the autumn of 1933, when Thelma, Lady Furness, sailed for New York, she asked her friend Wallis Simpson to "look after" the Prince while she was away. By the time she returned to London the following spring, the Prince had become infatuated with Mrs Simpson. Angered by reports of Thelma, Lady Furness's friendship with Prince Aly Khan, he soon broke with her. His final break with Mrs Freda Dudley Ward came at about the same time, as he fell more and more under Wallis Simpson's influence.

Royal biographer Frances Lady Donaldson wrote of this period: "Within a matter of weeks more gossip and scandal had been created than in the whole of his previous forty years. Until now . . . there is no doubt that the Prince had added more to the brilliance of the Crown, to the magic of the monarchy, than he had taken away. From now on he was to behave with a senseless recklessness in minor matters, an imperviousness to other people's opinions and feelings, which, carelessly and publicly proclaimed, could not for long have been covered by his

> **Classic One-Liners**
> Carlyle: "Four thousand people cross London
> Bridge daily, mostly fools."

Household and must in the end have undermined even his
extraordinary popularity . . ."

In August 1934 the Prince invited both Simpsons to join him
on holiday at Biarritz. Emest Simpson declined because of
business commitments. Mrs Simpson, who was therefore
obliged to decline also, later changed her mind and traveled to
Biarritz with her aunt, Mrs Bessie Merryman, as chaperone.
From Biarritz the Prince's party set sail on *Rosaura*, a yacht
owned by Lord Moyne (of the Guinness family), for a
fortnight's Mediterranean cruise. In the Duchess of Windsor's
own words years later, it was on this cruise that her association
with the Prince ". . . crossed the line that marks the indefinable
boundary between friendship and love." On their arrival at
Cannes he gave her a diamond and emerald bracelet charm, the
first in a cascade of precious stones he was to lavish on his new
love.

The Prince holidayed twice in Europe in 1935, the first time
at winter sports in Kitzbühel, followed by a visit to Vienna and
Budapest, then a leisurely summer vacation spent in the South of
France, Switzerland, Austria, and Hungary. On each occasion,
both Simpsons were invited to join him. Each time Ernest
Simpson declined while his wife accepted – and the inevitable
scandal grew. The second time Ernest Simpson sailed for the
USA to discuss his crumbling marriage with his wife's aunt,
Mrs Merryman. At Balmoral, George V met with the

Archbishop of Canterbury, the lugubrious Cosmo Lang, to mull
over the situation. In a later talk with his Prime Minister,
Stanley Baldwin, the King predicted with uncanny accuracy,
"After I'm dead the boy will ruin himself in twelve months." He
died on 20 January 1936; David became King Edward VIII –
and was on his way into exile, as ex-King, within the year.

Some observers, like his aide and cousin Lord Louis
Mountbatten, always maintained that the Prince would have
liked to discuss the possibility of marriage to Mrs Simpson
during the King's lifetime, but was too much in awe of his
disciplinarian father to do so. Once he was King himself, he was
free to marry whom he wished within the bounds of the Royal
Marriages Act. Given all that, there was still one major obstacle
to overcome before he could entertain any hope of marrying Mrs
Simpson: the fact that she was already married. At what stage
the first steps were taken to obtain that essential divorce – and at
whose instigation – has always been a subject of debate. Under
the divorce laws then obtaining in England, a successful appel-
lant would first be granted a decree nisi. (Literally "nisi" means
unless.) Then, if no evidence was brought within six months to
warrant the attention of the King's Proctor – evidence of collusion, perhaps, or some miscarriage of justice – the decree
became absolute and both parties would be free to remarry. That
unavoidable six months' interval would inevitably have been an
important consideration if, as some were beginning to suspect
and fear, the King intended to have Mrs Simpson crowned
Queen on 12 May 1937, the date set for his coronation.

American authors J. Bryan III and Charles J.V. Murphy state
categorically in their book *The Windsor Story* that:

"... the King stage-managed the divorce from beginning to
end. Wallis's attitude was depicted in her bland assurance ...

Boobs and Misprints

"Alleging the issue was stacked, Councillor Malcolm said the council had decided against the toilets prior to the meeting on the issue and 'just went through the motions'?"
New Zealand News Advertiser

"Mr Griffin said last night: 'I am very pleased alter this long wait that we are now able to get married. It has been a long time, but was worth every minute. The dispensation had to come from the Pope . . . Both my wife-to-be and myself were and still are active alcoholics, and will continue to be so.'"
Yorkshire Post

"The officer said that he and a colleague ran to the accused and found that he was exposed. Asked what he thought he was doing, he said: 'Nothing, nothing. I was just waiting for my wife.'"
Hendon Times

"A report in *The Age* on Monday said that up to six million dead had died in a gun battle in Sri Lanka. It should have read up to six militants died in a gun battle. This was a typographical error."
The Age

a few months later . . . that the divorce was 'at Ernest's instigation', and at no wish of hers. Precisely when the King
decided to start preparations for her suit is not clear. The
vague, but best available, date is 'one evening in February
1936'." A close friend revealed that he was present, at Ernest
Simpson's request, at a meeting between the two men at the
time. He said Simpson asked the King, "Are you sincere? Do
you intend to marry her?" and the King replied, "Do you
really think I would be crowned without Wallis by my side?"
At that, say the authors: "The bargain was struck. And kept."

Certainly the King's subsequent conduct would appear to
indicate that henceforth he took marriage to Mrs Simpson
almost for granted, although there has never been any suggestion
that either his own or Mrs Simpson's legal advisers were in any
way involved. On 27 May 1936 he gave a dinner party at St
James's Palace. The guests included the Mountbattens, Prime
Minister Stanley Baldwin and his wife, the Duff Coopers and
the Simpsons, husband and wife. Years later, as the Duchess of
Windsor, she wrote that the King said he was inviting the
Baldwins that night because "Sooner or later my Prime Minister
must meet my future wife . . ." What is beyond dispute, in the
light of the divorce action that was then being prepared, is that
the King's Mediterranean cruise that summer, with Mrs Simpson
in the royal party but not her husband, was positively reckless,
so much international publicity and speculation did it arouse.
Before the King left Britain, the Palace asked Fleet Street to
respect his privacy on holiday, as usual. No such obligation
rested upon the American and European press however.
Unfortunately no one could accuse the King of discretion. First
he hired a 250-foot luxury yacht, the *Nahlin*, complete with
crew of 50. When the royal party sailed in her from the

Yugoslav port of Sibenik, with two Royal Navy destroyers in attendance, a crowd of many thousands turned up to see them off, shouting "Zivila Ljubav!" (Long live love!).

The eccentric Bloomsbury hostess, Lady Ottoline Morrell, kept abreast of the 1930s social scene as well as the activities of all the literary lions she entertained at her home. In her journal in 1936 she recorded her chagrin that she and Virginia Woolf, her novelist friend, were not invited to a lunch with Mrs Wallace Simpson that had been arranged by Margot Asquith – "It wouldn't do my dear," said Margot. "You see, she has never opened a book in her life . . ."

"All England and the Commonwealth live in terror that he will marry her. She isn't a bad sort I hear but very common," reported Ottoline in her journal. Later as the abdication crisis deepened, she set down what she heard on the social grapevine about all the stresses the King was suffering – trying to cope with his constitutional responsibilities and more private obligations.

"It is said that he is very nearly mad. He had injections to make himself more virile and they affected his head and have made him very violent. He has remained shut up at Fort Belvedere . . . Poor little fellow – they also say that he has been drinking all these last weeks and has signed two abdications and torn them up."

True to its word, the British press, almost alone, made no open reference to Mrs Simpson's presence, although *The Times* was stung into commenting that a sovereign ". . . should be invested with a certain detachment and dignity . . ." Authors Bryan and Murphy summed up by saying: "The King returned to London no longer the invincible figure he had appeared when he left to join the Nahlin. The world publicity had done for him. Within the Establishment, his reputation was in ruins . . ."

Joke of the Day
Mom: "Sydney, there were two chocolate cakes in the larder yesterday, and now there's only one. Why?" Sydney: "I don't know. It must have been so dark I didn't see the other one."

Back in Britain, Mrs Simpson's name then appeared in the Court Circular as one of the King's house guests at Balmoral. On this occasion, however, it was not only members of his family and the Establishment who were offended; now it was the turn of the public. The King had been asked earlier, by the trustees of the Royal Infirmary at Aberdeen, to open a new hospital extension on his arrival on Deeside. He had refused on the grounds that the court would still be in mourning for his dead father. Since then he had been seen at Ascot and holidayed on the *Nahlin*; now, on the day that his brother, the Duke of York, deputized for him at Aberdeen, the King drove to Ballater railway station to meet Mrs Simpson on arrival there. This royal snub caused deep resentment, not only in Deeside but wherever the incident was related, in Scotland and south of the border.

Soon after the King's return from Balmoral to London, a date was set for the hearing of the Simpson divorce action – 27 October. Already the US newspapers were showing an almost obsessive interest in the royal romance. Those papers were finding their way into Britain and the Dominions, and angry letters of protest were reaching the leaders of the Establishment in London, at Downing Street, Lambeth Palace, and the Foreign

168

IT'S THE LAW

In California, community leaders passed an ordinance that makes it illegal for anyone to try and stop a child from playfully jumping over puddles of water.

In Connecticut you are not allowed to walk across a street on your hands.

In Asheville, North Carolina, it is illegal to sneeze on city streets.

In Florida, women may be fined for falling asleep under a hair dryer, as can the salon owner.

In Washington State it's illegal for a candidate to buy anyone a drink on Election Day.

In California it's forbidden to let phones ring more than nine times in state offices.

In Simsbury, Connecticu, it's illegal for a politician to campaign at the town dump.

A Minnesota tax form is quite thorough. Some would say too thorough. It even asks for your date of death.

In San Antonio, Texas, you can't honk a horn, run a generator, have a revival meeting or do anything else that disturbs the neighborhood and the city has a four-member noise police squad to enforce the law.

Office. Behind the scenes, pressure grew to try to have the divorce proceedings stopped but the King would have none of it. He told Prime Minister Baldwin that the divorce was the lady's private business, adding, "It would be wrong were I to attempt to influence Mrs Simpson just because . . . she happens to be a friend."

On 12 October 1936 Lord Beaverbrook, Canadian proprietor of the all-powerful *Express* group of newspapers, learned that the divorce was to be heard at Ipswich. He thereupon rang Mrs Simpson's solicitor, Theodore Goddard, and told him he intended to publish a report on the forthcoming petition in the *Evening Standard*. Goddard then called personally on Beaverbrook, to deny that the King intended to marry Mrs Simpson. Later the King invited Lord Beaverbrook to call on him and asked him not only to suppress all comment before the case was heard but for his help in limiting publicity afterward, on the grounds that Mrs Simpson was "ill, unhappy and distressed by the thought of notoriety . . . Notoriety would attach to her only because she had been his guest on the *Nahlin* and at Balmoral."

Lord Beaverbrook agreed and together with Esmond Harmsworth (son of Lord Rothermere, owner of the *Daily Mail* group), persuaded the rest of the British press to agree to this unprecedented voluntary pact of silence. Beaverbrook wrote later that:

> "While I was engaged in these activities directed to regulating publicity, I had no knowledge that marriage was in the mind of the King. He himself had given me no hint of the matter; and, at the same time, I had been told by Mrs Simpson's solicitor, Mr Theodore Goddard, that His Majesty had no such intention. I repeated that assurance to other newspaper proprietors. And I believed it . . ."

The divorce was heard at Ipswich where Mrs Simpson had taken up residence, presumably as a further deterrent to possible publicity. She was awarded a decree nisi against her husband, with costs, on the grounds of his adultery (with a professional co-respondent called Buttercup Kennedy but not named in court). As the former Mrs Simpson left with her solicitor, Theodore Goddard, so the courtroom doors were locked to keep the press inside. Outside, two photographers had their cameras smashed by the police as they attempted to photograph her. In the confusion, the King's chauffeur drove off with Mrs Simpson: yet next morning, as agreed, the divorce proceedings were reported without comment.

On 13 November, after a visit to the Fleet at Southampton where he was given a rousing ovation – the King returned to Fort Belvedere to find a terse, coldly polite letter awaiting him from his Private Secretary, Major Alexander Hardinge. In it the King was warned that the press was about to break its pact of silence and told that Prime Minister Baldwin had called a Cabinet to decide what action should be taken "to deal with the serious situation which is developing." Hardinge spoke of the possible resignation of the government and the damage which could result from an Election fought on the issue of the King's private life. His letter ended: "If Your Majesty will permit me to say so, there is only one step which holds out any prospect of avoiding this dangerous situation, and

Classic One-Liners
G. K. Chesterton: "The only way of catching a train I've discovered is to miss the train before."

that is for Mrs Simpson to go abroad without further delay and I would beg Your Majesty to give this proposal your earnest consideration before the situation has become irretrievable . . ." The King met with Prime Minister Baldwin and was told that his marriage to Mrs Simpson would not meet with the approval of the Cabinet. The King's response was that his mind was made up and that he was ready to abdicate if need be to marry her. Baldwin called it "grievous news". Later Queen Mary, Edward's mother, wrote to her son saying: "I do not think you have ever realized the shock which the attitude you took up caused your family and the whole nation . . . It seemed inconceivable to those who had made such sacrifices during the war that you, as their King, refused a lesser sacrifice . . ."

By now gossip was rife in the Commons. MPs, already restive under the self-imposed press censorship, were becoming increasingly concerned with the government's own deliberate attempts to hide the truth from the people. On 17 November 1936 Socialist MP Ellen Wilkinson put a leading question to Sir Walter Runciman, President of the Board of Trade, "Can the Right Honourable Gentleman say why, in the case of two American magazines of the highest repute imported into this country in the last few weeks, two and sometimes three pages have been torn out; and what is this thing the British public are not allowed to know?" To which Runciman replied equivocally, "My department has nothing to do with that . . ."

Next day the King put private cares aside, and carried out the tour by which he is still best remembered in Britain – through the distressed areas of the Rhondda and Monmouth valleys of South Wales. The unemployed, who knew nothing of the pending crisis, turned out in their thousands to cheer him and sing hymns of praise in Welsh. The King, who was deeply and visibly moved, declared passionately as he looked at all the poverty around him that, "Something must be done." If it was an empty promise, it was still the charismatic King at his best, establishing instant rapport with his subjects, so that he and his closest advisers were greatly impressed by the obvious public support he commanded.

Equally, no one who was aware of the fast-approaching constitutional crisis wanted the King to go, but most were determined that Mrs Simpson should not become Queen of England. Their objections had nothing to do with the fact that she was an American, or a commoner: they were that she was a twice-divorced woman, with her two ex-husbands still alive. Similarly, even those who supported the King's desire to marry the woman of his choice, believed his best course was not to challenge the Establishment head-on but to proceed with his coronation and then, at some unspecified future date, when Mrs Simpson had won public approval by example, to raise the issue again. This was unacceptable to the King, who felt it meant "being crowned with a lie on my lips." Instead, he approved the suggestion of a morganatic marriage, which meant that Mrs Simpson would become Consort of lesser rank (possibly Duchess), and with a proviso that their children, if any, could not enter the line of succession.

Again Prime Minister Baldwin, who knew what the answer must be, tried to dissuade the King from forcing the issue. He pointed out that the morganatic marriage proposal would have to be put, not only to the Cabinet at home but also to the governments of the Dominions. (Under the terms of the Statute of Westminster of 1931, ". . . any alteration in the law touching the Succession to the Throne or the Royal Style and Titles, shall hereafter require assent as well of the Parliaments of all the Dominions as of the Parliament of the United Kingdom.") Baldwin then asked the King if that was his wish: the answer

Fascinating Facts

The word "dunce" comes from one of the greatest of medieval philosophers, John Duns Scotus, born in 1265. Followers of Duns Scotus, knowns as "Duns men" or "dunces," opposed the new learning, and their opponents used the word "dunce" as an insult, meaning someone. who lacks learning.

The shrew, the smallest of all mammals, eats four times its own weight in 36 hours. It . . .

During the period for which he was world champion, boxer Jack Dempsey fought for only 138 minutes. This was because few opponents survived his savage style of fighting for more than a few minutes. On 8 February 1926, he knocked out four men in one round each, and repeated this feat again four days later.

In 1644, Danish author Theodore Reinking was given the choice of eating his own book or being executed. King Christian IV of Denmark thought the book too democratic in sentiment. Reinking chose to eat the book torn up in his soup.

The bagpipe was first introduced into Scotland by the ancient Romans.

Montana mountain goats can butt heads so hard their hooves fall off.

was "yes" and at once abdication loomed that much closer.

Lord Beaverbrook, who had been recalled from a transatlantic holiday by the King, immediately advised him to withdraw his request. Beaverbrook realized that if Baldwin's Cabinet colleagues advised against a morganatic marriage – and the King refused to accept that advice – then his ministers would have to resign. A General Election would then be fought on the very issue Hardinge had warned against, the King's marriage to twice-divorced Mrs Simpson and the title she should assume. However, after Lord Beaverbrook was telephoned by the King late that night and told, "Mrs Simpson prefers the morganatic marriage to any other solution . . ." he realized the battle was lost.

Baldwin, who was later accused of slanting the vital telegrams to the Dominion Prime Ministers, received the answer he expected. None was in favor of the morganatic marriage proposal, although some were less emphatic than others. From talks with Opposition leader Clement Attlee, Baldwin also knew that, with the exception of a few backbenchers, Parliament at home was against it. Since the voluntary "Pact of Silence" still held in the press, however, there had been no opportunity to sound out public opinion as late as the end of November. Then dramatically – and in all innocence, he later claimed – the silence was broken by the Bishop of Bradford, Dr Alfred Blunt, in an address to his diocesan conference. After a reference to the essential religious nature of the coronation ceremony, the aptly named Bishop went on to say, "The benefit of the King's coronation depends under God upon two elements – firstly, on the faith, prayer and self-dedication of the King himself. On that it would be improper for me to say anything except to commend him, and ask others to commend him, to God's grace, which he will so abundantly need – for the King is a man like any other –

175

if he is to do his duty properly. We hope he is aware of this need. Some of us wish that he gave more positive signs of such awareness . . ."

Although Dr Blunt later protested that at the time he had not heard of Mrs Simpson, the press clearly thought otherwise. The provincial newspapers examined the speech first. "Dr Blunt must have good reason for so pointed a remark," insisted the influential *Yorkshire Post*. "Most people by this time are aware that a good deal of rumour regarding the King has been published of late in the more sensational American newspapers. . . But certain comments which have appeared in reputable United States journals, and even we believe in some Dominions newspapers, cannot be treated with quite so much indifference. They are too circumstantial, and plainly have a foundation in fact . . ."

On the same morning the *Yorkshire Post* was published, the Cabinet in London formally rejected the proposal of a morganatic marriage between the King and Mrs Simpson. Prime Minister Baldwin called on the King that night to discuss the situation. In their varying accounts later of what took place at that meeting, both parties agreed on one thing: that Baldwin urged the King not to abdicate. However, he was obliged to point out that the King had three courses only left open to him. They were: to give up the idea of marriage to Mrs Simpson altogether, to marry against his government's advice – and

---

Joke of the Day
On which side does a chicken have the most feathers? On the outside.

plunge the country into constitutional crisis – or to abdicate, and marry. As the King considered his position, so Fleet Street joined in the great debate, at long last. Press reaction in the critical week that followed was mixed, with more newspapers against the marriage than for it. In the end the King, disheartened by press comment generally, and increasingly worried by anonymous threats made against Mrs Simpson, arranged for her to leave for the South of France accompanied by his Lord-in-Waiting, Lord Brownlow, and his personal bodyguard.

Before she left, Mrs Simpson suggested the King might borrow an idea from the American presidency and discuss his dilemma with his subjects direct – through a "fireside chat" broadcast. The King was enthusiastic but when he showed the proposed draft to Baldwin, the Premier warned him that, although he was willing to discuss the idea with his ministerial colleagues, he was in no doubt what their decision would be. He further pointed out that any such appeal to the public, over the heads of the elected government, would be unconstitutional. (Baldwin's opponents later claimed that he had already discussed the draft with his Cabinet who rejected it before he called on the King.)

According to Baldwin, the King replied, "You want me to go, don't you? And before I go, I think it is right for her sake and mine that I should speak." To which the Premier responded, "What I want, Sir, is what you told me you wanted: to go with dignity, not dividing the country, and making things as smooth as possible for your successor . . . You will be telling millions throughout the world – among them a vast number of women – that you are determined to marry one who has a husband living . . . You may, by speaking, divide opinion; but you will certainly harden it."

Shortly afterwards the King left Buckingham Palace for the

Boobs and Misprints

"Police are baffled as to why a naked woman, aged about fifty, was walking the streets of Pennant Hills early today with a garbage bin on her head. She was taken to Hornsby Hospital and treated for exposure."
Daily Mirror (Sydney)

"We learn that a tape recording taken in the Legislative Assembly has now established that the word spoken by Sir Seewoosagur was 'bolshy", and not 'bullshit'."

"Mr Kenneth Aylett, for Dearman, said to the jury that they may find the films 'Dirty, lewd, indecent, shocking, repulsive, revolting, outrageous, utterly disgusting or filthy', but added that those feelings did not mean that the videos were obscene."
Enfield Independent

"Borough arts liaison officer Marjorie Farley hopes that the bar, due to open in the next few weeks, together with proposed toilets, will attract a lot more people to Ruislip Halls – both as users and as spectators."
Uxbridge and Hillingdon Gazette

last time as sovereign and drove to Fort Belvedere. As always in critical moments in the nation's history, crowds began to gather outside the Palace and 10 Downing Street. Denied information for so long by press silence, their understandable confusion was reflected in the placards they carried: some for, some against the marriage. "After South Wales, You Can't Let Him Down . . . Come To The Palace Now!" Opponents of the marriage in their turn spread the crudest anti-Simpson jokes. "Heard about the King's new job? He wants to sign on as Third Mate on an American tramp!"

On 4 December, Baldwin told the House bluntly that there was no such thing as morganatic marriage in English law. "The lady whom [the King] marries . . . necessarily becomes Queen. The only way in which this result could be avoided would be by legislation dealing with a particular case. His Majesty's Government are not prepared to introduce such legislation." According to the *Daily Telegraph* (which was pro-Baldwin) the Prime Minister was cheered so loudly at this, "that for a little while, [he] could not continue . . ." Mrs Simpson telephoned from France and urged the King to "fight for his rights," but all to no avail. On the morning of 5 December he sent Walter Monckton, his barrister friend and adviser, to Downing Street to inform Baldwin officially that he intended to abdicate. When Beaverbrook heard the news he told Winston Churchill, the

---

Classic One-Liners
Oliver Edwards to Dr Johnson: "I have tried to be a philosopher, but cheerfulness kept breaking in."

King's political champion, "Our cock won't fight." On 7 December Churchill himself was howled down in the Commons when he sought an assurance from Baldwin that no "irrevocable" step should be taken by the government. Behind the scenes there were real fears that the King's Proctor might yet be asked to intervene and quash the decree nisi awarded to Mrs Simpson (and so thwart the intended marriage), but an attempt to have the divorce made absolute forthwith by Act of Parliament was resisted by the government, who believed that any such Bill could only provoke an even greater scandal.

Desperate eleventh-hour attempts were made to try to prevent the abdication. In Cannes, Mrs Simpson (under pressure, it was said, from Lord Brownlow) put out a press statement that read: "Mrs Simpson, throughout the last few weeks, has invariably wished to avoid any action or proposal which would hurt or damage His Majesty or the Throne. Today her attitude is unchanged and she is willing, if such action would solve the problem, to withdraw from a situation that has been rendered both unhappy and untenable." When told of its contents, the King, who was anxious that she should not be blamed for the crisis, said simply, "Go ahead if you wish. But it won't make any difference." Shortly afterwards Mrs Simpson's solicitor, Theodore Goddard, flew to Cannes to call on his client. Different reasons have since been given for his visit. One was that he had learned that an affidavit was about to be served on the King's Proctor, allegedly accompanied by "evidence" of collusion, by a private individual. Another, widely circulated within the Establishment, was that he had been requested to recover jewelery left by Queen Alexandra (wife of Edward VII), and since given to Mrs Simpson by the King. In the event, Mr Goddard telephoned the following message to the Prime Minister, after meeting with Mrs Simpson in Cannes: "I have today discussed the whole position with Mrs Simpson – her own, the position of the King, the country, the Empire. Mrs Simpson tells me she was, and still is, perfectly willing to instruct me to withdraw her petition for divorce and willing to do anything to prevent the King from abdicating. I am satisfied that this is Mrs Simpson's genuine and honest desire. I read this note over to Mrs Simpson who in every way confirmed it." It was signed by Mr Goddard, and counter-signed by Lord Brownlow.

In their turn the Cabinet sent a formal message to the King, asking him to reconsider his intention to abdicate. This he refused to do. "His Majesty has given the matter his further consideration but regrets he is unable to alter his decision." All that remained now was for the parties concerned to settle the King's future finances (never officially disclosed but said to be very considerable) and his rank. On Thursday, 10 December he signed the Instrument of Abdication. It read: "I, Edward the Eighth, of Great Britain, Ireland, and the British Dominions beyond the Seas, King, Emperor of India, do hereby declare My irrevocable determination to renounce the Throne for Myself and My descendants . . ." It was witnessed by his three brothers, Albert (York), Henry (Gloucester) and George (Kent).

On 11 December he sailed into exile. Only now that he was ex-King could he broadcast to his former subjects without first seeking government sanction. However, as a matter of courtesy, he sent an advance copy of his farewell speech to Number 10 Downing Street. Walter Monckton drove with him from Fort Belvedere to Windsor Castle, whence the broadcast was to be made. Sir John Reith, Director General of the BBC, introduced him, on the personal instructions of the new King, his brother George VI, as "His Royal Highness Prince Edward." It was a

ANIMAL SCIENCE

Despite its reputation for being finicky, the average cat consumes about 127,750 calories a year, nearly 28 times its own weight in food and the same amount again in liquids. In case you were wondering, cats cannot survive on a vegetarian diet.

Developed in Egypt about 5,000 years ago, the greyhound breed was known before the ninth century in England, where it was bred by aristocrats to hunt such small game as hares.

Dolphins sleep at night just below the surface of the water. They frequently rise to the surface for air.

During World War II, the very first bomb dropped on Berlin by the Allies killed the only elephant in the Berlin Zoo.

The average canary has about 2,200 feathers.

There are more chickens in the world than people.

The average robin lives to be about 12.

There is a type of parrot in New Zealand that likes to eat the rubber strips that line car windows.

moving, memorable speech and occasion, and his voice was heard wherever English was spoken:

"You all know the reasons which have impelled me to renounce the Throne. But I want you to understand that in making up my mind I did not forget the country or the Empire which as Prince of Wales, and lately as King, I have for twenty-five years tried to serve. But you must believe me when I tell you that I have found it impossible to carry the heavy burden of responsibility and to discharge my duties as King as I would wish to do, without the help and support of the woman I love."

Authors Bryan and Murphy described the scene 3,000 miles from Windsor Castle: "In New York, taxi drivers pulled over to the kerb and stopped, to hear him through. The whole English-speaking world all but stood still for seventy seconds. People wept. There never has been its match for pathos: a king – a king of England! – renouncing his imperial splendour for love alone . . ."

Amazing Engineering Facts

A Brief History of Radio and Television

Radio and television changed entertainment in the twentieth-century enormously. Suddenly, events from far away were brought into people's homes.

1900 – Tesla
In 1900, Nikola Tesla was granted a US patent for a "system of transmitting electrical energy" and another patent for "an electrical transmitter." Both devices resulted from his years of research into transmitting and receiving radio signals.

1901 – The First Transatlantic Radio Signal
Guglielmo Marconi picked up the first transatlantic radio signal in St John's Newfoundland. The signal was sent from a Marconi station in Cornwall, England. The message (the three dots for the Morse letter "s"), was sent by sending a copper wire aerial into the sky using a kite. Following on from this, Marconi built a business using radio as the new way to send Morse code.

1904 – The Vacuum Diode
The "Vacuum Diode" (a two-electrode radio rectifier) called an oscillation valve, was invented by British engineer Sir John

Ambrose Fleming. Based on Edison's lightbulbs, the valve reliably detected radio waves.

1906 – The Audion
American entrepreneur Lee De Forest expanded Fleming's invention by putting a third wire into a vacuum tube to create a highly sensitive receiver. He called his invention the "Audion." Eventually in 1917, it became possible to transmit transatlantic telephone calls.

1906 – Christmas Eve 1906, First Entertainment Broadcast
Reginald Fessenden a Professor of Engineering, transmitted a voice and music program in Massachusetts on Christmas Eve 1906. It was picked up as far away as Virginia.

1912 – The Invention of the Radio Signal Amplifier
Edwin Howard Armstrong, still a student at Columbia University devised a regenerative circuit for the triode that amplified radio signals.

1917 – The Superheterodyne Circuit to Improve Radio Reception
Edwin Howard Armstrong invented the superheterodyne circuit while serving in the US Army Signal Corps during World War I. The superheterodyne circuit consisted of an eight-tube receiver that dramatically improved the reception of radio signals by reducing static and increasing selectivity and amplification

1920 – The First Scheduled Commercial Radio Program
Station KDKA in Pittsburgh became radio's first scheduled commercial programmer broadcasting the Harding-Cox presidential election returns, transmitted at 100 watts from a

Joke of the Day
What's the difference between a coyote and a flea? One howls on the prairie, and the other prowls on the hairy.

wooden shack on the top of the Westinghouse Company's East Pittsburgh plant. Throughout the broadcast KDKA interspersed the election returns and occasional music with a message: "Will anyone hearing this broadcast please communicate with us, as we are anxious to know how far the broadcast is reaching and how it is being received?"

1925 – Televisor

Scottish inventor John Logie Baird successfully transmitted the first TV image (the head of a ventriloquist's dummy), at a London department store, using a device he called a Televisor. The televisor was a mechanical system based on a spinning disk scanner developed in the 1880's by German scientist Paul Nipkow. It required synchronization of the transmitter and receiver disks. The Televisor images were made up of 30 lines flashing 10 times per second and were so hard to watch they gave viewers a headache.

Meanwhile, Charles F Jenkins pioneered his mechanical wireless television that he called 'Radiovision' in downtown Washington, DC. Jenkins's radiovisor was a multi-tube radio set with a special scanning-drum attachment for receiving pictures (40 to 48 line), projected on a 6-inch-square mirror. Jenkins's system, like Baird's, broadcasted and received sound and visual images separately.

1927 – The Electronic Television System, The Cathode-Ray Tube

A 21-year-old farm boy from Utah called Philo T. Farnsworth transmitted images of a piece of glass painted black with a line scratched into its center. He positioned the glass between a bright carbon arc lamp and his own invention, a cathode-ray camera tube that he called an "image dissector." Viewers in the next room watched a cathode-ray receiver and as someone turned the glass 90 degrees the line moved. Cathode-ray tubes became the standard for transmitting and receiving pictures, overtaking the mechanical rotating-disk scanner.

1928 – Basic Colour Television "Televisor" System

John Logie Baird demonstrated that his Televisor system could produce images in crude color by covering three sets of holes in his mechanical scanning disks with gels of the three primary colors. First transmitted in a BBC experiment in 1929, the results were described as "as a soft-tone photograph illuminated by a reddish-orange light."

1929 – Television Cameras

Russian émigré, Vladimir Zworykin, moved to the USA in 1919. He demonstrated a cathode-ray-based television camera that he called an iconoscope that scanned images electronically, and a kinescope (a cathode-ray tube receiver) to send and receive filmed images.

1933 – FM Radio

The FM (frequency modulation) radio was developed by Edwin Howard Armstrong radio as a solution to the static interference problem that plagues AM radio transmission. Instead of increasing the strength or amplitude of the radio waves,

Boobs and Misprints

"Give away two kittens, six wks. Will do light mouse duties."
Gold Coast Bulletin

"NEWLY WEDS, AGED EIGHTY-TWO, HAVE PROBLEM"
West Briton

"At a meeting to discuss the route of a proposed ring road, the highways committee chairman said: 'We intend to take the road through the cemetery provided we can get the permission of the various bodies concerned.'"
West London Observer

"The launching ceremony was carried out by Mrs Lill Bull, wife of Mr Christian R. Bull, and despite her giant size, she moved smoothly into the waiting waters of the Mersey."
Birkenhead News

"Don't kill your husband. Let us do it for you. KC Landscaping."
Williamstown Advertiser

"Wanted: Babysitter, six months old, shift work, references necessary."
The Star (Qld)

IT'S THE LAW

Each year, the mayor of Danville, Kentucky., must appoint "three intelligent housekeepers" to the Board of Tax Supervisors.

An old federal law made it illegal to import tiny sponges, smaller than 4 inches in diameter.

It is illegal to loiter in the city morgue in Detroit.

A law passed in the 1950s by officials of Avignon, France, made it illegal for any flying saucer to land in the city.

Under the law of the state of Washington, any restroom with pay toilets has to have an equal number of free toilets. This law came to pass after the speaker of the state House of Representatives found himself in need of a toilet without any money.

In Boston it's illegal to post an advertisement on a public urinal. It's also against the law to hang a vending machine on a utility pole.

In Baltimore it's illegal to throw bale of hay (or of anything else) out a second-story window. The penalty is a $20 fine.

Armstrong changed only the frequency on which they are transmitted.

1947 – The Invention of the Transistor

John Bardeen, Walter Brattain, and William Shockley of Bell Laboratories co-invented the transistor, changing the future of broadcasting forever.

1950s – Television Monitors Improve

The rectangular cathode-ray tube (CRT) for television monitors was improved, eliminating the need for "masks" over the round picture tubes of earlier monitors. An average TV set now cost around $200 making them more accessible to the masses.

1953 – RCA's Commercial Colour System

CBS pioneered color television but RCA beat them when the National Television System Committee adopted RCA's new system for commercial color because CBS's system was not compatible with existing black and white TV monitors owned across the USA.

1954 – Coast to Coast Color Television

The New Year's Day Tournament of Roses in Pasadena, California, became the first coast to coast color television transmission (called a colorcast), broadcast by RCA's NBC network to 21 specially equipped stations. Six weeks later NBC's *Camel News Caravan* was transmitted in color, as was the first color sitcom, *The Marriage*, starring Hume Cronyn and Jessica Tandy on the same channel.

> **Classic One-Liners**
> Critic Eugene Field: "The actor who took the role of the king played it as though he expected somone to play the ace."

1954 – The First All-Transistor Radio
The TR-1 was the first all-transistor radio operating on a 20 volt battery and working immediately when switched on. The TR-1 cost $49.99, was the size of a pack of cigarettes and available in six colors.

1962 – Telstar 1
The $6 million communications satellite *Telstar 1* was launched into space by a NASA Delta rocket. It could transmit live transatlantic telecasts as well as telephone and data signals. The first international television broadcasts showed images of the American flag flying over Andover, Maine to the sound of "The Star-Spangled Banner."

1968 – 200 Million Television Sets Watched Worldwide
Up from 100 million TV's watched in 1960, by 1968 there were over 200 million TV sets watched around the world. The number reached 300 million by 1979 and over a billion by 1996.

1988 – Sony "Watchman"
Sony introduced the first small hand-held TV sets. Its Model FD – 210 had a 1.75 inch screen.

1990 – FCC Begins Testing for a Proposed All-Digital HDTV System
Zenith introduced the first HDTV-compatible front-projection television. Together, TV manufacturers and PC makers set an industry standard for digital HDTV. By the end of the Twentieth Century, digital HDTV was on the verge of offering fully interactive TV.

Science: How it Works

How Animation Works

When we watch an animation, we know that we're actually watching a series of still drawings but we don't see each drawing. Cartoons work because our eyes and brain can deceive us. Your brain holds on to a single image for a short time, even though the images appear and disappear quickly. The series of images begin to overlap in your brain so that the picture you are looking at seems to be moving.

People in History

Strange Historical Stories

Ghostblaster

It was 1803 and the citizens of Hammersmith, London, were all
very worried. One of the local residents had recently been
brutally murdered and the body had been recovered with the
throat violently slit. They were convinced that the spirit of the
murdered man was roaming along the banks of the River
Thames, a ghost of his former self. Tales abounded of sightings
of the terrifying, white monster with its horns and its howling
shrieks. One woman went out for a walk, caught sight of the
dreaded creature and instantaneously died of fright.

Two locals, Mr Smith, a highly respected customs officer, and
his friend Mr Girdler, the neighborhood watchman, were
determined to form a vigilante group and rid their streets of this
terrible threat. Mr Thomas Millwood was a bricklayer. On the
evening of 3 January 1804 he went to visit his parents, who
happened to live in Hammersmith, on his way home from work.
By the time he left it was quite late and he was still wearing his
normal work uniform which consisted of long white trousers and
a white shirt. Mr Smith and Mr Girdler were on their night-
watch when they caught sight of a ghostly white spectre ambling

Joke of the Day
What's the difference between a deer
running away and a small witch? One's
a hunted stag and the other's a
stunted hag.

slowly along the banks of the Thames. They immediately
concluded that this must be their prey and challenged the ghost
to fight them. Being a peaceable soul, mistakenly assuming
that he had just encountered two drunken men also on
their way home, Mr Millwood decided to turn the other
cheek and, ignoring their shouts, he walked on. Mr Smith
panicked and shot Mr Millwood who collapsed dead in front of
him. Seeing the blood, Mr Smith immediately realized his
terrible mistake and surrendered himself to a passing wine
merchant.

A mere ten days later he was up in the dock at the Old Bailey
accused of murder. Many of the good citizens of Hammersmith
came to give evidence about the terrifying reputation of the
ghost. Mr Girdler told the jury at great length that Mr Smith was
a generous and kind man and one of the best friends he had ever
had. Mr Smith himself made a short but moving speech
explaining that, whatever he had done, he had done it with the
interests of his beloved Hammersmith at heart. The judge, in his
summing up, explained to the jury that if they were satisfied that
Mr Smith had shot the victim intentionally then he was guilty
and there was no defence which could save him. He mistakenly
ignored the possibility that Mr Smith might have had the intention to shoot a ghost but certainly not a man. The jury had no
choice but to convict. The accused was sentenced immediately

to death on the following Monday with his body to be given to surgeons for medical experiments.

Fortunately for Mr Smith a pardon arrived in the nick of time. But the bricklayers of Hammersmith were thereafter very careful always to change into their own clothes before they went home from work.

Science: How it Works

Weight Distribution

Why are igloos dome shaped and not square? Have you ever been amazed at how a suspension bridge can hold the weight of hundreds of passing cars with little or no apparent support underneath it? Arches are used in architecture not only for aesthetic appeal – they also serve a very useful purpose. Arches are strong because they exert horizontal as well as vertical forces to resist the pressure of heavy loads. Even the crown of an eggshell can support heavy books because the weight is distributed evenly along the structure of the egg.

Fascinating Facts

The average blonde has thinner hairs than redheads and black haired women. The average blonde has about 150,000 hairs on her head, while redheads and black haired women have respectively 30,000 and 110,000.

It is claimed that Walt Disney had wooden teeth.

The shortest performance to achieve an Oscar nomination was by Sylvia Mills in *Midnight Cowboy*. She was in the film for only six minutes.

Finding fossilized dinosaur droppings is fairly common – they are called coprolites.

The microwave oven was invented after a researcher walked by a radar tube and a chocolate bar melted in his pocket.

The saying "raining cats and dogs" dates back to medieval times when family pets would sleep in the thatched rafters of a house. When it rained heavily they fled back down into the house.

In 1471 a chicken in the Alpine town of Basel, Switzerland, laid a brightly colored egg. The unnatural color of it upset local citizens to the point that it was burned at the stake for being a familiar of the devil.

Real Ghost Stories

The Living Dead

William Seabrook avidly studied the spirit religions of the West Indies in the 1920s. In his book The Magic Island he relates a strange tale told to him by a Haitian farmer. It seems that there was a bumper sugar cane crop in 1918, and laborers were in short supply. One day Joseph, an old headman, appeared leading "a band of ragged creatures who shuffled along behind him, staring dumbly, like people in a daze." They were not ordinary laborers. They were zombies – dead men whom Joseph had brought back to life by magic to slave for him in the fields.

Zombies must never taste salt according to the farmer's tale, so Joseph's wife fed them special unseasoned food. But one day she took pity on them and bought them some candy, not knowing it was made of peanuts. As soon as the zombies tasted the salty nuts, they realized they were dead. With a terrible cry they set off for their own village.

Stumbling past living relatives who recognized them in horror, they "approached the graveyard . . . and rushed among the graves, and each before his own empty grave began clawing at the stones and earth . . . and, as their cold hands touched the earth, they fell and lay there, rotting as carrion."

198

Classic One-Liners
Novelist William Dean Howells on guests: "Some people can stay longer in an hour than other people in a week.'"

The One-Minute Novel

Pride and Prejudice – **Jane Austen (1813)**
Mr and Mrs Bennet lived in a large beautiful house called
Longbourn in Hertfordshire, England. The problem was they
had five daughters but no son or male heir to inherit their
property. Without a man in the family the house would have to
pass on to a male cousin (called William Collins), because at the
time women were not allowed to own property themselves. A
very snobbish lady, Lady Catherine de Bourgh, was looking
after cousin William Collins. She had him move to a rectory
near where she lived in Kent and pestered him to get married to
a nice young wife.

Meanwhile everyone at Longbourn got new neighbors in the
form of Charles Bingley who bought nearby Netherfield a
similarly large house. Charles was unmarried but inclined to
enjoy life so brought his two sisters and his friend Fitzwilliam
Darcy to his house. The five young girls at Longbourn could
now look forward to having some fun.

Among all these shenanigans Charles Bingley and the eldest
Bennet daughter (Jane), fell in love. Mr Darcy also looked excitedly to this house of unmarried young girls and picked out the
next eldest daughter Elizabeth to chase around. However,
Elizabeth had heard some unsavoury tales about Mr Darcy
including one from an ex-employee and so decided to keep him

 # Boobs and Misprints

"POLICE IN IRELAND HUNT UNWANTED MAN"
Oman Observer

"Births: Gambardella, nee Bragg – warmest congratulations to Jeannie and Mark and Billy on the birth of their daughter."
Waltham Forest Guardian

"Drive carefully in the new year. Remember that nine people out of ten are caused by accidents."
Falkirk Herald

"Services: Mini Bouncer for hire; ideal for children's parties, playgroups."
The Swift Flash

"Business for sale. Urgent. Wagga fruit and vegetable shop with sandwich bar. No goodwill."
Murrumbidgee Irrigator (New South Wales)

"There is a fundamental difference between male and female homosexuality, which is that the former concerns men and the second women."
European Parliament Report

at arm's length. Her dislike intensified when Fitzwilliam Darcy tried to split up her sister Jane and Charles Bingley because Bingley's sisters thought that the Bennet girls and their mother were a bunch of badly behaved low-lifes on account of Mrs Bennet's urgency to marry off her daughters to the nearest available male.

To Mrs Bennet's delight William Collins, the cousin, asked Elizabeth Bennet to marry him. This would have solved the whole issue very neatly but Elizabeth was having none of it and refused. Desperate to marry anyone to get Lady de Bourgh off his back he then asked Elizabeth's friend Charlotte to marry him and she agreed. After they were married Elizabeth went to visit them at the rectory and who of all people should call round but Mr Darcy with Lady de Bourgh. Mr Darcy begged Elizabeth to marry him but she refused him on account of his being a no-good cad. He later wrote her a letter explaining why he thought he wasn't so bad.

Elizabeth, unable to escape from him, met him again at his place in the north of England, (she thought he was away at the time). He turned on the charm and eventually the chase was over when she agreed to marry him. (He had also helped to find another Bennet sister Lydia who had run off with the aforementioned employee sacked by Darcy). Luckily for a perfect ending, Jane and Charles Bingley got back together and everyone lived happily ever after.

202

 Joke of the Day
"How do dinosaurs pay their bills?
With Tyrannosaurus checks."

People in History

Strange Historical Stories

The Lunatic General

The appointment of Sir William Erskine as a senior commander during the Peninsular War was a mistake to rival the very best. The Duke of Wellington was astonished at the commission and wrote immediately to the Military Secretary in London to complain that Erskine was well-known to be barking mad. "No doubt he is a little mad at times," replied the Secretary by post, "but in his lucid intervals he is a jolly nice chap . . . though I must say that he did look a little mad as he embarked." Erskine's record wasn't too impressive either. His astonishingly bad eyesight had made him a complete liability at the battle of Sabugal in 1811, where he had led a charge away from the enemy by mistake.

At the battle of Almeida, all of Wellington's forebodings were fulfilled. The Iron Duke was closing in on the besieged French garrison and victory seemed assured. Aware of the dangers of placing too much on the madman's shoulders, Wellington asked him to perform the simple task of guarding the bridge of Barba de Puerca. There were no charges to be made and no pitfalls into which Erskine's loopiness or his short-sightedness could lead

In Berkeley, California, you can't whistle for an escaped bird before 7 a.m.

Baltimore has regulations governing the disposal of hog's heads, pet droppings, and oyster shells.

An old federal law made it illegal to import tiny sponges, smaller than 4 inches in diameter.

Under the law of the state of Washington, any restroom with pay toilets has to have an equal number of free toilets. This law came to pass after the speaker of the state House of Representatives found himself in need of a toilet without any money.

In Baltimore it's illegal to throw bale of hay (or of anything else) out a second-story window. The penalty is a $20 fine.

A regulation in San Francisco makes it unlawful to use used underwear to wipe off cars in a car wash.

him. He just had to stand there with a mixed battalion of cavalry and infantry and stop the French getting out.

Erskine was having dinner when Wellington's order arrived. His first response (madder than even Wellington could have anticipated), was to send a corporal and four men to guard the bridge. One of the other dinner guests was so shocked by this stupidity that he blurted out "Sir William, you might as well attempt to block up the bridge with a pinch of snuff."

This brosught on one of Erskine's famous moments of lucidity. He immediately wrote out an order to send a whole regiment to block the bridge. "Better safe than sorry," he added.

Unfortunately, this moment of lucidity was a particularly brief one. As soon as he had finished writing out the order, Erskine folded it up, put it in his pocket, and forgot about it. When the French realized the danger of their position and decided to retreat, they were amazed to find the bridge unguarded and escaped without a single casualty. Wellington called it "the most disgraceful military event that has yet occurred to us."

When Erskine subsequently committed suicide by jumping out of a window in Lisbon in 1813, his last words were "Why on earth did I do that?"

Classic One-Liners
Anonymous: "Alcohol does make you more attractive to the opposite sex. After they've drunk it."

Real Ghost Stories

Back From the Dead

In 1837 in Lahore, India [now in Pakistan] the yogi Haridas was buried alive for 40 days. British Colonel Sir Claude Wade, Dr Janos Honiborger, and the British Consul at Lahore all solemnly corroborated that he was locked in a box, placed in a sealed pavilion with doors and windows tightly blocked shut, and guarded day and night. After forty days, the box was opened.

Haridas had not gone into the tomb unprepared. For days before his burial he had no food but milk. On the burial day itself he ate nothing, but performed dhauti – a yoga purification practice that involves swallowing a long strip of cloth, leaving it in the stomach to soak up bile and other impurities, and then withdrawing it. Haridas then did another cleansing ritual. All the openings of his body were then sealed up with wax, and his tongue was rolled back to seal the entrance to his throat. Then he was buried.

When the box was opened the yogi's assistant washed him with warm water, removed the wax, and rubbed his scalp with warm yeast. He forced his teeth open with a knife, unfolded his tongue, and massaged his body with butter. After half an hour Haridas was up and about.

Fascinating Facts

It is commonly believed that carrying an acorn around with you for life will bring you good luck.

French painter Paul Gauguin worked briefly as a laborer on the Panama Canal during a trip to the South Sea islands.

The Hawaiian alphabet has only 12 letters.

Venetian blinds were actually invented in Japan.

The modern military salute dates back to the time when armored knights would raise their visors to identify themselves when they rode past the king.

A deaf footballer once used sign language to communicate with his team during a game of football. The team huddled around him so that the opposing team couldn't see what he was signing. This eventually became the modern "huddle."

There are no blue natural food groups. Blueberries are in fact, purple.

A male sea catfish holds the eggs of his young in his mouth to incubate them until they hatch. During this period, which can take several weeks, he will not eat until they have all hatched.

A dragonfly lives for only 24 hours.

People in History

Strange Historical Stories

Music of Irving Berlin

During World War II, Irving Berlin, the composer, had a massive smash hit with *White Christmas*. It was considered a tremendous morale boost for Allies everywhere. To celebrate he made a short trip to Britain.

One of Winston Churchill's aides noticed that Mr I. Berlin had arrived in the country and pointed out this heartening fact to the Prime Miruster, who was rather too busy to follow current trends in popular culture. The aide was thus surprised at the alacrity with which Churchill sprang into the air and positively urged him to invite the man to a special reception.

Irving Berlin was honored and flattered to be considered a man of such importance. He was frankly astonished on going into dinner to be seated right next to the great leader. He was interested in current affairs but he realized that he was a little out of his league on this occasion.

Churchill turned to him with a great air of concentration and leaning forwards over the soup, he said:

"So tell me, Mr Berlin, how do you think the war is going?"

> **Classic One-Liners**
> Philip Guedalla: 'History repeats itself; historians repeat each other.'

Irving was thrown. He didn't really feel in a position to respond; he really wasn't able.

"Come now," said Churchill, "a man of your stature. No false modesty here. Now tell me, if you were me, what would your next step be?"

Mr Berlin was silenced. He was at a loss for words. He raced his way through the remaining courses, desperately hoping that no one would notice his presence or ask him for an analysis of current military matters, about which he knew no more than the average popular music composer.

After the meal all of the guests departed. Winston Churchill turned around to his wife and his aide and remarked that the Berlin fellow was a remarkably thoughtful chap, terribly natural and unpompous given that he was one of the world's leading philosophical thinkers. His enthusiasm for his dinner guest had been fired by the wrong first name – not knowing anything about white Christmases, he had assumed that I. Berlin was Isaiah Berlin, the philosopher. Mrs Churchill thought it was all very amusing.

Amazing Engineering Facts

A Brief History of Computers

A relatively new invention, the first electronic computer did not appear until the mid-1930s. Even then it was capable of only the most basic tasks. Now, the twentieth-century is known as the computer age as all kinds of programable devices have begun to find their way into society.

1936 – "A Symbolic Analysis of Relay and Switching Circuits"

This was the title of the master's thesis of electrical engineer and mathematician Claude Shannon. He used Boolean algebra to establish a digital circuit in a paper that became the groundwork for all future telecommunications and computer industries.

1939 – The Atanasoff-Berry Computer (ABC)

John Atanasoff and Clifford Berry designed the first electronic computer at Iowa State College. This obscure project incorporated binary arithmetic and electronic switching. Atanasoff went to work for the National Ordinance Laboratory and never resumed his research, however, invited by Atanasoff, early computer pioneer John Mauchly of the University of Pennsylvania, visited Atanasoff in Iowa and saw the ABC demonstrated.

 # Boobs and Misprints

"Stories about a merger between Coca Cola and Pepsi Cola have been denied by spokesmen from both companies. It had been rumoured that the new advertising slogan would be: 'If you want a new sensation, have a Poke.'"
London Business News

"According to nature conservationist Mr Tony Joubert, poachers scatter maize pips soaked in pesticide solution near dams and on farmlands. Birds that eat the pips die within a short time, after which they are collected and slaughtered."
The Star (Johannesburg)

"The Hirsel has been renovated and made smaller, and one of the guests at the recent wedding reception of the family's youngest daughter Lady Diana, recalls that the house is 'beautiful, but very simple'. This, too, is the impression that many people gain from Lady Home herself. 'She is very attractive and charming', said Mrs V. E. Swinton."
Yorkshire Post

"The dead man is described as white, aged between thirty and forty, with an Irish accent."
Bradford Telegraph and Argus

1939 – The First Binary Digital Computers
Bell Labs' George Stibitz developed the Complex Number Calculator. It performed mathematical operations in binary form using on-off relays, and found the quotient of two 8-digit numbers in 30 seconds. Meanwhile, in Germany, Konrad Zuse developed the first programmable calculator, called the Z2, using binary numbers and Boolean algebra.

1945 – The Stored Program Computer
Mathematician's Briton Alan Turing and Hungarian John von Neumann had been working independently on the specifications of a stored program computer. Neumann worked on a computer on which data and programs could be stored and Turing worked on an Automatic Computing Engine based on speed and memory.

1946 – The First Electronic Computer
Towards the end of World War II, John Mauchly and John Presper Eckert developed the Electronic Numerical Integrator and Computer (ENIAC) at the University of Pennsylvania's Moore School of Electrical Engineering. It was used for ballistics computations, weighed 30 tons and included 18,000 vacuum tubes, 6,000 switches, and 1,500 relays.

1947 – The Invention of the Transistor
Three engineers, John Bardeen, Walter H. Brattain, and William B. Shockley of Bell Telephone Laboratories invented the transistor.

1949 – The First Stored-Program Computer
The first stored-program computer, known as the Electronic Delay Storage Automatic Calculator (EDSAC), was built

and programmed by British mathematical engineer Maurice Wilkes.

1951 – The First Business Computer

John Mauchly and John Presper Eckert, now owning their own company, designed the first business computer in the US. The device was known as the UNIVAC (Universal Automatic Computer) and its breakthrough feature was a magnetic storage system that replaced punched cards.

1955 – The First Disk Drive

Reynold Johnson led a team of IBM engineers in designing the first disk drive for random-access storage. The Model 305 Disk Storage unit, later called the Random Access Method of Accounting and Control, was released in 1956 with a stack of fifty 24-inch aluminum disks storing 5 million bytes of data.

1957 – FORTRAN

Fortran (for Formula Translation) was a programming language developed by IBM that became commercially available. Other programming languages quickly followed, including ALGOL, intended as a universal computer language, in 1958 and COBOL in 1959. Both dominated the computer-language world for the next two decades.

1964 – BASIC

The BASIC (Beginners All-Purpose Symbolic Instruction Code) was developed by John Kemeny and Thomas Kurtz who were professors at Dartmouth. Designed for non-computer-science students, it was easier to use than FORTRAN and was adopted by schools and universities. Computer companies began to provide BASIC manuals with their systems.

1968 – The Computer Mouse
The mouse was first exhibited in San Fransisco at a computer conference. Its inventor Douglas Engelbart received a patent for the mouse two years later.

1970 – The Palo Alto Research Center (PARC)
A team of researchers was put together in Palo Alto, California by the Xerox Corporation aiming to perfect a system of "the architecture of information." Over the next 30 years, the Palo Alto Research Center (PARC) created innovations such as Windows in 1972, Laser printers in 1973 and the concept of WYSIWYG (what you see is what you get) word processors in 1974 that led to the modern day computer screen interface.

1975 – The First Home Computer
Micro Instrumentation Telemetry Systems marketed the Altair 8800 considered by many to be the first home computer. There was no keyboard, monitor or programing language and data was input with a series of switches. It did however include an Intel microprocessor and cost only $400. Young computer entrepreneurs Bill Gates and Paul Allen set about writing a version of BASIC for this new computer and formed a company called Microsoft.

1977 – The Apple II
The Apple Computer was first formulated by Steve Jobs and Steve Wozniak. Their product The Apple II was a desktop computer for the mass market featuring a keyboard, mouse, monitor and in-built random-access memory (RAM). Independent manufacturers, mainly for the creative market created software for the Apple II.

ANIMAL SCIENCE

Emus have double-plumed feathers, and they lay emerald/forest green eggs.

Swans are the only birds with penises.

It takes 40 minutes to hard boil an ostrich egg.

Kiwi birds are blind, they hunt by smell.

The top knot that quails have is called a hmuh.

The bones of a pigeon weigh less than its feathers.

"Eat like a bird?" Many birds eat twice their weight a day.

Emus cannot walk backwards.

A bird requires more food in proportion to its size than a baby or a cat.

1979 – The First Laptop

William Moggridge of GRiD Systems Corporation in England created the first laptop. It had 340kb of memory and a foldaway screen in a light metal case. NASA used it in the early 1980s for its shuttle program and the "portable computer" was patented by GriD in 1982.

Joke of the Day
Caleb: "Dad, there's a man at the door
collecting for the new swimming pool."
Dad: "Give him a glass of water!"

1979 – The First Commercial Business Application
The first commercial business application was the VisiCalc
spreadsheet for the Apple II marketed by Harvard MBA
student Daniel Bricklin and programmer Bob Frankston.
VisiCalc was the sole application in the spreadsheet
market for nearly ten years before finally being overtaken by
Lotus 1-2-3, a spreadsheet program designed by a former
VisiCalc employee.

1981 – The IBM Personal Computer
The first IBM computer, with an Intel 8088 microprocessor and
an MS-DOS operating system designed by Microsoft was put on
the market costing $3,000.

1984 – The Apple Macintosh
The Macintosh was a low-cost, plug and play computer with a
central processor small enough to fit on a single circuit board.
It's easy-use graphics programs made it an essential tool in
graphics and publishing.

1984 – The First CD-ROM
Philips and Sony marketed the first CD-ROM (compact
disc read-only memory). The CD could store 300,000
pages of information including text, images, video and audio
files.

1985 – Windows 1.0

Windows 1.0 the prototype for Windows today, was released by Microsoft in 1985 and featured a Macintosh-like user interface including drop-down menus and technological support. However, most users still stuck to MS-DOS because the program ran too slowly on PC's at the time. Towards the end of the 1980's Microsoft began successfully marketing higher-powered microprocessors with Windows 3.0 and Windows 95.

1991 – The World Wide Web

Communicating by computer, what we know today as the Internet, began in 1991.

1999 – The Palm VII Connected Organizer

The Palm handheld organizer had 2mb RAM and cost less than $600. It weighed 6.7oz and operated for up to 3 weeks on two AAA batteries. With mobile phones and laptops the workforce had become more mobile and computer technology was innovated for this new market.

The One-Minute Novel

The Mayor of Casterbridge – Thomas Hardy (1886)

Michael Henchard got very drunk and sold his wife and child to
a sailor called Newson for five guineas at a local fair. Of course,
when he sobered up the next day he realised the error of his
ways and vowed never to touch alcohol again. He worked hard,
eventually becoming the wealthy Mayor of Casterbridge gaining
much respect from those around him.

Eighteen years later Henchard's wife came looking for him
with her daughter and told him that Newson was supposedly
dead. He was led to believe that the daughter (Elizabeth-Jane),
was his child but she was in fact Newson's. Things started going
wrong in Henchard's life. He quarrelled badly with Donald
Farfrae his assistant in the corn business, his wife died and he
learned the truth about who Elizabeth's father really was.

Meanwhile Farfrae had set himself up in business, as
Henchard's rival where he was successful not only in business
but in marrying the woman Henchard himself had hoped to win.
The story of how Henchard drunkenly sold his wife all those
years ago was revealed and Henchard became a ruined man.

Henchard's only comfort is his step-daughter but then
Newson returned and re-claimed her, taking her back with him.
Henchard ends up a desolate and lonely man dying in a hut on
Egdon Heath.

IT'S THE LAW

It's illegal in Boston to rummage through rubbish containers.

In North Carolina it's illegal to sell cotton lint at night. It's also legal to sell cottonseed at night.

It's illegal in New York to start any kind of public performance, show, play, or game until after 1:05 p.m.

A Boston mayor who disliked dancing and liked to retire early once banned midnight dancing in the Hub City.

Under an 1872 law still on the books, an alderman in Chicago can carry a gun.

In Hartford, Connecticut, it's illegal to plant a tree in the street.

In Boston, it's illegal to cut firewood or shoot a bow and arrow in the street.

In New York City, it's illegal to throw swill into the street.

San Francisco bans any "mechanical device that reproduces obscene language."

In Danville, Kentucky, it's illegal to throw slops or soapsuds in the street.

Beasts and Monsters

Modern Day Mammoths?

A Russian Hunter in 1918 was exploring the taiga – the vast
forest that covers nearly three million square miles of Siberia –
when he encountered huge tracks in thick layers of mud by a
lake in a clearing. They were about two feet across and about
eighteen inches long, and appeared to be oval. The stature was
obviously four-footed, and had wandered into the woods. The
hunter followed the tracks curiously, from time to time finding
huge heaps of dung apparently composed of vegetable matter.
The tree branches were broken off about ten feet up as if the
animal's enormous head had forced its way through. For days he
followed the tracks. Then he saw traces of a second animal, and
a trampling of the tracks, as if the two creatures had been
excited by the meeting. Then the two went on together.

The hunter followed. Suddenly, one afternoon, he saw them.
They were enormous hairy elephants with great white tusks
curved upward. The hair was a dark chestnut color, very heavy
on the hindquarters, but lighter toward the front. The beasts
moved very slowly.

The last of the mammoths are believed to have died more
than 12,000 years ago, and the hunter knew nothing about them.
But did he see mammoths?

Joke of the Day
Teacher: "I wish you'd pay a little attention." Girl: "I'm paying as little as possible."

Real Ghost Stories

The Vampire

Do vampires still walk in Romania? In 1974 a gypsy woman told of her father's death when she was a girl. According to custom, she said, the body lay in the house awaiting the ceremonial final dressing by the family. After this ceremony it would be carried to the grave uncovered, so that everyone could see that the man was truly dead.

When the family lifted her father's legs to put them in his burial clothes, the limbs were not stiff. Neither were his arms nor the rest of his body. Rigor mortis had not set in. The family stared horrified at him and at each other, and the fearful whispering began.

The story spread among the villagers – people who remembered, or thought they remembered, the vampires that used to roam in the darkness of night. One unmistakable sign of a vampire is an undecomposed body, kept lifelike by the regular feasting on the blood of the living. Fear licked through the village, and the inhabitants soon came to the house armed with a wooden stake.

The family – bewildered, uncertain, and grief-stricken – fell back. The men tore off the corpse's covering sheet and, in the traditional manner, thrust the stake through the dead man's heart. The vampire – if such it was – was vanquished.

Fascinating Facts

Penguins aren't very interested in sex. They only have sexual intercourse twice a year.

The memory span of a goldfish is three seconds.

The dot above the "i" in writing is called a tittle.

A peanut is not technically a nut – it is a legume.

It is impossible to sneeze with your eyes open.

You can't buy cashew nuts in their shell – this is because they are actually poisonous until they have been roasted.

Vietnamese currency has no coins, only notes.

A pig's orgasm lasts for 30 minutes.

Your skin is thickest on your back where it is a ⅙ inch.

Your forefinger is your most sensitive finger.

Panama hats actually originated in Ecuador rather than in Panama.

People in History

Strange Historical Stories

Knocking Shop

Elizabethan theaters were places of sex and scandal. The actors, who were always either men or boys, were therefore very keen to make time for interacting with members of the opposite sex at any available opportunity. Richard Burbage, who was Shakespeare's star actor, and generally considered to be a pretty damn sexy fellow, used to arrange assignations while he was performing on stage On one occasion, he managed to nip out in the interval of Richard III, in which he was playing the king, in order to experience a rendezvous with a particularly enthusiastic member of the audience.

Richard, who was naturally in a bit of a hurry, was surprised to find his way barred by an embarrassed servant, furtively guarding the door. The fan, it appeared, was already inside, pursuing her devotion with the Bard himself. Richard was furious at being so humbled and banged on the door loudly. Eventually, Shakespeare who was getting fed up with the interruption, sent down a note which bore the message "William the Conqueror comes before Richard III." The anonymous fan either didn't notice or didn't care.

Science: How it Works

Light

Light traveling in a straight line appears colorless. When light passes through a wedge shaped piece of glass called a prism, the light is separated into seven different, unique colors. These are the colors you see when light passes through rain or moisture producing a rainbow. This is what happens when various wavelengths of light are broken apart. Sunlight is comprised of seven different colors. A light bulb actually produces more red and orange colors. A fluorescent light has more blue and yellow.

Mysteries of the World

Loch Ness, Scotland

Loch Ness, the largest UK lake, is 22 miles long and about
1 mile wide; at its greatest depth, it is 950 feet deep. It is part of
the Great Glen, which runs like a deep crack right across
Scotland, from one coast to the other; it opened up between 300
and 400 million years ago as a result of earthquakes, then was
deepened by glaciers. At the southern end of the loch there is the
small town of Fort Augustus; at the northern end, Inverness.
Until the eighteenth century, the loch was practically inacces-
sible, except by winding trackways; it was not until 1731 that
General Wade began work on the road that runs from Fort
Augustus up the south side of the loch (although Fort Augustus
was not so christened until 1742). But this steep road, which
makes a long detour inland, was obviously not the shortest
distance between Fort Augustus and Inverness; the most direct
route would run along the northern shore. In the early 1930s a
road was finally hacked and blasted out of this northern shore,
and vast quantities of rock were dumped down the steep sides of
Loch Ness.

The road had only just been completed in April 1933, and it
was on the 14th of that month that Mr and Mrs John Mackay,
proprietors of the Drumnadrochit Hotel, were returning home
from a trip to Inverness. It was about 3 p.m. when Mrs Mackay

Boobs and Misprints

"Five-course dinner menu including a welcoming glass of red wine. Hot smoked mackerel with horseradish and black pepper. Curried eggs (two eggs filled with a delicate curried mouse). Melon balls marinated in ginger wine."
Harrogate Champion Shopper

"The incident happened at 2.10 a.m. when the sister was going to the ladies' toilet at the burns unit. The toilet sprang out and slashed her hand with a knife."
St Helens Star

"Meat Inspector: The successful applicant will be expected to ensure that no food fit for human consumption leaves the slaughterhouse for distribution to the general public."
Meat Trades Journal

"Talented, handsome, well-hung Persian/Burmese stud, preferably vegetarian non-smoker, needed for half Burmese female cat."
Loot (London)

"LESOTHO WOMEN MAKE BEAUTIFUL CARPETS"
Bangkok World

pointed and said, "What's that, John?" The water in the middle
of the loch was in a state of commotion; at first she thought it
was two ducks fighting, then realized that the area of disturbance was too wide. As her husband pulled up they saw some
large animal in the middle of the surging water; then as they
watched, the creature swam towards Aldourie pier on the other
side of the loch. For a moment they glimpsed two black humps,
which rose and fell in an undulating manner; then the creature
made a half-turn and sank from sight.

The Mackays made no attempt to publicize their story, but
gossip about the sighting reached a young water bailiff, Alex
Campbell, who also happened to be local correspondent for the
Inverness Courier; he called on the Mackays, and his report
went into the *Courier* on 2 May, more than two weeks after the
sighting occurred. The editor is said to have remarked: "If it's as
big as they say, it's not a creature it's a monster." And so the
"Loch Ness Monster" acquired its name.

This was not, strictly speaking, the first account of the
monster to appear in print. This distinction belongs to a *Life of
St Columba* dating from about AD 565. This tells (in vol. 6,
book 11, chap. 27) how the saint arrived at a ferry on the banks
of the loch and found some men preparing to bury a comrade
who had been bitten to death by a water monster while he was
swimming. The saint ordered one of his own followers to swim
across the loch. The monster heard the splashing and swam
toward him, at which the saint made the sign of the cross and
commanded the creature to go away; the terrified monster
obeyed . . .

Other reportings down the centuries are more difficult to pin
down. books Between 1600 and 1800 there were a number of
references to the "beast" or "water kelpie" (fairy) of Loch Ness.
A Dr D. Mackenzie of Balnain claimed to have seen it in 1871

or 1872, looking rather like an upturned boat but moving at great speed, "wriggling and churning up the water." Alex Campbell, the water bailiff, reported that a crofter named Alexander MacDonald had seen the monster in 1802 and reported it to one of Campbell's ancestors. But hearsay reports like this inevitably led sceptics to suspect that local people, particularly hoteliers, had a financial interest in promoting the monster, so that by the mid-1930s "Nessie" (as she was soon christened in the area) had become something of a joke.

In fact the first "modern" report of the monster had occurred in 1930; the *Northern Chronicle* reported that three young men who were out in a boat fishing on 22 July of that year, close to Dores, on the southern shore, saw a loud commotion in the water about 600 yards away, and some large creature swimming towards them just below the surface; it turned away when it was about 300 yards away. The young men commented that it was "certainly not a basking shark or a seal."

In 1971, British television journalist Nicholas Witchell interviewed Mrs Margaret Cameron, who claimed to have seen the monster on land when she was a teenager, during World War I; she said, "It had a huge body and its movement as it came out of the trees was like a caterpillar." She also described it as being about 20 feet long, and said that it had two short, round feet at

---

Classic One-Liners
Howard Hughes, speaking indignantly to a film producer who was asking for more money:
"Eight million dollars is a small fortune!"

the front, and that it lurched from side to side as it entered the water. She and her friends felt so sick and upset that they were unable to eat their tea afterward. Witchell also interviewed a man called Jock Forbes, who claimed to have seen the monster in 1919, when he was 12; it was a stormy night, and he and his father were in a pony and trap when the pony shied, and they saw something large crossing the road ahead of them, then heard a splash as it plunged into the loch.

In November 1933 "Nessie" was photographed for the first time. Hugh Gray, an employee of the British Aluminium Company, was walking on a wooded bluff, 50 feet above the loch, near Foyers. He had seen the monster on a previous occasion, and was now carrying a camera. It was Sunday, 12 November 1933, a sunny morning, and Gray sat down for a moment to look out over the loch. As he did so he saw the monster rising up out of the water, about 200 yards away. He raised his camera and snapped it while it was two or three feet above the surface of the water. It is not the clearest of all photographs – it is easy to focus attention on the dark shadow and to overlook the vague, greyish bulk of the creature rising from the water above it. This was only one of five shots; the others seem to have been even less satisfactory. Gray was so ambivalent about the sighting – afraid of being subjected to derision – that he left the film in his camera for two weeks, when his brother took it to be developed. It appeared in the Scottish *Daily Record* and the London *Daily Sketch* on 6 December 1933, together with a statement from the Kodak film company that the negative had not been retouched. But Professor Graham Kerr, a zoologist at Glasgow University, declared that he found it utterly unconvincing as a photograph of any living thing. It was the beginning of the "debunking" of the monster, in which major zoologists were to be prominent for many decades to come. And the sightings continued. The day after Hugh Gray had snapped the monster, Dr J. Kirton and his wife were walking down the hill behind the Invermoriston Hotel when they saw the monster swimming away from them. They saw a rounded back with a protuberance in the middle, "like the rear view of a duck in a pond."

That summer of 1933 was one of the hottest on record, and by the end of the summer the Loch Ness monster was known to readers all over the British Isles; it was still to become a world-wide sensation.

By now the monster had also been sighted on land. On a peaceful summer afternoon, 22 July 1933, Mr and Mrs George Spicer were on their way back to London after a holiday in the Highlands. At about 4 p.m. they were driving along the southern road from Inverness to Fort William (the original General Wade road) and were on the mid-portion between Dores and Foyers. About 200 yards ahead of them they saw a trunk-like object apparently stretching across the road. Then they saw that it was in motion, and that they were looking at a long neck. This was soon followed by a grey body, about five feet high (Mr Spicer said later "It was horrible – an abomination"), which moved across the road in jerks. Because they were on a slope, they could not see whether it had legs or not, and by the time their car had reached the top of the slope it had vanished into the undergrowth opposite. It seemed to be carrying something on its back. They saw no tail, and the drawing that Commander Gould made later under their direction justifies Mr Spicer's description of a "huge snail with a long neck."

On 19 April 1934 a Harley Street gynaecologist, Colonel Robert Wilson, was driving beside the Loch towards Inverness with a friend. His friend, Maurice Chambers, apparently saw a commotion in the water, and shouted, "My God, it's the

233

In New York City it's illegal to have a puppet show in your window and a violation can land you in prison for 30 days.

In Forest City, North Carolina, it's illegal to bring a pea-shooter to a parade. It's also illegal to shoot paper clips with rubber bands.

Take some elocution lessons if you're going to Joliet, Illinois, where it's against the law to mispronounce the city's name. Offenders can be fined up to $500 for not pronouncing the name properly.

In Salem, Oregon, it's illegal for patrons of establishments that feature nude dancing to be within two feet of the dancers.

"Dwarf-tossing," the strange practice of hurling dwarfs in padded suits, is outlawed in the bars of Springfield, Illinois, because it's "dangerous and exploitative." However, the practice is apparently allowed elsewhere in town with a special permit.

In Christiansburg, Virginia, it's illegal to "spit, expectorate or deposit any sputum, saliva or any form of saliva or sputum."

In Oakland, California, it is illegal to grow a tree in front of your neighbor's window and block his view. However, it is OK if the tree is one that town officials consider an attractive tree, such as a redwood or box elder.

monster." Wilson rushed to the car, came back with the camera, and managed to expose four plates in two minutes in such a hurry that he did not even look at what he was photographing. The serpentine head, not unlike an elephant's trunk, then withdrew gently into the water. Unsure as to whether he had captured anything, Wilson hurried to Inverness and took the plates to a chemist to be developed. They were ready later that day. Two proved to be blank; one showed the head about to vanish into the water. But the fourth was excellent, showing the dinosaur-like neck and tiny head.

On 12 December 1933 a firm of Scottish film producers, Irvine, Clayton and Hay, managed to film the monster in motion for a few seconds; unfortunately, the film shows little but a long dark shadow moving through the water.

The most famous photograph of the monster was taken in the following April – the celebrated "surgeon's photograph." On 1 April 1934 Robert Kenneth Wilson, Fellow of the Royal College of Surgeons, was driving northward with a friend; they had leased a wild-fowl shoot near Inverness, and meant to go to it and take some photographs of the birds. Wilson had borrowed a camera with a telephoto lens. It was early in the morning about seven and they stopped the car on a small promontory two miles north of Invermoriston. As they stood watching the surface, they noticed the signs of "considerable commotion" that seem to herald the arrival of the monster. After the initial excitement, most people were willing to accept the view of sceptics that the monster had been a cynical invention of people involved in the Highland tourist business; if so, it had certainly succeeded, for Loch Ness hotels were crowded throughout the summer.

Wilson sold the copyright of the photograph to the *Daily Mail* and it appeared on 21 April 1934, creating a sensation. It also aroused the usual roars of derision from the scientific establishment, who branded the photograph a fake, and pointed out that the "surgeon" (who had withheld his identity) could be an invention of the perpetrator of the fraud. In fact, Wilson soon allowed himself to be identified, and his name appeared in Commander Gould's book *The Loch Ness Monster and Others,* which came out later the same year, with the "surgeon's photograph" as a frontispiece. (The fact that the photograph was taken on 1 April may have increased the general skepticism.)

Many years later another monster-investigator, Tim Dinsdale, held the photograph at arm's length and noticed something that convinced him of its authenticity. When viewed from a distance, a faint concentric circle of rings is visible around the monster, while there is another circle in the background, as if some other part of the body is just below the surface. No one, Dinsdale pointed out, would take the trouble to fake a detail that is almost invisible to the eye. Another piece of evidence in favor of its authenticity emerged in 1972, when the photograph was subjected to the computer-enhancement process at NASA; the

Joke of the Day
One day Joshua's mother turned to Joshua's father and said, "It's such a nice day, I think I'll take Joshua to the zoo." "I wouldn't bother," said father, "If they want him, let them come and get him."

improved picture showed signs of whiskers hanging down from the lower jaw.

Dinsdale became a close friend of Torquil MacLeod, who had seen the monster almost out of the water in February 1960. MacLeod had watched it for nine minutes, and admitted being "appalled by its size," which he estimated at between 40 and 60 feet. It had a long neck, like an elephant's trunk, which kept moving from side to side and up and down, and "paddles" at the rear and front. In August 1960 MacLeod had another sighting from the shore, while a family in a motor yacht belonging to a company director, R.H. Lowrie, saw the monster at close quarters for about 15 minutes, taking a few photographs. At one point they thought the monster was heading straight for them and about to collide; but it veered away and disappeared.

It was also in August 1960 that Sir Peter Scott, founder of the Wildfowl Trust, and Richard Fitter of the Fauna Preservation Society, approached the Member of Parliament David James and asked for his help in trying to get government assistance for a "flat-out attempt to find what exactly is in Loch Ness."

In April 1961 a panel decided that there was a prima facie case for investigating the loch. The result was the formation of the Bureau for Investigating the Loch Ness Phenomena, a registered charity. In October 1961 two powerful searchlights scanned the loch every night for two weeks, and on one occasion caught an eight-foot "finger like object" standing out of the water. In 1962 another team used sonar, and picked up several "large objects"; one of these sonar recordings preceded an appearance of the monster on the surface.

In 1966 Tim Dinsdale's film was subjected to analysis by Air Force Intelligence, which reported that the object filmed was certainly not a boat or a submarine, and by NASA's computer-

Fascinating Facts

Urea is found only in human urine and, peculiarly enough, in dalmatian dogs.

The birth control pill also works on gorillas.

Dear Prudence by The Beatles was supposedly written for Mia Farrow's sister, Prudence, because she wouldn't come out and play with Mia and The Beatles during a religious retreat with the Maharishi in India.

There are no natural lakes in the state of Maryland.

In order to make sure they are ripe, cranberries must be bounced. A fully ripe one can be bounced continuously like a basketball.

When Charles Lindbergh made his famous transatlantic flight he only took four sandwiches with him.

A full moon always rises at sunset.

In the original plan for Disneyland, Lilliputland was intended to be built.

The "ZIP" in Zip Code stands for "Zone Improvement Plan."

Alexander the Great suffered from epilepsy.

Classic One-Liners
Austin O'Malley: "An Irishman can be worried by the consciousness that there is nothing to worry about."

enhancement experts, who discovered that two other parts of the body also broke the surface besides the main hump.

One of the most interesting sightings of 1934 went virtually unnoticed. On 26 May Brother Richard Horan, of St Benedict's Abbey, was working in the abbey boathouse when he heard a noise in the water, and saw the monster looking at him from a distance of about 30 yards. It had a graceful neck with a broad white stripe down its front, and a muzzle like a seal's. Three other people corroborated his sighting. In the December of the following year, a Miss Rena Mackenzie also saw the monster fairly close, and noted that its head seemed tiny, and that the underside of its throat was white.

A man named John Maclean, who saw the monster in July 1938, saw the head and neck only 20 yards away, and said that it was obviously in the act of swallowing food, opening and closing its mouth, and tossing back its head "in exactly the same manner that a cormorant does after it has swallowed a fish." When the creature dived Maclean and his wife saw two humps. They described it as being about 18 feet long, and said that at close quarters its skin was dark brown and "like that of a horse when wet and glistening." Each of these sightings enables us to form a clearer picture of the monster. And in July 1958 the water bailiff Alex Campbell had a sighting which confirmed something he had believed for many years – that there must be more than one of the creatures; he saw one lying quietly near St Benedict's Abbey while another (visible as a large black hump) headed across the loch, churning the surface of the water. (Many accounts indicate that the animals can move at high speed.)

During World War II interest in the monster (or monsters) waned, although sightings continued to be reported. In 1943 Commander Russell Flint, in charge of a motor launch passing through Loch Ness on its way to Swansea, reported a tremendous jolt that convinced the crew that they had struck some floating debris. In fact, they saw the monster disappearing in a flurry of water. His signal to the Admiralty, reporting that he had sustained damage to the starboard bow after a collision with the Loch Ness monster, earned him in response "a bit of a blast."

After the war, there came a new generation of "monster-hunters." In June, 1960, the first scientific expedition to Loch Ness embarked on a month-long investigation, with 30 student volunteers and a Marconi echo-sounder, as well as a large collection of cameras. A ten-foot hump was sighted in July, and the echo-sounder tracked some large object as it dived from the surface to a depth of 60 feet and back up again. The expedition also discovered large shoals of char at a depth of 100 feet – an answer to skeptics who said that the loch did not contain enough fish to support a monster; the team's finding was that there was enough fish to support several.

Dr Denys Tucker, of the British Museum of Natural History, who had organized this expedition, did not lead it as he had intended to; in June he was dismissed from his job – he claimed that it was because he had publicly expressed his belief in the existence of the monster.

Frank Searle, a manager for a firm of fruiterers in London, went to Scotland in 1958 and decided to camp by Loch Ness.

From then on he returned again and again. In June 1965 he was parked in a lay-by near Invermoriston and chatting to some hitchhikers when he saw a dark object break the surface, and realized he had at last seen the monster. His excitement was so great that in 1969 he gave up his job and pitched his tent by Loch Ness, where he was to remain for the next four years. In August 1971 he saw the tail at close quarters as the monster dived; his impression was of an alligator's tail, "seven feet long, dark and nobbly on top, smooth dirty white underneath." In November 1971 he got his first photograph of the monster – a dark hump in a swirl of water; he admitted that it was "inconclusive." But in the following five years he obtained at least ten of the best pictures of the monster taken so far, including one showing the swan-like neck rising out of the water, and another showing both the neck and one of the humps; these were published in his *Nessie: Seven Years in Search of the Monster* in 1976. During that time his tent had become a "Mecca for visitors" – mostly directed to him by the Scottish Tourist Board – and in 1975 he estimated that he had seen 25,000 in eight months.

On 7 June 1974, together with a girl visitor from Quebec, he had a memorable sighting. As they approached a barbed-wire fence near Foyers, they noticed a splashing sound. They crept up and peered over the fence, "and saw two of the strangest little creatures I've ever seen. They were about two feet in length, dark grey in colour, something like the skin of a baby elephant, small heads with black protruding eyes, long necks and plump bodies. They had snake-like tails which were wrapped along their sides, and on each side of the body, two stump-like appendages." When he tried to get through the fence, the small creatures "scuttled away with a kind of crablike motion" and were submerged in the loch within seconds.

 # Boobs and Misprints

"The Complete Cook of Budgerigars $17.95. Birchalls Book Department."
Launceston Examiner

"Detective Chief Inspector James Henderson said he had charged two 61-year-old youths with murder on 24 December and they had been remanded in custody."
Rochdale Observer

"HONEYMOON? IF WE CAN FIT IT IN, SAY COUPLE"
Northern Echo

"Mr Wedgwood Benn said: 'There is a great revolution under way in education. My education policy is to raise the school leaving age to 65."
Evening Post

"NURSE RAPED By Our Crime Staff"
Daily Telegraph

"Dr James Pike, who died recently in Israel, talks to Oliver Hunkin about psychic phenomena."
The Listener

In 1972, a team of scientific investigators led by Dr Robert H. Rines took some remarkable underwater photographs, one of which showed very clearly an object like a large flipper, perhaps eight feet long, while a 1975 photograph showed a long-necked creature and its front flipper; this was particularly impressive because the sonar evidence – waves of sound reflected back from the creature – made it clear that this was not some freak of the light or a piece of floating wreckage.

Despite the skepticism that tends to view the Loch Ness Monster as something of a joke, most people still regard the question of the monster's existence as an open one.

Strange Tales

Real Clairvoyants: Visions of the Future

At the age of 22 the German – Johann Wolfgang von Goethe had completed his studies in Strasbourg and was about to return home. While in Strasbourg he had fallen in love with the daughter of a pastor in a nearby village. He loved her but didn't want to be tied.

He paid one last visit to his Fredericka before leaving the town. "When I reached her my hand from my horse, the tears stood in her eyes and I felt sad at heart," he wrote in his autobiography. Then, as he rode away, he had a strange vision. "I saw, not with the eyes of the body, but with those of the mind, my own figure coming towards me on horseback, and on the same road, attired in a suit which I had never worn – pike grey with gold lace. As soon as I shook myself out of this dream the figure had entirely disappeared . . . eight years afterward, I found myself on the very road, to pay one more visit to Fredericka, in the suit of which I had dreamed."

Although the phenomenon of seeing one's doppelgänger is traditionally regarded as a death omen, Goethe did not interpret his experience in that way. "However it may be with matters of this kind generally, this strange illusion in some measure calmed me at the moment of parting."

The Abandoned Airfield

Air Marshal Sir Victor Goddard was lost. Flying over Scotland in a Hawker Hart biplane, he was caught in a heavy storm. He needed a familiar landmark to get his bearings, and so flew lower to see if he could sight Drem, an abandoned airfield whose location he knew. He did sight it – but instead of the deserted and dark scene he expected, he saw a busy scene in bright sunlight. Mechanics in blue overalls were hard at work on a group of yellow planes. He wondered that no one paid any attention to his low-flying plane, but, wondering, headed up into the clouds once more and went on toward his final destination. That was in 1934 when Drem was indeed nothing but a ruin. In 1938, however, the airfield was reopened as an RAF flying school in the face of the war threat. Between these two dates, the color of British training planes was changed from silver to yellow – a fact that Sir Victor could not have known at the time of his strange experience. Thus, in 1938, anyone flying over Drem would have seen exactly what Sir Victor had seen four years before it happened.

Lincoln's Dream

On an April night in 1865– with the trials of the Civil War still heavy on his mind – President Abraham Lincoln lay asleep and dreaming. In his dream, he was asleep in his huge bed in the White House. Suddenly he was wakened by sobbing. Getting up and following the sound of the weeping, Lincoln found himself in the East Room. There he saw people filing past a catafalque guarded by soldiers. The men and women were paying their last respects to a body laid in state.

245

IT'S THE LAW

In Oxford, Mississippi, it's illegal to "create unnecessary noises."

Balloons with advertising on them are illegal in Hartford, Connnecticut.

In Provincetown, Massachusetts, it's illegal to sell suntan oil until after noon on Sunday.

In Boston it's against the law to keep manure in a building unless the building is being used as a stable. If it is, you can keep up to two cords of manure. If you're overstocked, you need a permit to move the stuff. And you can't leave it in the street.

Perhaps anticipating telemarketing, the town fathers of Albany, Virginia, have for years prohibited peddlers from using the telephone to either sell things or raise funds.

Communism has been against the law in Haines City, since 1950.

In the late 1960s, there were so many hippies in Youngstown, Ohio, that a law was passed making it illegal to walk barefoot through town.

In Xenia, Ohio, it's illegal to spit in a salad bar.

In Jonesboro, Tennessee, a slingshot used to be classified by law as a deadly weapon.

Joke of the Day
Blake: "Do you have holes in your underpants?" Teacher: "No, of course not." Blake: "Then how do you get your feet through?"

The face of the corpse was covered from Lincoln's view, but he could see that those present were deeply affected by the person's death. Finally, he went to one of the soldiers and asked who was dead. "The President," was the answer. "He was killed by an assassin." With that horrifying reply came a loud outcry of grief from the group near the catafalque – and Lincoln woke up.

This troubling dream, which Lincoln told his wife Mary and several of their friends, turned out to be a prophetic one. In that very month, Lincoln went to the theater for a rare night away from his pressing responsibilities. Awaiting him there instead of a night of pleasure was a fatal bullet from an assassin's gun.

Real Clairvoyants: The Train Crash

Eva Hellström, a Swedish psychical researcher, once dreamed that she and her husband were flying over Stockholm and saw a traffic accident. She wrote the vivid dream down.

"I looked down and thought we were somewhere in the neighbourhood of the Kungsträdgarden . . . I said to myself, 'The green [train] ran into [the tram] from the back . . .' I saw an ordinary blue tram of the Number 4 type, and a green train . . . run into the tram."

Eva Hellström also made a sketch of the accident as it had appeared in her dream. At the time there were no green railroad cars in service. But when some months later a few green cars were introduced, she was sure her dream was accurate. She then wrote in her diary:

'The accident will happen when the train from Djursholm (a suburb of Stockholm) and the Number 4 trolley meet at Valhallavägen (a Stockholm street). This is a place where there have been accidents between autos and trains but so far as I know, never with a trolley . . .'

On 4 March 1956, nearly two years after her dream, a collision occurred at Valhallavägen between a Number 4 trolley and a green Djursholm train. The positions of the vehicles were exactly as in Mrs Hellström's sketch.

The Lift Operator

A foreboding dream saved Lord Dufferin, once the British ambassador to France, from possible death. His dream was related by Camille Flammarion, French astronomer and psychical researcher. Lord Dufferin dreamed that he went to the window of his room and looked out, compelled to do so by an overpowering apprehension. On looking down he saw someone walking by and carrying something. The figure looked up, and Lord Dufferin saw a hideous face. At the same moment he realized that the figure was carrying a coffin.

Years later during his service as ambassador, Lord Dufferin attended a public dinner in Paris. A staff member led him to the lift that would take him up to the dining room. When he saw the lift operator's face, Lord Dufferin gasped in alarm. It was the face of his dream.

Instead of getting into the lift, Lord Dufferin went away to try to find out the operator's name. He had not gone far when he heard a crash, followed by screams and moans. The lift had fallen down the shaft. Everyone in it was killed or seriously injured. But the ambassador had been saved by his fear of the face he had seen in his dream.

"I dreamed that I had in my hands a small paper with an order printed in red ink, for the execution of the bearer, a woman . . . The woman appeared to have voluntarily brought the order, and she expressed herself as willing to die, if only I would hold her hand."

The dreamer, Dr Walter Franklin Prince, was an American psychical researcher. In his own account of his dream he wrote that the woman was: "slender of the willowy type, had blonde hair, small girlish features, and was rather pretty. She sat down to die without any appearance of reluctance . . . Then the light went out and it was dark. I could not tell how she was put to death, but soon I felt her hand grip mine . . . and knew that the deed was being done. Then I felt one hand (of mine) on the hair of her head, which was loose and severed from the body, and felt the moisture of blood. Then the fingers of my other hand were caught in her teeth, and the mouth opened and shut several times as the teeth refastened on my hand, and I was filled with the horror of the thought of a severed but living head."

On the night after Dr Prince had his harrowing nightmare, a young mentally disturbed woman left her home on Long Island to pay a visit to her sister. The police later found her body near a Long Island railroad station. Her head had been cut off by a train. Near the body lay a note in which the woman stated that she was seeking decapitation in order to prove a theory that her body and head could live independently of each other. Her name

ANIMAL SCIENCE

There are more bald eagles in the province of British Columbia then there are in the whole United States.

Hummingbirds are the only animals that can fly backwards.

A flamingo can eat only when its head is upside down.

A group of larks is called an exaltation.

Big Ben was slowed five minutes one day when a passing group of starlings decided to take a rest on the minute hand of the clock.

A group of crows is called a murder.

A group of owls is called a parliament.

A robin's egg is blue, but if you put it in vinegar for thirty days it turns yellow.

A capon is a castrated rooster.

was Sarah Hand. On investigation Dr Prince learned that Sarah Hand, like the woman in his dream, was pretty, slender, and fair.

The Magic Whip

Bismarck, the Prussian statesman who unified the German states into an empire, fought three major wars to achieve his goal of unification. He became the chancellor of the German empire after the third of these, and King Frederick William IV of Prussia became Emperor Wilhelm I of Germany. Bismarck tells about one of his premonitory dreams of eventual victory in his book Thoughts and Memories.

In the dream he was riding on a narrow path in the Alps. On the right was a precipice, and on the left was smooth rock. The path got so narrow that his horse refused to go forward any further. Bismarck could neither dismount nor turn around in the space.

In this moment of trial, Bismarck struck the mountainside with his whip, and called upon God. Miraculously, the whip grew in length without end, and the "rocky wall dropped like a piece of stage scenery." A broad path opened out, giving a view of hills and forests that looked like the landscape of Bohemia. Prussian troops carrying banners dotted the area. They appeared to be victors of a bloody battle.

Three years later Bismarck was at war with Austria, and his troops marched through Bohemia on the way. They won – as in his dream.

The Young Hitler

In the third year of World War I on the Somme front, Bavarian and French troops faced each other in trenches across no-man's-land.

One day Corporal Adolf Hitler of the Bavarian Infantry woke suddenly from a fearful dream. In it he had been buried beneath an avalanche of earth and molten iron, and had felt blood coursing down his chest. He found himself lying unharmed in his trench shelter not far from the French front. All was quiet.

Nevertheless his dream worried him. He left the shelter, stepped over the top of the trench, and moved into open country between the armies. A part of his mind told him that he was being stupid because he could be hit by a stray bullet or shrapnel. But he went forward almost against his will.

A sudden burst of gunfire, followed by a loud explosion, made Corporal Hitler fall to the ground. Then he hurried back to the shelter but it was not there. In its place was an immense crater. Everyone in the shelter and that section of the trench had been buried alive. Only he survived.

From that day on, Hitler believed that he had been entrusted with a special mission which promised him a great destiny in world events.

The Crystal Ball

Dr Edmund Waller, an Englishman living in Paris in the early 1900s, was having a sleepless night. He wandered downstairs, and, finding the crystal his father had just bought, gazed idly into it. There, to his surpise, he saw the image of Mme D., whom he had promised to look after during her husband's out-of-town journey.

The next day, Waller again looked into the crystal, and again saw Mme D. – with a man. He rubbed his eyes, and looked once more. The pair remained in view, this time at a racecourse outside Paris. Agitated by all these visions, Waller went to the racecourse the next day – and there met Mme D. with a man whom he took to be the one he had seen in the crystal.

Waller continued to see Mme D., her husband, and the other man in the crystal. One scene showed the illicit lovers in a particular Paris restaurant. On the husband's return, Waller told him about the visions. The two men went to the restaurant revealed by the crystal, and there found Mme D. with her lover.

There was a tragic aftermath to Waller's visions: Mme D. ended in an asylum, a broken woman after her husband had divorced her.

Cathar Lover

Arthur Guirdham is an English psychiatrist. For over 40 years he was afflicted by a recurring nightmare in which a tall man approached him.

Then one day in 1962 a woman patient came to see him and descibed a nightmare similar to his own. Dr Guirdham did not tell her of his own dream; but oddly, it never recurred after that. As the woman, whom he calls Mrs Smith, continued treatment she revealed strange facts about her life: her ability to predict the future and her detailed dreams of life in the southern part of France during the Middle Ages as a member of a heretical sect

Boobs and Misprints

"Thousands of doves and multi-coloured balloons were released as 7800 athletes indulging 1500 women from five continents assembled in the second largest city of the United States."
Pakistan Times

"A large piece of green blotting paper rested on the seat of Prime Minister Harold Wilson today in the House of Commons. It was both symbolic and necessary."
The Times

"Atlanta Council's public safety committee voted with some argument – to 'upgrade womanhood' by requiring dancers in nightclubs to wear G-strings and pasties."
The News (Adelaide)

"I spent several days in a mental hospital and felt completely at home', Christopher Mayhew, MP, told a meeting of the Sheffield Branch of the Mental Health Association."
Daily Telegraph

"Wedding gown worn once by mistake. Size 9–10. Asking $20." *Oshawa Times*

called the Cathars. She did not at first tell the doctor that she immediately recognized him as her lover, Roger de Grisolles, in those dreams.

It is not unusual for a psychiatric patient to have sexual fantasies about the doctor. But Mrs Smith's recollections of medieval France, of the persecutions suffered by her co-religionists, and of being herself burned at the stake were extraordinarily detailed. Guirdham had details from them checked by medieval historians, and the most obscure of them were corroborated. Her memories struck a chord in the doctor's own psyche, and he is now convinced that he too lived as a Cathar in France.

Dolores Jay

Mrs Dolores Jay is an ordinary American housewife, married to a minister and the mother of four children. But when she is deeply hypnotized, Dolores Jay moves back through time past the time of her childhood and her infancy – deeper and deeper back until she whimpers in German. (When she is conscious, she neither speaks nor understands any German.)

It is 1870. She is Gretchen Gottlieb, a 16-year-old Catholic girl, terrified and in hiding from anti-Catholic fanatics in a forest. "The man made my mother dead," she says. She complains that her head aches, she talks about a glittering knife, and then, desperately, evades questions. "Gretchen can't," she finally wails. And there it ends. Gretchen presumably was killed, and Mrs Jay remembers nothing until her own life began in 1923.

Dolores Jay herself can't account for it. She doesn't believe in reincarnation. She has only heard fragments of the taped hypnosis sessions, but she can't understand the language. She has never been to Germany. She has never heard of the little town of Eberswalde where Gretchen says she lived, and which exists in what is now East Germany close to the Polish border. But Eherswalde was the scene of Germany's last stand against the Soviet Union in 1945, and the town was almost completely razed. The records that once might have proved whether or not there was such a person as Gretchen Gottlieb have been destroyed.

Who can explain it? Not the modern middle-aged woman who, under hypnosis, becomes the young nineteenth-century German girl – a girl who remembers her dolls, her home, and her own death.

Seeing the Past: Tina

Tina was born in 1940 in Brazil, but she has clear memories of a previous existence as a child in France and of her own murder by a German soldier early in World War II. She gave an account of her death to the Brazilian Institute for Psychical Research.

"I don't think there was anyone at home that day," she wrote, "because it was I who answered the door. It must have been

---

Classic One-Liners
Rose Macaulay, on a novel: "It was a book to kill time for those who like it better dead."

about ten in the morning and the weather was cloudy." A soldier entered, wearing a round helmet and olive-green uniform. He carried what looked like a rifle and fired it at her heart.

"I remember," she continued, "asking for water before I died, but I don't remember if they gave me any. I can see myself lying on the floor on my back, wearing a light dress. I don't remember seeing any blood."

Tina has had from birth two distinct marks, on the front and back of her left side, precisely where a bullet aimed at the heart would have gone in and out. She has other memories too. In the interval between her death in France and her rebirth in Brazil she was present in the house of her parents-to-be. As soon as she could talk she correctly described all the furnishings in the house before her birth.

Strange Powers: The Bank Job

Wolf Messing was a stage mind reader who fled for his life from Poland to the Soviet Union during World War II. He had been in danger not only because he was a Jew, but also because he had predicted Hitler's death if the German dictator 'turned toward the East'. Hitler, a believer in fortune telling, put a price on Messing's head.

In the USSR Messing faced another dictator's challenge when Josef Stalin set a test for him. It was not an easy one. Messing was to enter Stalin's country house – a place bristling with guards and secret police – without a pass.

One day as Stalin sat working in the office of his country home, a man walked coolly into the grounds and then into the house. All the guards and servants stood back respectfully as he

Fascinating Facts

A bat's leg bones are so thin that they cannot walk. They shuffle using their wings.

You can't fold a piece of paper in half eight times, no matter how big, small or thin the paper.

The Grateful Dead were once called The Warlocks.

Although we refer to it as "paper money," money notes are generally not made out of paper – instead they are made out of linen.

A banana tree is not actually a tree – it is an herb.

Half of the world's oxygen supply is produced by the Amazon rainforest.

The collective noun for a group of kangaroos is a "mob."

Animal horns are made from the same substance as their hair.

The hearts of shrimps are found in their heads.

Short men are more likely to show dictatorial tendencies when given power. Stalin was only five feet, four inches tall.

passed. He walked to the doorway of Stalin's study. When the dictator looked up, he was astonished. The man was Messing!

The celebrated psychic's explanation was this: by mental suggestion he had made the guards think he was Lavrenti Beria, the much-feared head of the secret police at that time. So strong were his powers that, even though Messing looked nothing like Beria, the guards were convinced it was he.

On another occasion, Stalin suggested to Messing that he rob a bank by telepathy.

Messing chose for the experiment a big Moscow bank in which he was not known. He calmly walked in and handed the teller a blank piece of paper torn from a school notebook. He placed his case on the counter, and mentally willed the clerk to give him 100,000 roubles.

The bank clerk looked at the paper, opened the safe, and took out piles of banknotes until he had stacked 100,000 roubles on the counter. He then stuffed the money into the bag. Messing took the case, walked out of the bank, and showed the money to Stalin's two observers to prove his success as a bank robber. He then went back to the clerk and began handing the bundles of banknotes back to him. The teller looked at him, looked at the money, looked at the blank paper – and collapsed on the floor with a heart attack.

Fortunately, Messing reported, the clerk recovered.

Possessed by a Surgeon?

José Arigó was a simple man of little education who suddenly began to do skilful surgery in a small town in Brazil. His first operation was witnessed only by the patient. Arigó, who had been in a trance at the time, didn't believe the story himself when told about it. But his second operation took place in public.

It happened when an old woman lay dying, surrounded by her family, friends, and the Catholic priest who had just given her the last sacrament. Arigó was among the friends present. All at once he drew a large kitchen knife and ordered everyone to stand back in a strong German accent and voice that were not his own. He then plunged the knife into the woman's stomach. The onlookers, terrified he had gone mad, stood transfixed. He slashed through the stomach wall, cut out a growth the size of an orange, and closed the incision by pressing the sides of the cut together. The incision closed immediately without a scar. A moment later he was himself again – the plain, somewhat bumbling man his neighbors knew. Arigó had no memory of the episode, though soon the woman who had been on the point of death was walking around the room, recovered.

Real Clairvoyants: The Spectral Doctor

Dr William Lang died in 1937, but he is practicing today in a town just north of London – or so say many who have consulted him. Patients who come to see him meet him in a curtained room. He talks to them, diagnoses the complaint, and then, if necessary, operates on them. Because Dr Lang operates on the spirit body, the patient remains fully clothed. His hands move swiftly and surely, although his eyes are closed, to correct the difficulty in the patient's body – and such correction enables the physical body to function properly.

Patients may have met the medium George Chapman before

> ### Joke of the Day
>
> "Waiter, this lobster's only got one claw." "It must have been in a fight, sir." "Then bring me the winner."

he went into the trance that allows Dr Lang to appear, but they report that he is quite unlike the formerly well-known surgeon. Dr Lang's voice is a little quavery and high-pitched. and his shoulders are stooped. Those who knew him in life say it is unmistakably Dr Lang.

Patients report that they can feel Dr Lang at work. During the operation his warm friendly manner sometimes grows sharp, and he snaps his fingers peremptorily to indicate which instruments he wants passed by his spirit assistants. Patients say they feel safe in Dr Lang's hands – though the hands are unseen.

Psychics: The Missing Girls

Gerard Croiset Junior, son of the world-famous Dutch psychic who helped police solve many baffling cases, inherited his father's strange powers. He demonstrated this when he assisted in the case of two missing girls in South Carolina – and he did it from thousands of miles away. It all started when one of the girls' desperate mother, having heard about the Croisets' miraculous ability to locate missing persons, wrote to them in Holland with a plea for help. Croiset Junior replied.

The two teenage girls had gone for a walk on Folly Beach near Charleston, South Carolina, and they hadn't been seen

IT'S THE LAW

A 1950 anti-obscenity law in Irondale, Alaska, prohibited any showing of anyone nude or "in a substantially nude state" except a babe in arms.

In Olympia, Washington, minors are prohibited from frequenting pool halls.

In Washington State it's illegal to sell to minors comics that might incite them to violence or depraved or immoral acts.

In Washington, it's illegal to pretend you're the child of a rich person.

Wyoming required that every inmate of the state's training school for girls be issued with crinoline bloomers.

Under a 1959 ordinance, stubborn children were considered vagrants in Jupiter Inlet Colony, Florida.

In North Carolina it's against the law to dig ginseng on other people's property between the months of April and September, according to an 1866 law.

If you happen to own a marl bed in North Carolina, the law demands that you put a fence around it. A marl bed is actually a kind of rock quarry, not a place where you sleep.

The city council of West Palm Beach, Florida, once decreed that the roofs of all outhouses be fireproof.

since. In his reply to the mother, Croiset drew a map of Folly Beach – which he had never seen – including such details as a bus stop and a parked bulldozer. He also wrote a page and a half of comments. The accuracy of the map convinced skeptical police to take him seriously.

In the letter Croiset said: "The girls will be there [on the beach], they will be together." The police found the girls where Croiset indicated. And they were together – buried in shallow graves in the sand. They had been murdered.

Real Clairvoyants: Mrs Guppy's Trance

Two London mediums, Frank Herne and Charles Williams, were holding a joint seance with a respectable circle of sitters. The voices of the spirits John King and his daughter Katie were heard, and Katie was asked to bring something to the sitters – which she willingly agreed to do. One sitter perhaps jokingly suggested that Katie produce Mrs Guppy, a well-known medium of majestic dimensions. Katie chuckled and said she would. John King shouted out, "You can't do it, Katie," but she declared "I will." The sitters were all laughing when there came a loud thump on the table, and a couple of people screamed. Someone lit a match – and there was Mrs Guppy, her considerable bulk deposited neatly on the seance table. She was in trance and held a pen and an account book.

When Mrs Guppy was gently awakened, she was somewhat upset. The last she remembered she had been sitting comfortably in her own home – about three miles away – writing up her accounts. Several sitters escorted the medium to her house, where an anxious friend waited. According to the friend, the two had been in Mrs Guppy's room together when, suddenly, Mrs Guppy was gone "leaving only a slight haze near the ceiling."

Real Clairvoyants: The Living Piano

During the presidency of Abraham Lincoln the vogue for the new Spiritualism was at its height among fashionable people. Even the President – a far from fashionable man – was drawn into it. Colonel Simon F. Kase, a lobbyist who had several times met Lincoln to discuss a railroad project with him, tells of encountering the President at a seance in the home of Mrs Laurie and daughter Mrs Miller. She was known for making a piano beat time on the floor as she played while in trance. Kase said of the occasion that Mrs Miller began to play, and the front of the piano in truth rose off the floor and beat the time of the tune with heavy thuds. Kase asked if he could sit on the instrument so that he could "verify to the world that it moved." The medium composedly answered that he and as many others as wished could sit on the piano. Four men did: Kase, a judge, and two of the soldiers who were accompanying Lincoln. Mrs Miller again began to play and the piano – heedless of its load – began to rise and thump, lifting at least four inches off the floor. Kase concluded ruefully: It was too rough riding; we got off while the instrument beat the time until the tune was played out.

Real Clairvoyants: When Spirits Attack

During his investigation of the powers of Eusapia Paladino, the Italian medium noted for highly eventful seances, Professor P. Foa tried to use a photographic plate to register radiations. Eusapia Paladino's spirits apparently resented the interference. As the medium sat in trance outside the curtained cabinet, a hand shot out and tried to snatch the plate. Dr Foa seized the hand as it retreated behind the curtains and felt the fingers, but the hand wriggled loose and hit him squarely.

The spirits then turned their attention to a table, which they sailed over the heads of the company. When the sitter attempted to approach it, the spirits whisked it behind the curtain where it began to break up noisily. Dr Foa saw the table turn over on its side, and one leg snap off. At that point it shot back out of the cabinet and continued to break up noisily under the fascinated gaze of the entire circle.

One of the sitters asked for a handshake, and Eusapia Paladino invited him to approach the cabinet. He had hardly reached it when he felt himself attacked by hands and pieces of wood.

The entire circle heard the noises of the blows, and saw the hand moving in the ghostly half-light.

Real Clairvoyants: A Dozen Roses

It was evening in Benares, India. The legendary Madame Blavatsky – the small, dumpy Russian mystic and medium with a strangely magnetic personality – was surrounded by several Indian scholars, a German professor of Sanskrit, and her devoted disciple Colonel Olcott.

The professor observed with regret that the Indian sages of old were supposed to have been able to perform amazing feats, such as making roses fall from the sky; but that people said the days of such powers were over. Madame Blavatsky stared at him thoughtfully. "Oh, they say that, do they?" she demanded. They say no one can do it now? Well, I'll show them; and you may tell them from me that if the modern Hindus were less sycophantic to their Western masters, less in love with their vices, and more like their ancestors in many ways, they would not have to make such a humiliating confession, nor get an old Western hippopotamus of a woman to prove the truth of their Shastras!

She set her lips together firmly, and made a grand imperious sweep of her right hand. With a swish, exactly one dozen roses came cascading down. Madame Blavatsky returned calmly to her conversation.

Real Clairvoyants: Automatic Writing

Unlike most automatic writers, who received their messages from the spirits, the nineteenth-century British journalist William Stead got messages from the living – and saved them the bother of writing themselves. He would ask mental questions and his hand would write the answers automatically – sometimes he would learn more than the friends wanted him to.

Once he had arranged a lunch engagement with a woman who had been out of town over the weekend. He mentally inquired whether she had returned to London yet, and his hand wrote a long note. It described an unpleasant encounter she had had on the train. According to the message, she had found herself alone

 # Boobs and Misprints

"A migrant woman thought she had been sent home 'to die' when the hospital told her to go home 'today'. A Migrant Resource Centre spokeswoman said the misunderstanding underlined the need for improved interpreting services in Queensland hospitals."
The Herald (Melbourne)

"The artificial insemination of animals is taken for granted to improve the breed and product. Human insemination is a different ball-game."
Catholic Register (Canada)

"During the war the Queen was presenting awards to a Polish fighter pilot who, during the Battle of Britain, had shot down a record number of Fokkers. She asked him about his most hair-raising exploit.

'I came out of a cloud and found three Fokkers waiting for me. I dived under one of them and shot him down, then another Fokker came up behind me, and I did a left turn and shot him down, then, as the other Fokker dived down on me, I looped the loop and sent him down in flames.'

The Queen nodded admiringly. 'And what were they – Messerschmitts?'"

in a compartment with a strange man. He came over, sat close to her, and when she tried to push him away, attempted to kiss her. Struggling furiously, she thumped him with his umbrella, which broke. Then the train unexpectedly stopped and the man took flight.

When Stead sent his servant to his friend's house with a note condoling her on the assault, the woman was taken aback. She replied: "I had decided not to speak of it to anyone." She added, "The umbrella was mine, not his."

Science: How it Works

Sinking and Floating

Have you ever wondered how a submarine can manage to sink to the bottom of the ocean and then rise again upon command? The answer lies in the pressure inside the submarine. By increasing the pressure and thereby increasing the density the submarine will sink. Reduce the pressure and the submarine will rise again. If the average density of the submarine is less than that of the water then the submarine will float. If the average density of the submarine is more that that of the water then the submarine will sink (or dive in submarine terminology).

Royal Scandal

The Buckingham Palace Security Scandal

House break-ins have become so common in London that it has become a genuine oddity to see one reported in the media. Yet in the summer of 1982 one particular break-in caused such a furore that questions were asked in the House of Commons and calls were made for the resignations of both the Chief of the Metropolitan Police and the Home Secretary. Oddly enough, the cause of so much fuss was not a burglar or a spy, but an unemployed labourer trying to do Queen Elizabeth a favor.

Thirty-two-year-old Michael Fagan broke into Buckingham Palace twice in the months of June and July 1982 and might have gone undetected both times if he had not felt it was his duty to tell Her Majesty that her palace security was shockingly poor.

Fagan later claimed that he had noticed that Buckingham Palace's security was "a bit lax" during a sightseeing trip with his two young children. He became increasingly disturbed by this risk to the royal family – for whom he had great admiration – and eventually decided to break into the palace as an act of public-spiritedness. "I wanted to prove the Queen was not too safe," he said later.

Fascinating Facts

Armadillos sleep for around 18.5 hours of a day - they can also walk underwater.

The earth is the only planet in our solar system that doesn't have a ring.

The reflective dots in the middle of roads are called Botts dots.

Impotence is legal grounds for divorce in 24 American states.

The US Declaration of Independence was written on paper made from hemp.

The longest word in the English language that contains only one vowel is "strengths".

Of all the bones in your body, almost half are in your hands and feet.

A caterpillar has about 248 muscles inside its head.

The gestation period for an elephant is nearly two years.

A regulation golf ball contains 336 dimples.

Fagan must also have been inspired by the fact that a year before, in the summer of 1981, three West Germans had been found peacefully camping in the palace grounds. When questioned by police they said that they had arrived in London late at night and had climbed over the palace railings in the belief they were entering a public park. They had camped there totally undisturbed until the next morning. A rueful palace spokesman later admitted that this was not the first time that this sort of thing had happened.

On the night of 7 June 1982, Fagan clambered over the iron railings that surround the palace and wandered into Ambassadors Court. Here he found a sturdy drain pipe and proceeded to shin his way up to the roof. On the way he paused to look in at a lighted window. The occupant, housemaid Sarah Jane Carter, was reading in bed and happened to look up when Fagan was looking in. He moved on quickly and the housemaid, shaken and partially convinced that she had been seeing things, called security. They decided not to investigate.

After climbing 50 feet – no small feat in the dark – Fagan reached a flat roof that adjoined the royal apartments. He opened a window and climbed in. Over the next half hour he wandered about quite freely, crossing several infrared security beams as he did so. These had been fitted incorrectly, like the window alarm, and failed to go off.

During his walk-about he paused to admire the various royal portraits and had a brief rest on the throne. He also came across some royal bedrooms – those of Mark Phillips and the Duke of Edinburgh – the first he decided not to bother and the second turned out to be elsewhere. He then entered the Post Room and found a fridge containing a bottle of Californian white wine. Expecting to be arrested at any moment, he decided to relax a bit first. He had drunk half the bottle by the time he realized that

> **Classic One-Liners**
> Sidney Smith: "It was so hot that I found there was nothing for it but to take off my flesh and sit in my bones."

nobody was coming to get him, so he put it down and left by the risky way he had entered.

Just over a month later, on the night of 9 July, he drank a fair amount of whisky and set out to repeat his performance. Once again he entered the palace with no difficulties. This time though, he was clearly suffering from stress and too much booze. He smashed a royal ashtray with the intent of cutting his wrists with the jagged edge, but in doing so cut his hand. Thus, looking for a suitable place to kill himself and dripping blood on the carpet, he came across a door that pronounced itself to be the entry to the Queen's bedroom.

Her Majesty awoke to find Michael Fagan sitting on the edge of her bed, nursing his wounded hand and mumbling in a quiet voice. Speaking reassuringly to him she quietly reached for the alarm button by her bed, but unfortunately it had been incorrectly wired and failed to work. When she realized that nobody was coming, she marshalled considerable courage and picked up the bedside telephone – this apparently didn't bother Fagan in the least. The telephone connected her directly to the palace switchboard and she asked them to put her through to security. Unfortunately the police guard had already finished for the night and nobody else in the vicinity could be raised. Her footman was out in the grounds walking the royal corgis and the nightmaid was working in a room out of earshot of a telephone. The Queen kept a brave face in what must have been a night-mare situation and kept on chatting with the intruder.

Eventually Fagan asked for a cigarette and the Queen, pointing out she was a non-smoker, said she would go and get one from a member of staff. By this time the footman, Paul Whybrew, had returned from walking the dogs and quickly went in to confront the intruder. Fagan quietly insisted that all he wanted to do was talk with his Queen. Whybrew said that was fine, but in all fairness he should let her get dressed first. Fagan agreed and went with the footman and a maid to a nearby pantry. He waited there quietly until the police eventually arrived and arrested him.

Despite the fact that Michael Fagan gave a full and detailed confession of both break-ins, the police and crown prosecution faced a difficult problem. It is a peculiarity of English law that entering another person's property is not a criminal offence unless it can be proved that it was done with an intent to commit a crime (Fagan could have been charged with trespassing, but that would have merely been a civil offence). Thus, rather ridiculously, Fagan was tried in the Old Bailey for the theft of half a bottle of wine (valued by the court at £3) that was technically owned by the Prince and Princess of Wales.

The trial contained some farcical scenes. When Mrs Barbra Mills, acting for the prosecution, asked Fagan: "It wasn't your drink was it?" he replied: "It wasn't my palace either." "It was not your right to drink it," she insisted, to which Fagan countered: "Well, I'd done a hard day's work for the Queen, showing her how to break her security." He went on to point out that Her Majesty was lucky that somebody as public-spirited as himself had broken into her apartments: "I mean, I could have been a rapist or something!"

IT'S THE LAW

In Los Angeles, many years ago it was legal to cook in your bedroom, but not to sleep in your kitchen.

An old law in Columbus, Georgia., made it illegal to sit on your porch in an indecent position.

In San Francisco, it's illegal to beat a rug in front of your house.

A Kennesaw, Georgia. law makes it illegal for every homeowner not to own a gun, unless you are a convicted felon, conscientious objector or disabled.

In Ballwin, Mo., the only place you can use vulgar, obscene or indecent language is in your home.

In Washington State it's illegal to sleep in an outhouse without the owner's permission.

In New York City it's illegal to shake a dust mop out a window.

In Colorado it's now legal to remove the furniture tags that say, "Do Not Remove Under Penalty of Law."

In Washington State, until quite recently, you could have been fined up to $500 for removing or defacing the label on a pillow.

Joke of the Day
A little firefly was in school one day
and he put up his hand. "Please may I
be excused?" "Yes," replied the
teacher, "when you've got to glow,
you've got to glow."

The jury acquitted Fagan of the crime of theft, but he was
held in custody on an unconnected charge of taking and driving
away a car without the owner's permission, to which he had also
admitted. His second trial took place that October and after he
had pleaded guilty, the judge ordered him to be placed in the
care of a high-security mental hospital. Despite the fact that it
was pressed by several doctors that he should be held without
time limit, he was given the right to appeal.

In January of the following year, the psychiatric review board
found that he was "not fully recovered," but on the grounds that
he offered no threat to the community allowed his release.
Perhaps predictably, angry questions were asked in the House of
Commons.

The mortified police officers in charge of palace security
might have hoped for a bit of peace and quiet in which to put
their house in order, but this was not to be. Fagan's break-in
indirectly sparked off another, if unconnected, scandal involving
one of their most senior officers.

Michael Holroyd, the biographer, was once invited to a state
banquet with members of the royal family. He was very well
positioned, opposite one particularly distinguished lady member of
the clan. She began to demonstrate a great ability to mimic accents.

First she did an incredibly accurate imitation of a Yorkshire accent. Michael Holroyd clapped in admiration. Next she managed an absolutely perfect rendition of an Irish lilt. Mr Holroyd murmured in appreciation. Her powers of mime were truly wonderful. Finally she did a third accent, quite brilliantly, and the biographer had to burst into spontaneous applause. He burst out laughing and congratulated Her Majesty heartily. Now that one, he commented, was truly superb. An absolutely priceless imitation of an accent. The table fell silent and the lady stared. She had been speaking in her own voice.

Amazing Engineering Facts

A Brief History of the Telephone

Invented by Alexander Graham Bell in 1877 the telephone expanded over the twentieth century to reach across continents and oceans, eventually becoming wireless. By the start of the twenty-first century, more than a billion people worldwide had mobile phones.

1900 – Telephone Transmission
The American Telephone and Telegraph Company's (AT&T) George Campbell and Michael Pupin of Columbia University invented "loading coils" or inductors to be placed along telephone lines to reduce distortion or loss of signal power. First used in New York and Boston they made cross-city or inter-city telephone conversation a reality.

1904 – Fleming and the Vacuum Diode
The "Vacuum Diode" (a two-electrode radio rectifier) called an oscillation valve, was invented by British engineer Sir John Ambrose Fleming. Based on Edison's lightbulbs, the valve reliably detected radio waves. Lee De Forest's 1907 patent of the triode made successful transcontinental telephone service possible using a three element vacuum tube it electronically amplified signals for long-distance usage.

 # Boobs and Misprints

"Family & Children's Services Region of Waterloo invites applications to post of: Child Abuse Co-ordinator."
Globe and Mail (Toronto)

"The judge said that when the organist started to spend a lot of time at the rectory, Mr James (the vicar) warned his wife 'not to get into a position from which it might be difficult to withdraw'."
Evening Standard

"ONE LEGGED ESCAPEE RAPIST STILL ON THE RUN"
Weekend Australian

"FIRE MAY HAVE CAUSED BLAZE"
Barnet Borough Times

"Hundreds use our service. They know no better."
Windsor Express

"Marketing Executive: Post-secondary education –
Kowledge in marketing research – Good command in written Engliqh ald Ahilese – Illiterate and Creative."
South China Morning Post

1915 – The First Transcontinental Telephone Call
The first transcontinental telephone call was made by Alexander Graham Bell in New York to Thomas Watson in San Fransisco using De Forest's triodes to boost the signal. The world's longest telephone wire was made from 2,500 tons of copper wire and 130,000 telephone poles.

1919 – Rotary-Dial Telephones
Bell Systems began installing rotary dial telephones to make it easier for customers to dial without an operator. The wheel of the dial interrupted the current and created pulses that corresponded to the digits of the number being dialed.

1947 – The North American Numbering Plan
The North American Numbering Plan was developed by AT&T and Bell Labs and assigned telephone numbers to US customers and its territories as well as Canada and the Caribbean. The first three digits indicated the area being called and the next three identified the local area switching office with the last four digits representing the line number.

1949 – The First Phone With a Ringer and Handset
The Model 500 telephone was introduced by AT&T. It was a classic black rotary phone with a volume control for the bell. The classic shape became a cultural icon.

1951 – Direct Long-Distance Telephone Calls
Beginning in Englewood, New Jersey long-distance calls in the USA could be made without an operator. It would be 1961 before long-distance was available across the continent.

1956 – The First Transatlantic Telephone Cable

The TAT-1 was the first transatlantic telephone cable and was installed from Scotland to Nova Scotia, providing telephone service between North America and the United Kingdom. It was eventually extended to Western European countries including Germany, France, and the Netherlands. The project took three years and cost $42 million to plan and install and used 1,500 nautical miles of cable. It could handle up to 36 calls at any one time and worked with existing telegraph and radiophone links.

1962 – Digital Transmission

Bell Systems introduced the first commercially available paging system at the Seattle World's Fair. A signal alerted customers to call their office or homes from a regular phone. Bell called it the Bellboy.

1962 – Telstar 1

The $6 million communications satellite *Telstar 1* was launched into space by a NASA Delta rocket. It could transmit live transatlantic telecasts as well as telephone and data signals. The first international television broadcasts showed images of the American flag flying over Andover, Maine to the sound of "The Star-Spangled Banner." Later the same day AT&T chairman

Joke of the Day
Just before the Ark set sail, Noah saw his two sons fishing over the side. "Go easy on the bait," he said, "Remember I've only got two worms."

Fred Kappel made the first long-distance telephone call via satellite to Vice President Lyndon Johnson.

1963 – The Touch-Tone Telephone
The Western Electric 1500 touch-tone telephone featured 10 push buttons that replaced the standard rotary dial. A 12-button model featuring the * and # keys came out soon afterward and replaced the 10-button model.

1968 – Calling 911
The first 911 call was made in Haleyville, Alabama on 16 February 1968. In 1967, Congress passed legislation for a single nationwide emergency number for people to report fires and medical emergencies. A similar system (999) had been in place in Britain since the 1930s. The numbers 911 were chosen because they were easy to remember and did not include three digits already in use in any US or Canadian area code.

1973 – The First Portable Cell Phonecall
Martin Cooper of Motorola made the first portable phone call to research rival Joel Engel at Bell Labs. Cooper's team at Motorola was awarded a patent in 1975.

1978 – A New Cellular Phone System
The first public tests of what would be today's cellular phones took place in Chicago by AT&T and Bell Labs. This test was followed by a trial in 1981 in the Washington-Baltimore area by Motorola and the American Radio Telephone Service. A commercial cellular phone service was approved by the Federal Communications Commission in 1982. The service was available in most of the USA by the late 1980s.

ANIMAL SCIENCE

The penguins that inhabit the tip of South America are called jackass penguins.

If NASA sent birds into space they would soon die, they need gravity to swallow.

Many species of bird copulate in the air. In general, a couple will fly to a very high altitude, and then drop. During their descent, the birds mate.

Ancient Romans ate flamingo tongues and considered them a delicacy.

Crows have the largest cerebral hemispheres, relative to body size, of any avian family.

An ostrich's eye is bigger than its brain.

If you feed a seagull Alka-Seltzer, its stomach will explode.

Mockingbirds can imitate any sound from a squeaking door to a cat meowing.

Elephant tusks grow throughout an elephant's life and can weigh more than 200 pounds. Among Asian elephants, only the males have tusks. Both sexes of African elephants have tusks.

Lovebirds are small parakeets who live in pairs.

1990s – Voice Over Internet Protocols

Voice Over Internet Protocols (VOIP), that allowed people to make voice calls over the Internet, gained ground because users could call long-distance for the same price as a local call since the call went through the local telephone exchange system.

2000 – 100 Million Cellular Telephone Users

From only 25,000 in 1984, the number of people with a cellular phone grew to over 100 million. Cellular phones shrunk in size over this period and began to be used as cameras, diaries and handheld computers.

Fascinating Facts

Whenever he sensed trouble on the way, the dictator Benito Mussolini would touch his testicles in order to ward off evil spirits.

It takes about seven minutes for the average person to fall asleep.

John Adams lived to be the oldest of all the American presidents so far. He was 91 years old when he died.

The IRS has a manual for collecting taxes after a nuclear war.

Over 50% of the world's population have never made nor received a telephone call.

The number of bacteria in your mouth is larger than the number of people in the world.

When exiting a cave or their homes bats always turn left.

There is more protein in an avocado than in any other fruit.

Beasts and Monsters

The Inscrutable Yeti?

In the decade after World War II Slavomir Rawicz, a Polish refugee living in England wrote about his experiences in *The Long Walk*. In this book he claimed that he and six others escaped from a Siberian prison camp and walked 2,000 miles to freedom. During their grueling journey to India they crossed the Himalayas. It was there, one day in May 1942, that he said they saw two massive Yeti.

"They were nearly eight feet tall and standing erect," Rawicz wrote. "The heads were squarish and . . . the shoulders sloped sharply down to a powerful chest and long arms, the wrists of which reached the knees." One was slightly larger than the other, and Rawicz and his companions concluded they were a male and female. The unknown creatures looked at the humans, but appeared – completely indifferent. Unfortunately, the beasts were in the middle of the most obvious route for the refugees to continue their descent, and the men were disinclined to approach much closer in spite of the apparent lack of interest.

The refugee party finally moved off by another route. Behind them the Yeti watched their retreat with obvious unconcern, and then turned away to look out over the magnificent scenery.

Joke of the Day

A woman is having a terrible day at the casino in Vegas. With only $100 left at the roulette table, she cries, "What dreadful luck! What shall I do now?"

A man next to her, trying to be nice, loudly suggests, "I don't know . . . Maybe you should play your age?"

He goes on his way, but hears a commotion at the roulette table behind him. Turning back to the table, he is amazed to see the lady lying prostate on the floor, with the croupier leaning over her. He asks, "What happened? Is she OK?"

The croupier says, "I really don't know what happened . . . She put $100 on 29. The ball landed on 35, and then she screamed and fainted!"

People in History

Strange Historical Stories

Art Botch

Dr Abraham Bredius, a Dutch art-historian, was very boastful about his expertise in the seventeenth-century artist, Vermeer. In 1938, he discovered a new painting by his hero called *The Disciples on the Road to Emmaus*, which was immediately bought by the famous Boymans Museum in Rotterdam for the huge sum of £58,000.

Unfortunately, *The Disciples* was actually the work of Hans van Meegeren, an art student, who had specifically painted the picture to expose Bredius and the art cognoscenti in The Netherlands. Bredius was later taken in by ten other paintings by van Meegeren and the fraud was only discovered when the latter owned up to selling an imitation Vermeer to Goering in 1945 and subsequently confessed all.

Bredius' influence was so powerful that nobody believed van Meegeren until he painted another *Vermeer, Jesus and the Scribes*, under their very noses.

Joke of the Day
"What's green and red and goes at 170 miles an hour?" "A frog in a blender."

Amazing Engineering Facts

Healthcare and Medical Technology

*Within a century between 1900 and 2000, life expectancy in
the United States almost doubled. From the birth of the X-ray
in 1895 to other more complicated diagnostic tools like the
electrocardiograph, CAT scan, and MRI, the developments in
medical technology together with new life-saving medications
the medical world advanced rapidly.*

1903 – The First Electrocardiograph Machine
The first electrocardiograph machine was designed by Willem
Einthoven, a Dutch physician and physiologist. It was capable of
measuring tiny changes as the heart contracted and relaxed.
Electrodes attached to both arms and the left leg allowed
Einthoven to record the heart's wave patterns. Einthoven was
awarded the Nobel Prize for medicine in 1924.

1927 – The First Respirator
The first respirator was made from an iron box and two vacuum
cleaners by Harvard medical researcher Philip Drinker. Known
as the iron lung, its first users were polio sufferers whose chests
had been paralyzed.

Boobs and Misprints

"Counterfeit fifty-dollar Federal Reserve notes seized in Milan, Italy, bore the words, 'redeemable in awful currency of the United States Treasury."
New York Times

"Question: I have an Irish terrier bitch, which ignores the doorbell. How can I train her to be a watch?
Answer (the vet): Each time the doorbell rings, jump up excitedly and bark yourself."
Evening Telegraph

"He pushed what looked like the barrel of a gun into my chest and told me he was going to blow my brains out."
Manchester Evening News

"East German swimmer Sylvia Ester set a world 100-metres record of 57.9 seconds in 1967 – but officials refused to recognize it because she swam in the nude."
The West Briton

"People who travel on trains without a reasonable excuse will be summonsed and may face fines of up to $200."
Newcastle Herald

1930s – The Artificial Pacemaker
The first artificial pacemaker was developed by Albert S.
Hyman, a New York cardiologist. It was constructed from a
hand-cranked apparatus with a spring motor that rotated a
magnet in order to supply an electrical impulse to the heart.
Despite being patented, the device never gained popularity in the
medical community.

1933 – Kouwenhoven Cardiovascular Research
William B. Kouwenhoven and neurologist Orthello Langworthy
at Johns Hopkins University, discovered that a low-voltage
shock to the heart can restore natural rhythm. Kouwenhoven's
research into the effects of electricity on the heart led to the
development of the closed-chest electric defibrillator and the
technique of external cardiac massage today known as
cardiopulmonary resuscitation, or CPR.

1945 – Kidney Dialysis
Dutch physician Willem J. Kolff successfully treated a dying
man with an artificial kidney. The purpose was to literally
"clean" and oxygenate the blood. In the course of his research,
Kolff had noticed that blue, oxygen poor blood that passed
through the artificial kidney became red and oxygen rich outside
the body and could then be pumped back into the body.

1948 – The Plastic Contact Lens
The plastic contact lens designed to cover only the cornea was
patented by Kevin Touhy. The design was developed two years
later by George Butterfield so that it was molded to fit the
contour of the eye rather than sit flat on top of it.

Classic One-Liners
C. A. Leisure, film critic, reviewing a film called *Tokyo Rose*: "No wonder."

1950s – The First Artificial Hip Replacement
The artificial hip was invented by English surgeon John Charnley. By applying engineering principles to orthopedics, he developed a low friction, high-density polythene to create artificial hip joints. The same technology was subsequently used for other joint replacements such as the shoulder or knee.

1951 – The Artificial Heart Valve
Albert Starr at the University of Oregon along with electrical engineer Lowell Edwards designed a two-cage structured heart valve in which the outer cage separated the valve struts from the aortic wall. Starr's design incorporated a silicone ball inside a cage made from an alloy of cobalt, molybdenum, chromium, and nickel. Named the Starr-Edwards heart valve it is still in use today.

1952 – The First Successful Cardiac Pacemaker
The initial cardiac pacemaker was a bulky piece of equipment worn externally on a patients belt. It was designed to plug into a wall socket, stimulating the heart through two metal electrodes placed on the bare chest.

1953 – Open-Heart Bypass Surgery
The first heart surgery patient was 18-year-old Cecelia Bavolek. During the surgery, her heart and lungs were supported by a

heart-lung machine developed by the surgeon, Philadelphia physician John H. Gibbon. Today heart bypass surgery is one of the most common operations in hospitals.

1954 – The First Human Kidney Transplant
Physician Joseph E. Murray led the first team of doctors ever to perform a human kidney transplant. Murrays took a healthy kidney from donor Ronald Herrick and implanted it inside his twin brother Richard who was dying of renal disease. Both donor and recipient were perfectly matched and the operation was a success.

1960 – The First Internal Pacemaker
The first internal pacemaker was constructed from two commercial silicon transistors. When implanted into ten dying patients, the first recipient lived for 18 months, another one of the ten lived another for 30 years.

1963 – Laser Eye Treatments
The first laser eye treatment was developed in order to help patients with diabetic retinopathy, a complication of diabetes. Francis L'Esperance, of the Columbia-Presbyterian Medical Center pioneered the treatment, eventually working with Bell researchers Eugene Gordon and Edward Labuda designing an argon laser for eye surgery. Treatment of the retina by laser was successful and is still in use today.

1971 – The First Soft Contact Lens
The first soft contact lens was called Softlens and was licensed in the 1970s by Bausch & Lomb. The product was initially developed in Czechoslovakia by scientists Otto Wichterle and Drahoslav Lim. They invented a "hydrophilic" gel that was

compatible with living tissue. The new soft contact lenses allow more oxygen to reach the cornea resulting in much greater comfort for the wearer.

1978 – The First Cochlear Implant Surgery

New advances in receiver technology enabled Australian Graeme Clarke to design a multiple electrode receiver stimulator the size of a quarter to be inserted inside the ear canal. Clarke carried out the first cochlear implant in 1978.

1982 – The First Permanent Artificial Heart Implant

The first permanent artificial heart was given to Seattle dentist Barney Clark. Clark survived for 112 days with his new pneumatically driven heart made from silicone and rubber. The device was invented by Robert Jarvik, Don Olsen, Willem Kolff, and William DeVries at the University of Utah.

1987 – First Laser Surgery on a Human Cornea

The first laser surgery on a human cornea was performed by New York City ophthalmologist Steven Trokel. In the USA, by 1996, the first computerized laser, the Lasik, was approved to correct refractive error myopia.

1990 – The Human Genome Project

The goal of the human genome project was to identify all of the approximately 30,000 genes in human DNA to determine the sequences of the three billion chemical base pairs that make up human DNA. The project fostered many new medical applications including isolating genes responsible for genetic illnesses and inherited breast and colon cancer.

295

IT'S THE LAW

Because people were using them for cheap furniture, it's now illegal in North Carolina to take and sell labeled milk crates.

In Baltimore it's illegal to play professional croquet before 2 p.m. Sunday. The law also applies to professional quoits.

In Hawaii it's illegal for a shooting gallery to offer liquor as a prize in case the shooter might want to come back after drinking the prize and try again.

Both Massachusetts and New Hampshire had old laws that penalized gamblers who lost money. You'd get fined in Massachusetts if you had any money left. In New Hampshire you are prohibited from pawning the clothes off your back to pay off gambling debts.

In the state of Washington it's illegal to catch a fish by throwing a rock at it.

Delaware prohibits horse racing of any kind on Good Friday and Easter Sunday.

Under Delaware law, any person of good moral character may keep and operate a bowling alley. No gambling, however, is allowed.

In Las Vegas you can bet on any team—except The University of Nevada at Las Vegas.

296

Joke of the Day
What was written on the
hypochondriac's tombstone? "I told
you I was ill."

Hollywood Tales

A Little Night Music

Hollywood writers Ben Hecht and Charles MacArthur formed a Hollywood chamber music group, which included Harpo Marx and composer George Antheil. Groucho Marx, who played mandolin, was excluded. On the evening the group met to rehearse in an upper room of Ben Hecht's house, Groucho interrupted the session by flinging open the door and shouting "Quiet, please." When he was gone, the group speculated what he was up to, the general view being that he was jealous. Soon after, the door opened again, and Groucho shouted: "Quiet, you lousy amateurs." He disappeared downstairs, and minutes later the house was shaken by the sound of the Tannhauser overture played at full volume. They rushed downstairs to find that the complete Los Angeles Symphony Orchestra – about a hundred men – had been squeezed into Hecht's sitting room, and that Groucho was conducting them with sweeping gestures. He had sneaked them into the house one by one during the evening.

The chamber music group decided it would be less trouble to admit Groucho and his mandolin.

The Bridle Path

Peter Sellers once went to a party in the country at which he danced all night with a very beautiful stranger. He was quite

captivated by her charming looks and personality and
determined to accompany her home. They left the party together
and Peter thought his luck was in. There was a full moon and
the evening was warm. Perhaps, suggested Mr Sellers
tentatively, he might be allowed to accompany his lovely
companion along the bridle path?

"Oh no, I'm terribly sorry," was her immediate and frank
response, "it's far too early to be thinking about marriage."

Moby Jane?

When Ray Bradbury was working with John Huston on the film
script of Moby Dick, Huston came in one day waving a telegram
signed "Jack Warner" which declared: "CANNOT PROCEED
WITH FILM UNLESS SEXY FEMALE ROLE ADDED."
Bradbury almost became hysterical. "Has the man gone insane?
We can't have a woman on the ship . . ." "That's Hollywood,
Ray," said Huston, shaking his head. "Maybe Ahab could have
an affair with Gina Lollobrigida as a disguised stowaway." Just
as Bradbury looked like having apoplexy, Huston flung himself
on the couch, doubled up with laughter, and Bradbury realized it
was a practical joke.

The Quack

Robert Benchley's doctor was an indefatigable inventor of new
cures, and the obliging Benchley allowed himself to be used as a
guinea pig. One day the doctor asked his cooperation to try out a
pill for restoring sexual potency. The day after he had taken the
pill, the doctor called to ask if he had noticed any change, and
put him through a catechism: temperature, sexual excitement
etc. To each question Benchley replied in the negative. "There
must have been some change," said the disappointed doctor.
"Only this," said Benchley, dropping his pyjamas, and revealing

Joke of the Day
Two fleas went to the cinema. When they came out, one said to the other, "Shall we walk or take a dog?"

a sprouting of cock tail-feathers at the base of his spine. Benchlcy had glued them on with the help of his actor friend Roland Young.

The Chess Match
Charles MacArthur regarded himself as a formidable chess player. One day some friends told him they had met a Spaniard called José Raùl, who wanted a match. MacArthur agreed immediately.

An unusually large number of friends appeared to watch the match. It was not until he was some way into the game that MacArthur guessed from his opponent's formidable skill – that he was actually the world chess champion Capablanca.

War And No Sleep
Arthur Sheekman, a Hollywood writer, tells of a fellow writer who, late one afternoon, received a note signed "Jack Warner." It explained that he was considering making a film of *War and Peace*, and asked the writer to read it overnight and make a quick assessment.

The writer learned that it was a practical joke only when he went into Warner's office – after a sleepless night – and asked if Warner needed a story outline.

The Card

Robert Benchley was part of a school of card players in the
Algonquin Hotel. Asked if he didn't mind that another player
went to the lavatory so often, he replied: "No, it's the only time
I know what he's got in his hand."

The Radio Theme

Victor Young went to enormous lengths to play a practical joke
on fellow film-composer Max Steiner. Young happened to be in
the studio when the orchestra was trying out the love theme of
Now Voyager ("Would It Be Wrong To Kiss"), and jotted it
down. A few evenings later, Steiner came to Young's house to
play cards. At 11 p.m., someone suggested turning on the radio
to get the local news. After the announcer had introduced the
programme, there came a blast of music – Steiner's love theme.
Steiner leapt to his feet with a howl of anguish. "That's my
theme – they've stolen my music." "That's impossible," said
Young, "that programme has been on for years and they've
always used that theme to introduce it." "I tell you it's my
theme" howled Steiner, now almost hysterical. At that point
Young admitted what he'd done: how he had orchestrated the
theme and had it recorded by the orchestra for whom he was
then writing a score, and finally how he had cut the recording
into a tape of the local news programme, recorded the previous
day.

Real Ghost Stories

The Wounded Vampire

The nineteenth-century diarist Augustus Hare recounts the following story:

"Groglin Grange was an English manor house that overlooked the nearby church in the hollow. It was rented by two brothers and their sister. One night as the sister lay in bed she became uneasily aware of something moving across the lawn toward the house.

Mute with horror, she saw a hideous brown figure with flaming eyes approach. It scratched at her window with bony fingers, and one pane fell out. It reached in, unlocked the window, and before she could scream, sank its teeth into her throat. Her brothers were wakened by the commotion, but by the time they reached her room the creature had vanished and the girl lay unconscious and bleeding. One brother tried to follow the attacker, but lost it. The girl recovered and bravely insisted on returning to the house. Nearly a year later, she again woke to see the creature scratching at the window. Her brothers, who since the first attack slept armed, came running. They found the creature in flight. One brother fired and hit it, but it escaped into the churchyard. When the two men entered the churchyard vault, they discovered all the coffins broken open except one. In that coffin was the vampire – and it had a bullet wound in its leg."

 # Boobs and Misprints

"In the Nuts (unground) (other than ground nuts) Order, the expression nuts shall have reference to such nuts, other than ground nuts, as would but for this amending Order not qualify as nuts (unground) (other than ground nuts) by reason of their being nuts (underground)."
Amendment to British Parliamentary Act

"The court was told that soon after the party came into Maloney's Bar, Milligan spat at O'Flaherty and called him a stinking Ulsterman'. O'Flaherty punched Milligan, and Rourke hit him with a bottle. Milligan kicked O'Flaherty in the groin and threw a pint of beer in Rourke's face. This led to ill-feeling, and they began to fight."
County Louth (Eire) newspaper

"English Spanish shorthand Typist. Efficient. Useless. Apply Otherwise."
Advertisement in Spanish newspaper

The One-Minute Novel

Of Mice and Men – John Steinbeck (1937)
Two migrant workers, Lennie Small and George Milton had
recently escaped from a farm where Lennie, a mentally deficient
yet docile man, was wrongly accused of rape when he touched a
woman to feel her soft dress. They went to a new place of
employment, a local ranch. George wanted them both to raise
enough money to buy a patch of land, where they would have a
small farm with a vegetable patch and a rabbit hutch. The rabbit
hutch was the only detail of the plan that Lennie consistently
remembered and he liked the sound of it. George told Lennie
that, if he got into trouble as he did before, he should return to
the brush near the river and wait for George to find him.

When George and Lennie reached the bunkhouse at the ranch,
an old man named Candy showed them their beds and told them
that the boss was angry that they didn't show up the night
before. The boss later questioned George and Lennie and found
them suspicious because George spoke for Lennie. He could not
understand why George would travel with Lennie until George
explained that Lennie was his cousin. After the boss left, his son
Curley entered the bunkhouse. Curley had a young wife who
everyone knew was not exactly faithful. His wife visited the
bunkhouse later that night searching for Curley, and flirted with
the other men. Later, Curley returned looking for his still-

missing wife again, and confronted George in an attempt to start a fight.

After a day of work, the men return to the bunkhouse. Slim, whose dog had a new litter of puppies, gave Lennie one of them. When George told Candy about the house that they wanted to have, Candy said that he knew about an available house that they could have if the three men pooled their money. Curley came in searching for his wandering wife again, and fought with Lennie when he suspected that Lennie was laughing at him. Lennie didn't fight back until George gave him permission and then he crushed Curley's hand, and did not stop until George told him to do so.

The next morning, when Lennie was playing with his new puppy, he accidentally killed it by bouncing it too hard. Curley's wife found him in the barn with the dead puppy, and when she allowed him to feel how soft her hair was, he handled her too forcefully. When she screamed, Lennie covered her mouth and, as she tried to struggle he snapped her neck. Lennie escaped the ranch and Candy and George found the body and immediately realised that Lennie killed her. Candy alerted the other men, and Curley formed a party to search for Lennie. Curley intended to murder him. In the interim, George stole Carlson's gun, leading the other men to think that Lennie actually took it before he escaped.

George, pointed Curley and the other men in the wrong direction, and found Lennie in the brush where he knew he would be. Lennie had been having hallucinations of a giant rabbit and his Aunt Clara. George warned Lennie that Curley would be angry with him for killing his wife and that he would lose the possibility of having a house with a rabbit hutch. George began to tell Lennie about the plans for a house and rabbit hutch during which time he shot Lennie in the back of the head with

Carlson's gun. Upon hearing the gun shot, the other men found George and Lennie. George told them that Lennie had stolen the gun and he himself had shot Lennie when he got the gun back from him after capturing him.

Science: How it Works

Gyroscopic Inertia

Riding a bike is easy, even with just two narrow tires one is able to travel almost effortlessly. But it's impossible, or very difficult to balance on the bike when it's not moving. This is because of the principles of gyroscopic inertia. Gyroscopic inertia is a force common all around us. It explains how we are able to ride a bike, how planes navigate, and how a figure skater is able to do those lightning fast spins.

Gyroscopic inertia is the property of a rotating object to resist any force that would change its axis of rotation. Something that is set spinning at an angle perpendicular to the ground, will go on to resist any forces (such as gravity) that try to change that angle.

Fascinating Facts

The most powerful electric eel in the world lives in the rivers of Brazil, Columbia, Venezuela, and Peru. A shock from one produces 400–650 volts.

The average car produces a pound of pollution per 25 miles.

The only land on the planet that is not owned by any country is Antarctica.

You can legally marry a dog in India.

The parrot and the rabbit are the only two animals that can see behind them without turning their heads.

You are more likely to be bitten by a German Shepherd than by any other type of dog.

The names of the three wise monkeys are; Mizaru (see no evil), Mikazaru (hear no evil) and Mazaru (speak no evil).

The tip of a whip moves faster than the speed of sound. This is why it makes a cracking sound.

A kangaroo cannot walk backwards – this is because of the size of its hind legs.

Rats bite approximately 24,000 Americans every year.

Amazing Engineering Facts

A Brief History of Spacecraft

The Soviet Union launched the first spacecraft on 4 October 1957 from Kazakhstan. The spacecraft carried a 184-pound satellite called **Sputnik.** *Man's fascination with space has been a constant feature across the centuries. The Hubble Space Telescope made it possible for us to study faraway galaxies and stars and an abundance of satellites have made it possible to have up-to-the-minute weather information, communications and navigation systems. All of this stems from man's first forays into space.*

1903 – Liftoff with Liquid Fuels is Demonstrated as Possible on Paper

In 1903 Konstantin Tsiolkovsky published a paper in Russia that mathematically demonstrated how to achieve liftoff with liquid fuels. He proposed using multistage rockets, which would be jettisoned as they spent their fuel and guidance systems using gyroscopes and movable vanes positioned in the exhaust stream. His formulas for adjusting a spacecraft's direction and speed to place it in any given orbit are still in use today.

> **Classic One-Liners**
> Film critic Hedda Hopper, reviewing another
> film: "For the first time in my life I envied my
> feet – they were asleep."

1915 – A Rocket to the Moon
In 1915, Robert Goddard used reaction propulsion in a vacuum
to establish that it is possible to send a rocket into space.
Goddard launched the first liquid-fueled rocket in1926.

1942 – The Successful Launch of a V-2 Rocket
The V-2 rocket was realized by a German ballistic missile
technical director called Wernher von Braun. They were used
heavily in World War II but the guidance system was imperfect and
many never reached their targets. American scientists developed
early rocket research techniques from a captured World War II V-2
rocket, creating a smaller version capable of reaching an altitude of
244 miles and able to obtain data on high altitudes.

1957 – *Sputnik I*
A liquid fueled rocket built by Sergei Korolev was launched by
the Soviet Union. The first artificial Earth satellite was about the
size of a football and weighed 184 pounds. It completed an orbit
of the Earth in 98 minutes. *Sputnik II* was launched a month
later with a heavier cargo including a dog called Laika.

1958 – Launch of First US Satellite
Explorer 1 was the first US satellite in space, weighing 30.8lbs.
On board was an experiment created by James A. Van Allen, a

physicist at the University of Iowa, designed to document the existence of radiation zones circling the Earth within its magnetic field. The Van Allen Radiation Belt dictated the electrical charges in the atmosphere and measured the solar radiation that reached Earth. The National Aeronautics and Space Administration (NASA), was formed and authorized by congress later the same year.

1959 – The *Luna 3* Probe
The Soviet Union's *Luna 3* probe took the first pictures of the far side of the moon. This satellite carried an automated film-developing unit that relayed the pictures back to Earth via video camera.

1960 – *TIROS 1*
In 1960, a weather satellite called *TIROS 1* was launched to test the creation of a global meteorological satellite information system. It weighed in at 270 pounds, was made of aluminum and stainless steel, measured 19inches high and was covered with 9,200 solar cells to charge the onboard batteries. Its launch was a success and the earth's weather systems began to be surveyed from space.

1961 – Yuri Gagarin the First Human in Space
Cosmonaut Yuri Gagarin became the first human in space in 1961 aboard *Vostok I*. Launched on 12 April from Baikonur Cosmodrome, he completed one orbit of the Earth in a cabin providing him with three small portholes. The flight took 108 minutes and the spacecraft was operated by ground crews. He successfully parachuted to safety in Kazakhstan.

1961 – Alan B. Shepard, Jr. the Second Human in Space
US astronaut Alan B. Shepard, Jr., became the second human in space 23 days later on 5 May 1961 onboard the *Freedom 7*.

ANIMAL SCIENCE
All swans and all sturgeons in England are property of the Queen.

A Cornish game hen is really a young chicken, usually 5 to 6 weeks of age, that weighs no more than 2 pounds.

A father Emperor penguin withstands the Antarctic cold for 60 days or more to protect his eggs, which he keeps on his feet, covered with a feathered flap.

Most father penguins lose about 25 pounds while they wait for their babies to hatch.

A woodpecker can peck twenty times a second.

Parrots, most famous of all talking birds, rarely acquire a vocabulary of more than twenty words, however Tymhoney Greys and African Greys have been know to carry vocabularies in excess of 100 words.

By feeding hens certain dyes they can be made to lay eggs with varicolored yolks.

Macaroni, Gentoo, Chinstrap and Emperor are types of penguins.

Owls have eyeballs that are tubular in shape, because of this, they cannot move their eyes.

The spacecraft was launched from Cape Canaveral by a Mercury-Redstone rocket, the first of its kind to be piloted. *Freedom 7* reached an altitude of 115 nautical miles and a speed of 5,100 miles per hour before landing in the Atlantic. Sheperd Jnr. enjoyed a 15-minute sub-orbital flight in which he showed how a vehicle could be controlled during weightlessness and high G-force stress.

1962 – John Glenn the First American to Circle Earth

John Glenn made three orbits of earth in *Friendship 7* a Mercury spacecraft. Due to an autopilot failure, Glenn flew parts of the last two orbits manually and during re-entry to the Earth's orbit had to leave the normally jettisoned retro-rocket pack attached to his capsule because of a loose heat shield. Glenn was welcomed back on Earth as a hero.

1965 – The First American Spacewalk

Gemini IV, the second piloted Gemini mission, stayed in space for four days. Astronaut Edward H. White, Jr. performed the first extravehicular activity (EVA) by an American. This task needed to be perfected before man could land on the moon.

1968 – *Apollo 8* Flies to the Moon

Apollo 8 took off from the Kennedy Space Center on 21 December 1968. Onboard were three astronauts Frank Borman, James A. Lovell, Jr., and William A. Anders. The astronauts had a portable television camera that they focused on the Earth as their ship traveled out into space. For the first time humans could now see their planet as it looked from space. After reaching the moon on Christmas Eve the crew fired the booster rockets for the return journey home on Christmas Day, landing in the Pacific Ocean two days later.

1969 – Neil Armstrong the First Man on the Moon

Apollo 11 lifted off on 16 July 1969 carrying three astronauts Neil Armstrong, Michael Collins and Edwin E. (Buzz) Aldrin. On 20 July the lunar module landed on the Moon's surface with Armstrong and Aldrin onboard whilst Collins orbited overhead in the command module. Armstrong and Aldrin spent more than 21 hours on the Monn's surface before successfully returning to the command module. They left behind scientific instruments, an American flag and a plaque bearing the inscription: *"Here Men From Planet Earth First Set Foot Upon the Moon. July 1969 A.D. We came in Peace For All Mankind."*

1971 – *Salyut 1* the First Space Station

Salyut 1 was launched by the Soviet Union in 1971 and was the world's first space station. Two years later in 1973, the USA sent *Skylab* into orbit where three different crews worked on scientific projects before *Skylab* was abandoned in 1974. The Soviet Union continued to explore long-stay space projects and launched the *Mir* space station in 1986.

1972 – Pioneer 10

Pioneer 10 was the first spacecraft destined for the outer solar system. Launched by an Atlas-Centaur rocket. *Pioneer 10* made a close approach to Jupiter in December 1973 before finally being powered on a trajectory that would take it out of the solar system. *Pioneer 11* gave scientists their closest view of Jupiter from just 26,600 miles above Jupiter's clouds in 1974. In 1979, *Pioneer 11* reached Saturn and sent back images of the planet's rings before travelling out of the solar system in the opposite direction to *Pioneer 10*. *Pioneer 10* actually sent more data back to NASA in 2002, 30 years after being launched. The link was switched off in 2003.

Joke of the Day
"Waiter, you have your thumb on my steak!" "I know sir, I don't want it to fall on the floor again!"

1975 – NASA to Mars
On 20 August, NASA sent space probe *Viking 1* to Mars. Later the same year in November it sent another probe *Viking 2*. Both probes had an orbiter and a landing vehicle. *Viking 1* landed on Mars in July 1976, *Viking 2* in September 1976. Both space probes sent back images of Mars. Contact with the Viking probes ended in 1982 when all efforts to contact the space probes failed. Scientists at NASA closed down the mission in 1983.

1977 – *Voyager I* and *Voyager 2*
Both *Voyager 1* and *Voyager 2* were sent to Jupiter and Saturn. Over the next three years these space probes sent information back to NASA. Amongst their discoveries were 22 new satellites, (3 at Jupiter, 3 at Saturn, 10 at Uranus, and 6 at Neptune) rings on Jupiter and the knowledge that Saturn's rings contained structures that are not just gases. They also discovered that Jupiter's moon Lo had active volcanism, the only planet other than Earth discovered so far with such activity.

1981 – Space Shuttle *Columbia*
Columbia was the first reusable winged spacecraft. The first astronauts to fly *Columbia* were John W. Young and Robert L. Crippin who safely landed the spaceship at Edwards Air Force Base in Southern California. *Columbia* was the first space vehicle to use both liquid and solid propellant rocket engines.

314

IT'S THE LAW

Riverboat gamblers in Iowa have a $5 maximum bet.

The state of Washington doesn't allow marathon dancing, or marathon skipping, sliding, gliding, rolling, or crawling.

In North Dakota, charitable groups can hold stud poker games to raise money, but only twice a year.

In San Francisco it's illegal to play poker in public or gamble in a barricaded room.

In Maine it's illegal to catch lobsters with your bare hands.

In Indiana a sports agent is supposed to give a college 10 days notice before luring a star athlete into the professional ranks.

In Idaho, it's illegal to hunt from the back of an animal.

In Iowa, it is illegal to hunt from an aircraft.

It's against the law in Fairbanks, Alaska, to give a moose a beer.

The game of crackaloo is illegal in Fairfield, Ala.

In Mooresville, North Carolina, it's illegal to attach anything to a pool table.

1986 – Space Shuttle *Challenger*
Space Shuttle *Challenger* was destroyed during its launch from
the Kennedy Space Center on what was to be the 25th shuttle
flight. Astronauts Francis R. (Dick) Scobee, Michael Smith,
Judith Resnik, Ronald McNair, Ellison Onizuka, Gregory Jarvis,
and Sharon Christa McAuliffe were all killed when an explosion
destroyed the spaceship 73 seconds into the launch. A leak in
one of the two solid booster rockets ignited fuel in the main fuel
tank. It was two years before a space shuttle was sent into orbit
again.

1990 – The Hubble Space Telescope
The Hubble Space Telescope was sent into orbit on 25th April
by the crew of the Space Shuttle *Discovery*. The mission was a
cooperative project by the European Space Agency and NASA.
The telescope was equipped with many special features
including 76 handholds with a 15-year design life intended to be
a space-based observatory.

1998 – The International Space Station
Astronauts from the Space Shuttle *Endeavour* joined together
the first two sections of the International Space Station during a
number of space walks. Cables were connected between two
modules, *Zarya* from Russia and one from the United States.
Hatches between the two spacecraft were opened allow for easy
access between the two.

2000 – Expedition One of the International Space Station
Expedition One of the International Space Station was launched
on 31 October 2000. The crew spent 6 months in space
conducting experiments before returning home on 21 March
2001.

Classic One-Liners
Arthur Bloch: "The man who can smile when things go wrong has thought of someone he can blame it on."

Royal Scandal

King George III: The Fat Philanderer

In the last days of October 1788, King George III began to lose his reason. The signs were familiar to those around him, for he had hovered on the brink of madness on a number of occasions. These episodes had, of course, been carefully hidden from the British public.

The symptoms that began appear that October were more disturbing than in the earlier attacks. It started with back pains and convulsions, then the king began to suffer from hallucinations. A page saw him holding a conversation with an oak tree, apparently under the delusion that it was the King of Prussia. After that, the king's urine turned brown, his eyes became bloodshot, and he began to foam at the mouth. The royal household did its best to remain calm and stoical, but there was an increasing sense of panic.

The problem, quite simply, was who would succeed him. For Prince George, the heir to the throne, was one of the most habitual drunks and profligate spendthrifts in the country. When, in 1762, King George III's firstborn proved to be a son, there had been rejoicing throughout the land. King George was a level-headed and modest man, obsessed by the notions of royal duty and clean, healthy family life, and he would eventually father fifteen children.

Boobs and Misprints

"Danish police are trying to trace women who own 577 panties, bras and stockings of all shapes and sizes stolen from clotheslines at Holstebro in western Denmark. A thirty-four-year-old man has been charged with theft."
Western Morning News

"An overstressed traffic policeman in Bangkok Thaland was taken to mental hospital after switching all the lights green and dancing amid the ensuing chaos. The twenty-five-year old officer, stationed at one of the city's worst crossroads, nicknamed Hell Intersection, was diagnosed as suffering from severe stress."
Western Morning News

"Quote: 'Quoting the Queen, Sir Norman admitted that last year had been an 'anus horibilis'."
Daily Telegraph

"A tenant found a unique way to keep his council house as warm as toast – insulating the loft with Edam cheese. Workmen calling to insulate the home in Loughton, Essex, were amazed to find the work already done with several thousand pieces of the Dutch cheese's distinctive red coating."
Western Morning News

Everyone hoped that his son, Prince George, would in due course make as good a king as his amiable father. Unfortunately, as the young man matured, this began to look increasingly doubtful. Even as a child the prince displayed a taste for flattery and a fondness for overeating, flaws that were encouraged by his uncles, whom the boy admired rather more than he did his father. For the king's austere morality was not shared by his siblings. The Dukes of Gloucester and Cumberland in particular were notorious drunks and womanizers, who enjoyed disgracing the House of Hanover in drinking establishments and gambling clubs all over London. Young George greatly preferred them to his incredibly dull father. His main ambition seemed to be to develop into a world-class seducer and alcoholic.

At the same time as he was losing his son to wine and women, King George was losing America to its rebel colonists. His high-principled, moralistic attitudes, which created a sense of stability in times of peace, only aroused irritation in people with grievances, like the over-taxed Bostonians. For all his good intentions, the king seemed doomed to cause misunderstandings.

Prince George's first public affair began when he was 18. Seated in the royal box with Lord Malden, at Covent Garden, watching a performance of *The Winter's Tale*, George was dazzled by the beauty of the actress playing Perdita. Whenever she approached his side of the stage, the prince would lean out of the box and, to the amusement of the audience, gaze at her with forlorn adoration.

Her name was Mary Robinson, she was just 21, and George learned from his chaperon Lord Malden that she was married to a young clerk in a law office. Brushing aside this complication, George called for pen and ink, and wrote her a love letter, which he signed Florizel, the name of Perdita's lover in the play. Robinson refused to see him. The prince persisted.

However, in spite of a series of charmingly written love letters, Mary Robinson declined to meet Prince Florizel. She was flattered and not a little tempted for George was a handsome young man, and his waistline was still under control but she feared the reaction of the king. The prince's scandalous sexual adventures were already common knowledge, and so was his father's disapproval. The prince could not compel her into his bed, but the king could destroy her acting career, which was the only thing that stood between her and debtors' prison she had only recently escaped.

Recognizing that his tender pleas were a waste of time, George decided to offer a more substantial inducement. In his next letter, among the passionate protestations of undying love, he offered her £20,000 if she would become his mistress. This, the practical Mary thought, was a bit more like it. She agreed immediately, explaining her hange of heart by declaring that she had finally succumbed to "the irresistible sweetness of his smile, the tenderness of his melodious yet manly voice." But before fulfilling her part of the bargain, she made sure that George signed an undertaking to pay her the £20,000 as soon as he came of age because until then he had to make do with a small allowance. So Mary Robinson settled in a house whose rent was paid by the prince, and George finally had his way with her.

Classic One-Liners
Jerome K. Jerome: "It is always the best policy to speak the truth, unless; of course, you are an exceptionally good liar."

There was no hint of intrigue about the affair. Everyone knew about it from the start. Cartoons portraying Perdita and Florizel drawn to look like the pair were displayed in London shop windows. Mrs Robinson, previously only moderately well-off, now rode around London in a four-horse carriage with two servants perched on the back. Moreover, she wore a picture of George around her neck in public. She found that being a royal mistress was more fun than she had expected.

George, on the other hand, was already regretting the bargain. He was too young to realize that, after so much anticipation, even a night with Cleopatra would have been an anticlimax, and like all spoilt and selfish people was inclined to put the blame on the lady. Within weeks he was tired of her, and transferred his attentions to a Mrs Grace Dalrymple, the divorced wife of a Harley Street doctor.

Trusting to the postal service to end the affair, just as it had begun it, George wrote Mrs Robinson a brief letter in which he explained that they could never meet again, since he had learned that she had insulted one of his friends in public. But Mary had no intention of being abandoned.

Their correspondence continued, but it had now deteriorated into accusations and counter-accusations. And when she realized that there was no chance of getting him back, Mary finally hinted to Lord Malden that she would make use of the document promising her £20,000, and the prince's love letters, which made it clear why he felt she was worth so much.

This hint of public exposure sobered the prince. The problem was that he had no way of laying his hands on such a vast sum. Lord Malden was authorized by George to offer £5,000. Mrs Robinson scoffed at the offer. Her debts, she said, amounted to six hundred pounds more than that.

In the end George had to give in. The £5,000 was accepted,

Fascinating Facts

Liquor can be good for you. Almost half of all alcoholic beverages contain all of the 13 minerals essential to human life.

Collectively, Americans eat a hundred pounds of chocolate every second.

At birth, a baby giraffe falls six feet without being hurt.

Venus is the only planet that rotates clockwise.

The person who created the Nike symbol only got paid $35 for their work.

A hurricane can release more energy in 10 minutes than all the nuclear weapons in the world.

All Dalmatian puppies are spotless and white when born.

All birds except for the owl raise their lower eyelids to blink. The owl drops its upper eyelid.

The first Harley Davidson used a tomato can for a carburetor and was built in 1903.

The name of the lion that roars in the MGM logo is Volney.

accompanied by a pension of £500 a year for life. On Mrs Robinson's death, her daughter would continue to receive half that amount for life. The letters would be returned, along with a letter from George agreeing that the papers had not been sold, but given freely.

Now the problem was to raise the £5,000. George was forced to tell his father the whole story. Since the king did not have the money either, he had to go to his Prime Minister, and beg him to try and raise it. Lord North solved the problem by quietly adding the figure to that year's Secret Service budget, in effect, embezzling the taxpayer. The king dug in his heels about Mrs Robinson's pension, declaring that his son could find that out of his own allowance.

So Mary received her pay-off, and the first instalment on her pension, and went off to live in Paris. This episode finally convinced King George that his son was totally irresponsible. George now spent his evenings drinking and whoring around London with disreputable members of the peerage. His love affairs were conducted openly, and he ran up enormous debts that he had no hope of paying.

At age 22, George was involved in his maddest love affair so far. The lady was a beautiful widow named Maria Fitzherbert. She was 28, six years George's senior, and had been twice married. George fell instantly and violently in love with her when he saw her sitting in a friend's box at the opera, and pursued her with his usual single-mindedness. But Mrs Fitzherbert was more a difficult catch than Mary and others like her. George pursued her with the same wild passion he had shown for Mary Robinson. She was flattered, found him likeable, but had no intention of becoming his mistress. George found it incomprehensible that anyone could refuse to give him his own way. Mrs Fitzherbert decided it would be simplest if she left England.

When he heard about it, George collapsed on his couch in an agony of grief. No previous conquest had ever been this difficult. In a grand romantic gesture George attempted suicide by falling on his sword. He was found, bloody but only superficially wounded, lying on his couch.

Four royal equerries went to Mrs Fitzherbert's house and finally prevailed on her to see him. She was reluctant, but Mrs Fitzherbert agreed to see him on condition she could take some lady of unassailable reputation with her. The Duchess of Devonshire was persuaded to go, and they found the prince lying on the settee, his chest covered in blood. When George showed her his wound, she was shaken, and began to feel that his threats of suicide were serious after all. George declared that he would make another attempt unless Mrs Fitzherbert agreed to marry him, and accepted a symbolic ring. Mrs Fitzherbert allowed herself to be convinced; she borrowed a ring from the Duchess of Devonshire, and placed it solemnly on her finger.

Back at home, Mrs Fitzherbert decided that it had all been a charade. The next day she left England, leaving no address.

George flew into another hysterical frenzy. Then he decided to pursue her to Europe. He finally obtained Mrs Fitzherbert's address, and kept up a stream of love letters.

After 16 months of separation from his beloved; George wrote to her proposing marriage. She knew the idea was insane, that it would be illegal, and that no priest would dare to marry them. But George's devotion had finally convinced her that she loved him, and in late November 1785, she returned to London. A few weeks later, she and George were married at a secret ceremony by a priest who had been released from Newgate debtors' prison. They then went off for a honeymoon at Richmond.

The marriage was soon the gossip of the London drawing

rooms. But although the couple waas often seen at the same
social gatherings, even sitting at the same table, their relationship publicly seemed to be one of friendly politeness. George's
friends noted that he seemed more contented than he had ever
been. Mrs Fitzherbert moved to a house in St James's Square,
which was closer to Carlton House.

Unfortunately, George's new-found happiness did not curtail
his extravagance. By the end of 1785, he owed more than
£250,000. His father showed no sign of wanting to persuade
Parliament to pay off his debts. Something had to be done.
George persuaded an independent Member of Parliament to
raise the question in the House. The response of the Tory
spokesman was that this was a delicate subject, because it
involved matters concerning the Church and Constitution, a
clear hint at the marriage with Mrs Fitzherbert. The loyal
Sheridan rose to ask what they were hinting at. Mr Pitt, the
Prime Minister, replied that if this matter of the prince's
finances was pursued, he might be obliged to reveal something
he would prefer to conceal. Sheridan replied that in that case, he
should explain what he meant. Mr Pitt realized that he was
treading on the edge of an abyss, and replied lamely that he was
merely referring to the prince's debts.

Typically, the prince wanted to tell Mrs Fitzherbert that it
might be necessary to deny their marriage in public, but was too
much of a coward to do it.

IT'S THE LAW

An old Washington law sent duelists to jail for ten years, assuming they didn't lose the duel.

It's illegal to clean salmon along Maine's upper Kennebec River. Enforcement of this law has been made easier for many years by the fact that, because of a dam, there are no salmon on the upper Kennebec River.

An old law in Texas made it illegal to go to church in disguise.

It used to be a $200 fine in Vermont to deny the "existence or being of God."

It's illegal in Nevada to have a "house of ill fame" within 400 yards of a church or school.

A recent proposal that ministers walk the beat with police officers in Belmont, North Carolina, notes "the ministers will carry a Bible instead of a gun."

It's against a Key West, Florida, ordinance to spit on a church floor.

In Spokane, Washington, it used to be illegal to interrupt a religious meeting by having a horse race.

And it was at this point that the bombshell exploded. The king began to show unmistakable signs of insanity, and Parliament realized that this probably meant that Prince George would become king or at least regent, the temporary guardian of the throne. The thought appalled everybody. If this drunken, womanizing spendthrift came to the throne, he would bankrupt the country, and probably cause a revolution.

Prince George hurried to see his father, and was himself shocked by his ravings. In his misery, the king abandoned all pretence of even liking his son. During dinner, he leapt to his feet, dragged George out of his chair, and hurled him against the wall. The prince was not as upset as he might have been. At least his father's feelings were out in the open, and he could also drop the pretence of loving the irascible old man. His parties at Carlton House became bigger, noisier and more expensive, and he achieved a new level of bad taste by entertaining his guests with imitations of his father's ravings.

What no one realized at the time was that the king was suffering from an illness called porphyria, which involves a problem with the creation of haemoglobin, the oxygen-carrying red component of blood. As a result, there is a buildup of brownish pigment one of haemoglobin's components which shows up in urine as a brown discoloration. Other symptoms are extreme sensitivity of the skin, and mental confusion. In effect, the sufferer's own body is poisoning him to death.

By now, the equerries who attended King George were exhausted. He did not sleep for more than a few hours at a time, which meant that the equerries had to sit in the king's bedroom all night. If he woke and found himself unattended, the king was likely to escape from the palace and wander around the grounds. The sensitivity of his skin also meant that shaving irritated him badly. On one occasion, having been persuaded by long

Fascinating Facts

Liquor can be good for you. Almost half of all alcoholic beverages contain all of the 13 minerals essential to human life.

Collectively, Americans eat a hundred pounds of chocolate every second.

At birth, a baby giraffe falls six feet without being hurt.

Venus is the only planet that rotates clockwise.

The person who created the Nike symbol only got paid $35 for their work.

A hurricane can release more energy in 10 minutes than all the nuclear weapons in the world.

All Dalmatian puppies are spotless and white when born.

All birds except for the owl raise their lower eyelids to blink. The owl drops its upper eyelid.

The first Harley Davidson used a tomato can for a carburetor and was built in 1903.

The name of the lion that roars in the MGM logo is Volney.

argument to sit still and be shaved, the king jumped up and ran off halfway through the operation. For the rest of the day he wandered the palace with half a beard.

The doctors guessed, correctly, that the problem was some kind of poison in his system, and they tried to cure it by blistering the king's legs, hoping the "evil humours" would run out through the sores. This only made the king hate his doctors.

In his illness, the king's conversation tended more and more towards sex, particularly how much he used to enjoy sex with the queen. One afternoon in late December, Willis decided that the king was calm enough to benefit from a visit from his wife. A courtier named Greville reports that, while standing guard outside the door, he heard George weeping. The proud and highly moral king had lost all his self-control and tried to rape his wife.

Meanwhile, back at Windsor, Prince George had taken control of the court. As everyone had feared, increased responsibility had no effect upon him. He was drinking and spending more heavily than ever. It was also clear that he was beginning to enjoy power. He wanted to be declared regent on the grounds that the king was incapacitated.

Understandably, Prime Minister Pitt disagreed. He was hoping against hope that the king would recover.

Boobs and Misprints

"With more than sixty sashes of honour in Prince Philip's dressing room, it was perhaps an accident waiting to happen. But few could have expected the embarrassment of his attendance at the funeral of King Baudouin of Belgium last month.

Instead of the deep purple of Belgium's Grand Cordon of the Order of Leopold, he wore the green, red and gold of Zaire's Order of the Leopard. To make matters worse, although Zaire was once a Belgian colony the two countries no longer have any links.

Baudouin is even said to have ordered that President Mobutu of Zaire should be barred from the funeral.

Onlookers at the service, attended by royalty and heads of state from all over the world, were astonished at the blunder.

And the Prince is said to be furious with the member of his household responsible for the mix-up.

Buckingham Palace claimed yesterday that the sash was that of the military division of the Order of Leopold from the former Belgian Congo. But there is no mention of any such honour in a detailed record in Debrett's of sixty-three decorations awarded to him."

Western Morning News

Finally, in February 1789, Pitt knew he could go on no longer.

It was time for Parliament to vote whether the prince would become Prince Regent. And, to Pitt's inexpressible relief, he won. The House voted that Prince George did not have an automatic right to power because his father was ill, and that the queen would remain head of the royal household.

Within weeks, it had become clear that the bill had been unnecessary. The king's doctors reported that he was beginning to recover. The prince refused to believe it, suspecting that it was all a plot to keep him out of power. Finally, he and his brother Frederick managed to set up an appointment to see the king. The old man looked frail and exhausted, but there could be no doubt that he was no longer mad.

In their disappointment, George and Frederick went to Brooks's Club, and told everyone that the king was as ill as ever. Word got back to the queen, who was enraged. Next time they tried to visit the king, they were refused admittance.

In an attempt to raise money for his creditors, George had allowed himself to be dragooned into marrying a princess named Caroline of Brunswick. When he saw her for the first time he was horrified; she was fat, coarse, and personally unhygienic. At the marriage ceremony he was drunk. Even so, Parliament refused to pay his debts – now £600,000. England was at war with France and could not afford such a sum. After dutifully impregnating her, the prince found himself unable to remain in the same room with her, let alone continue to sleep with her, and within a year wrote her a letter explaining that "our inclinations are not within our power," and made sure she moved elsewhere.

When the prince separated from Caroline, she made sure that the British public knew how badly she had been treated, and her husband's popularity declined to such an extent that he did not

Joke of the Day
"Five dollars for one question!" said the woman to the fortune teller, "That's very expensive, isn't it?" "Yes. Next!"

dare to show his face in London for fear of being attacked by the mob.

In 1810 the king's mind collapsed again, and George was finally sworn in as regent. He immediately enraged the Whigs by refusing to keep any of his promises.

In 1820 the Prince Regent finally became King George. To his embarrassment, Caroline reappeared and demanded her rights as queen. The country supported her, and George's popularity reached a new low when she was locked out of Westminster Abbey at his coronation. Her death less than a month later resolved the situation, but as her body was taken through London to Germany, there were riots in the streets.

As King George, he was less bad than expected largely because age had reduced his capacity for debauchery. He confined his extravagance to projects like modernizing Windsor Castle, building the British Museum and National Gallery, and planning the royal home that would become Buckingham Palace. An attempt to interfere in international politics was foiled by his Prime Minister George Canning, but he solaced himself with a new mistress, Lady Conyngham, and began spending much of his time in a "cottage" in Windsor Park, which he preferred to the Castle. In the last six years of his reign, his excesses caught up with him, and he began to spend most of his time in bed with gout and bladder problems. In June 1830, his strength began to fade, and on 26 June, to the relief of most of his subjects, he died at the age of 67.

Science: How it Works

To Keep Energy Levels High, Make Sure You're Getting Enough Iron

If you are feeling tired and weak, it may be because your body is short of iron. Oxygen is transported through your body in your blood and iron is required in the blood for the oxygen to cling too. The oxygen attaches itself to the iron and is carried throughout your body to all of the individual cells. If you do not consume enough iron, your body will be short on oxygen and you will feel tired.

Strangely enough, having too much iron in your body can also be a problem, as it can lead to a condition called hemochromatosis. Some people supplement their diet with vitamins and minerals including iron. Taking in too much iron overloads the body. The symptoms of this iron overload are very similar to the symptoms of an iron shortage – feeling tired and weak.

Fascinating Facts

It cost $200,000,000 to make the film *Titanic* and only $7,000,000 to build the original ship.

In 1957, the Shipping port Atomic Power Station in Pennsylvania, the first nuclear facility to generate electricity in the United States, went on line. (It was decommissioned in 1982.)

Those plastic tips on the ends of your shoelaces are called aglets.

In a game of soccer, an average player runs about seven miles.

The first ship ever to use the radio SOS system was the *Titanic*.

A diamond will not dissolve in acid. The only thing that can destroy it is intense heat.

A lump of pure gold the size of a matchbox can be flattened into a sheet the size of a tennis court.

Absolutely pure gold is so soft that it can be molded with the hands.

An ounce of gold can be stretched into a wire 50 miles long.

People in History

Strange Historical Stories

Christopher Columbus

Born in 1451 in the Italian port, of Genoa, Christopher
Columbus was attracted to water. He went to sea as a pimpled
youth, proceeded to marry the daughter of a Portuguese
navigator, and settled down happily in Lisbon.

Christopher was very highly influenced by his reading of a
fashionable book of the period, Ptolemy's *Geography*. From this
work Columbus learnt two main facts: (1) that the world was a
perfect sphere (which is clearly a mistake) and (2) that the
known world extends in a continuous land-mass from the
western extremities of Europe to the easternmost limit of Asia
and that between the two ends of this landmass on the other side
of the sphere, there was one single intervening ocean (which
was clearly also a mistake). Theoretically, it would thus be
possible, according to Ptolemy, to cross from Europe to Asia via
the Atlantic Ocean.

Ptolemy also reckoned that the proportions of land to ocean were
identical and therefore the Atlantic would be too wide for any
vessel in existence at the time to be able to cross it. Columbus
didn't like this part of the book so he dismissed it as incorrect.

With the assistance of his brother and expert chart-maker, Bartholomew Columbus, Christopher, a most charming and sophisticated fellow, used the parts of Ptolemy which supported his argunent, to acquire the support of Ferdinand and Isabella of Spain in his mission to discover the other route to the Indies.

On 3 August 1492, Columbus embarked from the port of Palos in his trusty boat the Santa Maria and set sail for a destination due west. On 12 October 1492, after quelling a potential mutiny on board by sheer force of personality, he landed in the Bahamas, believing himself to be in China. He kept notes on the native people, as if he were making notes about the Chinese, and he explored Haiti. He returned to Barcelona to a hero's welcome.

In September 1493, Columbus once again set sail, landing this time in Puerto Rico which he considered to be an island in the Indian Ocean. This is when things began to go badly wrong. A large number of colonizers had sailed with Columbus, thinking that they were about to get rich on gold. Columbus, however, was very keen that they should all plant vegetables. The unhappy Spaniards seized most of the boats and returned to Spain. Those who remained were disgusted to discover that the local food was horrible, the weather was lousy, and there wasn't a nugget of gold to be found.

Columbus wasn't a man to be easily deterred by the big

things in life. It was during his third voyage to the East Indies that Magellan and Da Gama actually did reach the Orient, thus discrediting Columbus completely whilst he was still claiming that Honduras was, in fact, Japan. Two years later, he returned to Spain, a broken man, but still pretty wealthy.

IT'S THE LAW

Idaho and other states allow members of the Native American church to use the hallucinogenic plant peyote in religious services.

A law in Chicago, Illinois, makes it illegal to serve liquor to the feeble-minded.

It's against the law in Vermont for vagrants to procure food by force.

At the Mardi Gras in New Orleans it's against the law to throw food from a float.

In New Orleans you may not fall over and block the sidewalk.

It used to be legal in Minnesota to sell rolled candy on Sunday, and illegal to sell flat candy.

It used to be against the law to go to the theater in Gary, Indiana, after eating garlic.

An old law in Waterloo, Nebraska, discouraged barbers from eating onions on the job.

You may deserve a break today, but you won't get it in Bloomfield, Connecticut., if you can't wait to get home from your local fast food emporium: It's against the law to eat in your car.

The One Minute Novel

A Christmas Carol – **Charles Dickens (1843)**
Scrooge was a miserable old bloke who hated Christmas and
general merry-making. One Christmas Eve he was visited by the
ghost of Marley, his recently deceased partner in business.
Marley took him on a journey showing him Christmas's past,
present, and future including a vision of what his own death
would be like unless he changed his ways.

   Stunned by these events, Scrooge woke up on Christmas
morning and decided to start there and then mending his ways.
Much to the shock of his employees and acquaintances he
suddenly revelled in Christmas good tidings, sending a goose to
Bob Cratchit, someone he had previously treated badly. He ran
around town giving charitable handouts to anyone who looked
like they needed a little help. In general he subscribed to all the
Christmas charities he could and from then on became the
complete opposite of his old self. By the end of the book he was
a genial, charitable, and kind old man and everyone responded
in kind.

Science: How it Works
Flotation and Buoyancy

How does a boat or ship carrying a heavy load float while that same load would sink to the bottom of the ocean if dumped overboard? When you're in a swimming pool and you stretch your body out flat, why is it that you float. And on the other hand, why is it that if you wrap your arms around your legs and curl up into a ball you sink?

It all depends on how much water is pushing against you. It is the scientific principle known as buoyancy or flotation. When you stretch out flat more water pushes against you because your body is laid out flatter.When you curl up into a ball, less water is pushing against you.

If the total area of the object that makes contact with the water is large enough, the object floats. The object must make room for its own volume by pushing aside, or displacing, an equivalent (or equal) volume of liquid. The object is exerting a downward force on the water and the water is therefore exerting an upward force on the object. Of course the floating object's weight comes into play also. The solid body floats when it has displaced just enough water to equal its own original weight.

This principle is called buoyancy. Buoyancy is the loss in weight an object seems to undergo when placed in a liquid, as compared to its weight in air. Archimedes' principle states that an object fully or partly immersed in a liquid is buoyed upward by a force equal to the weight of the liquid displaced by that object. From this principle, he concluded that a floating object displaces an amount of liquid equal to its own weight.

Beasts and Monsters

Bigfoot in Canada

Albert Ostman, a Canadian lumberjack, in 1924 combined a holiday with a bit of gold prospecting. He came near the head of the Toba Inlet opposite Vancouver Island, spent a week exploring, and decided to stop in a lovely glade under some cypress trees. The second night there he awoke to find himself being carried away in his sleeping bag like a sack of potatoes. He saw a huge hand around the partly open neck of the bag.

When Ostman was later dumped out on the ground, he was in the middle of a family of four big-footed monsters – the Sasquatch or Bigfeet. They were all enormous and hairy: father, who had kidnapped him; mother; a nearly adult son; and a younger daughter. The father was eight feet tall, the mother about seven. For six days Ostman was held prisoner, though no harm was done him. He observed that they were vegetarians, eating the grass, roots, and spruce tips gathered mainly by the mother and son. The daughter and father kept an eye on Ostman, but grew increasingly trustful of him. Finally he got the chance to escape. Fearing to be locked away as a madman, Ostman said nothing publicly about his adventure for many years.

ANIMAL SCIENCE

Pet parrots can eat virtually any common "people-food" except for chocolate and avocados. Both of these are highly toxic to the parrot and can be fatal.

The average adult male ostrich, the world's largest living bird, weighs up to 345 pounds.

The fastest bird is the Spine-tailed swift, clocked at speeds of up to 220 miles per hour.

The hummingbird is the only bird that can hover and fly straight up, down, or backward!

The hummingbird, the loon, the swift, the kingfisher, and the grebe are all birds that cannot walk.

The largest bird egg in the world today is that of the ostrich. Ostrich eggs are from 6 to 8 inches long.

The most frequently seen birds at feeders across North America last winter were the Dark-eyed Junco, House Finch and American goldfinch, along with downy woodpeckers, blue jays, mourning doves, black-capped chickadees, house sparrows, northern cardinals, and European starlings.

The turkey was named for what was wrongly thought to be its country of origin.

People in History

Strange Historical Stories

Spaced Out

On 28 July 1962 the *Mariner I* space probe was launched from Cape Canaveral headed directly for Venus. Never before had this been attempted in so technical a way.

The craft would cruise at over 25,000 miles an hour and in only 100 days Mariner would be circling the great planet with the mysterious cloudy rings.

A mere four minutes after take-off Mariner I hurled headlong downward and straight into the Atlantic Ocean.

A subsequent inquiry revealed that the cause of this accident was the absence of a minus sign which had unfortunately, been omitted from the computer program.

This oversight was a result of human error and cost NASA a staggering £4,280,000.

Joke of the Day
"What do you call a pig that does karate? A pork chop."

Amazing Engineering Facts

A Brief History of Nuclear Technology

Opinion is divided on whether nuclear technology is for good or ill. Its opponents would tell you that given it's hugely destructive potential it is almost too dangerous to use. Its proponents insist that it is a clean and powerful new source of energy.

It was the ancient Greeks who first put forward the idea that everything was made up of tiny particles or atoms but it was not until the twentieth century that scientists realized that the atom could be split leading to investigation into nuclear fission.

1905 – The Special Theory of Relativity

Albert Einstein introduced his special theory of relativity in 1925. Einstein held that the laws of nature are the same for all observers and that the speed of light is not dependent on the motion of its source. His most famous equation $E = mc^2$ demonstrated that energy equals mass multiplied by the speed of light squared and introduced the idea that mass can be converted into energy. Einstein won the Nobel Prize for physics in 1921.

1932 The Discovery of the Neutron

Following on from the work of New Zealander Ernest

# Boobs and Misprints

"Rats and cockroaches raiding the stores – not unscrupulous policemen with an eye for resale value – accounted for the loss of £17,000 worth of illegal drugs seized from addicts in the Philippines, a police chief said."
Western Evening News

"A glossy American cookbook coritained a recipe for Silky Caramel Slices: put an unopened can of condensed milk in a pot and leave it on the stove for four hours. The publishers later recalled all the books at vast expense, when they realized they had just invented the first exploding pudding – they had forgotten to mention that the pot should first be filled with water."
Readers Digest

"Intersection Six is still being planned,' said a spokesman for the Department of the Environment. Asked where it was going to be, the spokesman replied: 'We aren't quite sure but I imagine it would be between Intersection Five and Intersection Seven."
Manchester Evening News

Rutherford, who demonstrated the existence of protons, Chadwick, an English physicist, discovered the neutron by exposing the metal beryllium to alpha particles (consisting of two protons and two neutrons). Alpha particles are positively charged and are released by some radioactive materials. The neutron came to be seen as one of the three subatomic particles along with the positively charged proton and the negatively charged electron.

1932 – Splitting the Atom
In 1932, British physicist John Cockcroft joined forces with Irish scientist Ernest Walton to split the atom using protons accelerated to high speed. They won the Nobel Prize in 1951.

1939 – Splitting Uranium Atoms
Four physicists, Otto Hahn and Fritz Strassmann of Germany, along with Lise Meitner of Austria and her nephew Otto Frisch, developed a process known as fission to split uranium atoms. They proved Einstein's theory by demonstrating that some of the atoms converted into energy.

1939-1945 – The Manhattan Project
Although known as the Manhattan Project, this top-secret energy program run by scientists from the US army was based in Los Almos, New Mexico. Physicist J. Robert Oppenheimer led a team in developing the first transportable atomic bomb.

1945 – Hiroshima and Nagasaki
During World War II, Hiroshima was an important army depot and port. Nagasaki was a coastal city where the Mitsubishi torpedoes used in the attack on Pearl Harbor were made. The United States wanted to force the Japanese to surrender to end

the war and so dropped atomic bombs on both cities – hundreds of thousands of citizens were killed.

1946 – The Atomic Energy Commission
The Atomic Energy Commission replaced the Manhattan Project and was set up by US Congress. The Atomic Energy Commission had the responsibility for overseeing the development of nuclear technology in the postwar era.

1948 – The Commercialization of Nuclear Power
Two US companies, the government's Argonne National Laboratory operated by the University of Chicago, and the Westinghouse Corporation's Bettis Atomic Power Laboratory in Pittsburgh, made plans to produce nuclear powered electricity for commercial use.

1954 – The Atomic Energy Act of 1954
The 1946 act was amended in 1954 to allow private companies to use nuclear materials under license and so build and operate nuclear power plants. Also included in the new act was President Dwight D. Eisenhower's Atoms for Peace Program promoting peaceful use of nuclear energy.

Joke of the Day
A woman walked into a pet shop and said, "I'd like a frog for my son." "I'm sorry, madam," said the shopkeeper, "We don't do part exchange."

1955 – BORAX-III
Arco, Idaho became the first town in the world to be supplied solely with nuclear energy. The BORAX-III provided power from a nuclear reactor for more than an hour.

1955 – The First Nuclear-Powered Submarine
The Soviet Union's USS *Nautilus SSN 571*, was the world's first nuclear-powered submarine. The ship was built by the Electric Boat Company of Groton, Connecticut, and fitted with a pressurized water reactor. The *Nautilus SSN 571* later became the first submarine to sail under the North Pole in 1958.

1957 – The International Atomic Energy Agency
The International Atomic Energy Agency was formed by eight member companies in order to promote the peaceful use of nuclear energy. By the year 2000 it had 130 members worldwide.

1974 – The Energy Reorganization Act of 1974
The Energy Reorganization Act of 1974 divided up the Atomic Energy Commission into the Energy Research and Development Administration (ERDA) and the Nuclear Regulatory Commission (NRC). From now on each sector had different responsibilities. ERDA managed the development and refinement of nuclear power and the NRC managed and researched the safe use and disposal of nuclear materials.

1979 – Three Mile Island
A malfunctioning water pump in a secondary cooling system caused a major failure at the nuclear facility at Three Mile Island near Harrisburg, Pennsylvania. A relief valve became stuck causing a partial meltdown at the core of the plant but only a minor amount of radioactive material was released into the atmosphere.

Fascinating Facts

Colored diamonds are caused by impurities such as nitrogen (yellow), boron (blue). Red diamonds are due to deformities in the structure of the stone, and green ones being the result of irradiation.

Prussic acid, in a crystalline powder called Zyklon B, was used to kill in Nazi Germany's gas chambers. The gas paralyzed the victim's lungs, suffocating them.

Diamond is the hardest naturally occurring substance, and also one of the most valuable natural substances. They are formed almost entirely of carbon. Since it is so hard, the diamond is the most enduring gemstone known to man. Their rarity is due to the fact that only four significant diamond fields have ever been found – in Africa, South America, India, and the Soviet Union.

In 1982, in the first operation of its kind, doctors at the University of Utah Medical Center implanted a permanent artificial heart in the chest of retired dentist Dr. Barney Clark, who lived 112 days with the device.

Mercury is the only metal that is liquid at room temperature.

The mineral deposits in caves that grow upward are stalagmites, the ones growing downward are stalactites.

1986 – Chernobyl

One of the worst ever nuclear disasters occurred at Chernobyl in the Ukraine. Radioactive particles drifted over much of the European continent after four pressurized water reactors overheated releasing the water as steam. The hydrogen in the steam caused two major explosions and a fire. The site is radioactive to this day.

2000 – World Record Reliability Benchmarks

The world record reliability benchmarks were intended to promote the safe use of nuclear energy. In the USA over one hundred nuclear power plants operated at more than 90 per cent capacity during the 1990s, the equivalent of 2,024.6 gigawatt-years of safe reactor operation. Nuclear power energy production began to grow across the world most notably in the Far-East in China, Korea, Japan, and Taiwan.

Fascinating Facts

The most abundant metal in the Earth's crust is aluminum.

The only rock that floats in water is pumice.

The three most common elements in the universe are:
1) hydrogen; 2) helium; 3) oxygen.

The US government keeps its silver supply at the US Military Academy at West Point, New York.

352

Joke of the Day
"What do you get if you cross a chicken with a cement mixer? A brick layer!"

Real Ghost Stories

The Red Scratch Case

Mr F.G., a traveling salesman from Boston, had returned to his hotel room one afternoon. As he sat working he suddenly became aware of someone in the room.

Glancing up he was astounded to see his sister, who had died nine years before. "I sprang forward in delight, calling her by name," he said, "and as I did so, the apparition instantly vanished . . . I was near enough to touch her, had it been a physical possibility . . . She appeared as if alive." Yet there was one noticeable change in her appearance: her right cheek bore a bright red scratch.

Disturbed by this experience, F.G. went to see his parents with the story. When he mentioned the scratch, his mother was overcome with emotion. She revealed that she had made the scratch accidentally while tending to her daughter's body. Two weeks after this, his mother died peacefully.

Psychical researcher F.W.H. Myers pointed out that the figure was not "the corpse with the dull mark on which the mother's regretful thoughts might dwell, but . . . the girl in health and happiness, with the symbolic red mark worn simply as a test of identity." He suggested that the vision was sent by the spirit of the girl to induce her brother to go home and see his mother.

IT'S THE LAW

It's illegal to carry an ice cream cone in your pocket in Lexington, Kentucky.

Tomatoes are actually a fruit, but legally speaking, they're a vegetable. Ruling in an 1893 tariff case, the US Supreme Court said that because tomatoes are normally eaten during a meal and not afterward, they are legally vegetables.

One of the early Occupational Safety and Health Act laws in effect prohibited the use of ice in drinking water. It's been repealed.

The Iowa Legislature once passed a resolution ordering the state cafeteria to start serving cornbread.

In Nevada until the 1960s it was illegal to sell liquor at religious camp meetings, within a half-mile of the state prison, in the State Capitol Building or to imbeciles. Also, bar keepers had to publicly post the names of habitual drunkards if so requested by the local sheriff or members of the imbiber's immediate families.

California only fairly recently legalized the sale of alcoholic beverages in nudist colonies.

It's illegal in Florida for an unmarried man and woman to live together in "open and gross lewdness." Connecticut once had a similar law, but only the woman was penalized.

Royal Scandal

The Scandalous Princess

On 30 August 1997, Princess Diana was on a cruise along the coast of Sardinia, in the yacht *Jonikal*, owned by tycoon Mohammed al-Fayed, together with the new man in her life, al-Fayed's son Dodi. As usual, they were being observed by hordes of paparazzi, including two who were following the yacht in a rubber dinghy with a powerful engine. Sick of being pursued, Dodi decided to fly to Paris. They left by a Harrods Gulfstream jet at 1:45 p.m., and when they arrived at Le Bourget an hour and a half later, they were driven to a villa that had been owned by the Duke of Windsor, now the property of Mohammed al-Fayed.

Although they had been followed there by paparazzi on motorcycles, the ever-restless Diana decided that they would leave the security of the villa and go on to the Ritz Hotel in Paris, also owned by al-Fayed, so she could go shopping for presents for the birthday of her son Harry. Once in the Imperial Suite, Diana went to have her hair done. She also rang a friendly reporter on the *Daily Mail* to say she intended to quit public life for good. He would mention in his story a rumor that she and Dodi Fayed intended to announce their engagement.

Dodi now decided to go to his apartment in the Champs-

> **Classic One-Liners**
> S.J. Perelman: Love is not the dying moan of a
> violin. It's the triumphant twang of a bedspring.

Elysées to change for dinner – once more followed by
photographers, and by two bodyguards in a Range Rover. Later,
finding that a bistro where they had intended to eat was
surrounded by photographers, they returned to the Ritz, and
started to eat a meal there. But, nervous about having their
privacy invaded by photographers, they left it unfinished and
returned to their suite, where they finally ate dinner.

For some reason, Dodi then decided he wanted to return to his
apartment. And he decided that his regular chauffeur, Philippe
Dourneau, should drive off in a Range Rover to mislead the
paparazzi, while Henri Paul, who had met them off the plane,
should take them to the Champs-Elysées apartment, leaving the
Ritz by the back way. Paul had been off duty, expecting a quiet
evening. He had undoubtedly been drinking.

The paparazzi were at the back door too, and lost no time in
revving their machines. Henri Paul decided to outrun them, and
was soon driving at 60 miles an hour. And as they plunged into
the steep Alma tunnel, a 142-metre underpass, the car went out
of control and smashed into a concrete pillar. Dodi al-Fayed and
Henry Paul were killed outright; and Diana was so badly injured
that she died later in hospital. Only the bodyguard employed by
al-Fayed, Trevor Rees-Jones, survived, his life saved by an air
bag.

The sense of shock was tremendous. Since the announcement
of the engagement to Prince Charles in February 1981, Diana

had been the British public's favorite member of the royal family, her beauty and shy demeanor turning her into a media goddess. Crowds would wait all day outside her home, Kensington Palace, to catch a glimpse of her. Rumors of her marital problems created widespread anger. The marriage broke up in 1992, and public sympathy soon swung in Diana's favor when Andrew Morton's book *Diana: Her True Story* revealed that the cause of the split had been the long-standing love affair between Prince Charles and Camilla Parker-Bowles.

The lack of public grief displayed by the royal family undermined even the Queen's popularity, and it may have been in response to the rising tide of criticism that the royal family took the unusual step of arranging for the funeral to be televised internationally.

Sixteen years earlier, on 29 July 1981, 750 million people had watched the marriage of Prince Charles, the Prince of Wales to Lady Diana Spencer, and a frenzy of media attention had followed the ceremony. The diffident bride-to-be had been pursued everywhere by gangs of reporters, and the curiosity of the British public was fed to bursting by daily stories in competing tabloid newspapers. In the battle for circulation each one was desperate to outdo the others with pictures of the couple taken in private, or stories of their courtship wheedled from close friends. Diana's face smiled from the cover of nearly every magazine on the news stands.

The British public's delight at the prospect of a royal wedding had been mingled with relief. During the late 1970s, Charles's name had been linked with many eligible socialites – Davina Sheffield, Princess Marie-Astrid of Luxembourg, Susan George, Sabrina Guinness, Amanda Knatchbull, Anna Wallace, Jane Ward (the latter the manageress at the Guards Polo Club where the prince regularly played) but every time the gossip-column

Boobs and Misprints

"All meat in this window is from local farmers killed on the premises."
Sign in a Somerset butcher's shop

"A restaurant that gave a new meaning to atter-dinner sweets has been ordered by health officials to use plates – and not the bellies of its topless waitresses – to serve dessert. The restaurant in Perth, Australia, invited diners to eat fruit salad and cream off the stomach of a waitress."
Western Morning News

"A Minneapolis suburb has been buzzing with the news that a housewife was seen holding hands with the mailman on her front porch. True, the lady in question calmly admits, it was the best way she could think of to convince her dog that postmen aren't burglars."
"Almanac" in Minneapolis Tribune

"Western Morning News was wrongly illustrated with a picture of another hallucinogenic fungus, the fly agaric, which is extremely poisonous if eaten and can prove fatal. We apologise for the error."
Western Morning News

writers predicted that a royal wedding was in the offing, their
hopes had been frustrated. "Sources" close to the prince would
report that the relationship was over, or had never even
happened. The general opinion among royal observers was that
Charles, at 31, was taking rather longer than necessary to sow
his wild oats.

So when his engagement to Diana was announced on 24
February 1981, the same royal observers agreed that his choice
showed excellent taste. The bride to be was attractive,
charmingly shy in front of the cameras, and most importantly,
from the right background: Diana was the third daughter of Earl
Spencer. In the tradition of the British royal family, she was not
formidably intellectual – she had left school with only two "O"
levels, and had then taken a course in cookery and worked as a
child minder. Clearly Diana was not intended to take up a
professional career. She had "wife of the gentry" written all over
her.

What no one realized until later was that Prince Charles
himself was not entirely happy about the idea of marrying Diana
Spencer. He had finally given way to family pressure to settle
down and provide an heir – pressure from his mother and father,
his Uncle Dickie (Lord Louis Mountbatten), and from the Queen
Mother, who virtually chose Diana herself.

In fact, Diana had not had the happy, sheltered life everyone
assumed. When she was three, her mother had fallen in love
with another man, and the Spencers were divorced three years
later. She had been brought up by her father. The divorce
disturbed her deeply, and it may have been in reaction that she
began to devote much attention to sick animals. It also seems to
have been responsible for a tendency to overeat that made her
plump and – to her own eyes – unattractive. As a teenager she
had worked at a kindergarten in Pimlico, and shared a flat with

three friends. But although she had boyfriends, she remained –
according to her flatmates – sexually inexperienced; one
commentator says this was because she saw sex as the cause of
the breakup of her parents' marriage, and was afraid of it.

Charles, on the other hand, had had three serious sexual relationships in the year before the engagement was announced. Since the
mid-1970s, many women had been to dinner in his flat in
Buckingham Palace and stayed the night. The prince's valet,
Stephen Barry, later told a gossip columnist how he had frequently
retrieved items of ladies' underwear from under the bed or behind
the cushions of the settee. If the owner was known, these were
laundered and returned to her in an Asprey gift box; if not, they
might be presented to members of the palace staff – occasionally
gentlemen. (The same gossip columnist remarks that many of the
male staff at Buckingham Palace are homosexual, since homosex-
uals have no wives to divide their loyalties, and tend to enjoy the
protocol of palace life.) Prince Andrew is reported to have told a
girlfriend that his brother was trying to emulate actor Warren
Beatty, who had the reputation of having slept with every attractive
starlet in Hollywood.

According to gossip columnist Nigel Dempster, there was
even a "slush fund" that had been set up to pay off the women
who objected to being one-night stands, a few of whom received
a dollar cheque running to six figures. Unlike the Prince Regent,
described in an earlier chapter, Charles seems to have had no
problem financing his high turnover of mistresses.

Charles had also had a brief romance with Diana's sister
Sarah (who later insisted it had remained platonic), and so the
general assumption was that Diana had begun to feel an interest
in Charles at this time – many girls develop a crush on their
elder sisters' boyfriends. (Sarah had apparently been finally
rejected by Charles's vetters because she suffered from anorexia

Joke of the Day
What's furry, has whiskers and chases
outlaws? A posse cat.

and was a chain smoker – her sister called her "fagash Lil.") The
only slight problem seemed to be the difference in the ages of
Charles and Diana: at 20, Lady Di was more than ten years
younger than her royal husband-to-be.

On 29 July 1981, St Paul's Cathedral was the focus of the
world's attention. In the surrounding streets, many were
unashamed to weep with joy at the sight of their future king and
queen. When the couple kissed on the balcony of Buckingham
Palace after the ceremony, the crowds that jammed the Mall
screamed their approval. Despite the economic recession and
Britain's declining importance in the league of world powers,
the nation was proud; there had been nothing so romantic since
Prince Rainier married Grace Kelly in Monaco.

Perhaps it was the feeling of anticlimax that followed the
wedding that started the reaction. Newspapers that had whipped
their readership into a frenzy of nationalism with massive
souvenir pull-outs and photo specials found it difficult to simply
drop the story and return to more mundane and depressing news.
Even if the newspapers' editors had wanted to, competition
would not allow it. A paper with a new picture of Diana outsold
its Dianaless rival. The publicity was unrelenting: every minor
occasion at which the Prince and Princess of Wales appeared in
public received blanket attention. In the fever of interest in the
future queen, Charles was sometimes forgotten. At public
appearances, it was clear whom the crowds had turned out to

see. Charles seemed to take the implied affront in good part, apologizing to crowds in Wales that he only had one wife.

Soon the purely descriptive news items, praising Diana's dress sense and cooing about the happy couple, began to sound a little repetitive. Clearly, while the public's appetite for royal gossip was undiminished, every tabloid editor sensed that they were beginning to get bored with positive stories. To vary the diet, feature writers began turning out pieces expressing concern about Diana's well-being. They pointed out that in February, when the engagement was announced, Diana had been a rosy-cheeked, healthy-looking girl who looked as if she played hockey every morning before breakfast. By the time of the wedding, she had shed considerable weight, and her cheeks were no longer so rosy. No doubt she had been dieting for her wedding day – but could it be that she was overdoing it?

When, in the months following the wedding, the princess seemed to go on losing weight, the newspapers clucked and worried like maiden aunts. Their anxiety communicated itself to the public, who responded by buying the newspapers that sounded most concerned. So when, on 21 November 1981, the palace announced that Diana was pregnant, everyone heaved a sigh of relief – not least the newspaper editors, who now had an excuse for beginning the party all over again.

In February 1982, five months into Diana's pregnancy, the Waleses holidayed on Windermere Island in the Bahamas. For many years there had been an unspoken agreement between Fleet Street and the palace that royal holidays were no-go areas. This tradition soon fell a victim to the circulation war, and newspaper photographers secretly photographed Diana in her bikini. These pictures revealed that, although pregnant, she was still obviously underweight.

Fascinating Facts

Natural gas has no odor. The smell is added artificially so that leaks can be detected.

You have to walk up 1,792 steps to get to the top of the Eiffel Tower.

Sea water, loaded with mineral salts, weighs about a pound and a half more per cubic foot than fresh water at the same temperature.

Ten per cent of the salt mined in the world each year is used to de-ice American roads.

The air we breathe is 78per cent nitrogen, 21.5 per cent oxygen, 0.5 per cent argon and other gases.

The Chinese were using aluminum to make things as early as 300 AD. Western civilization didn't rediscover the substance until 1827.

The Cullinan Diamond is the largest gem-quality diamond ever discovered. Found in 1905, the original 3,100 carats were cut to make jewels for the British Crown Jewels and the British Royal family's collection.

The largest hailstone ever recorded was 17.5 inches in diameter – bigger than a basketball.

The largest gold nugget ever found weighed 172 pounds, 13 ounces.

The publication of these pictures brought a strong rebuke from the palace. It was, said the spokesman, "one of the blackest days in British journalism." Such a criticism from the royal family was unheard of, mainly because long-established guidelines of good taste had previously governed what could be printed. But in Fleet Street, times were changing. The struggle for circulation meant that such tacit agreements were luxuries that could no longer be afforded.

All this prying and intrusion involved a slow change in the attitude of reporters toward Prince Charles. The tacit agreement that had operated since the time of Queen Victoria meant that reporters addressed the Prince of Wales as "sir" and treated him with respect. They still continued to address him as "sir," but the respect was eroding. Charles's admission that he talked to his plants in order to encourage them to grow resulted in acres of ridicule in the tabloids. Taken in combination with his avowed liking for the mystical writings of Sir Laurens van der Post, Charles was made to appear to be a kind of blue-blooded hippy. Yet he had many sympathizers when, in 1983, he attacked plans for an addition to the National Gallery in Trafalgar Square, describing it as a "carbuncle on the face of a much-loved and elegant friend." (The plans for the extension were then dropped.)

The couple certainly had to endure trial-by-camera. Every time they appeared together, the expressions on their faces were analysed and discussed in the captions, and sometimes they had to endure intrusion by long telephoto lens. (Charles had been sensitive about such matters ever since he had been photographed, in May 1960, lying on a blanket by the river at Balmoral with a girlfriend named Anna Wallace.) Moreover, the smallest physical contact between Charles and any other woman who happened to be in the entourage was subjected to the same minute analysis.

There was also an attempt to humanize the royal couple with
"chatty" (i.e. disrespectful) and "homely" (i.e. impertinent)
stories – for example, after the Wales's second son, Harry, was
born, the newspapers revealed that William and Harry were
known by their parents as the "heir and spare."

Now in their fourth year of marriage, Charles and Diana were
granted a respite. Finally starved of new material for gossip, the
tabloids had turned their attention on to Prince Andrew,
Charles's younger brother. Andrew's relationships with women
provided more substantial fare than the diet of innuendo and
rumor in the stories about Diana. Andrew was portrayed as
libidinous and cheeky, a convenient contrast to the intellectual
and contemplative Charles. Andrew played up to the "Randy
Andy" tag. He attempted to get TV presenter Selina Scott's
phone number while being interviewed by her for Terry Wogan,
and was often photographed "out on the town" with one-time
soft-porn actress Katherine "Koo" Stark.

But by 1985, Andrew was twenty-five, the age when royal
tradition dictated that he should be thinking of marriage. Then,
during the Royal Ascot week party at Windsor Castle, the
invited guests were surprised to see Andrew handfeeding
profiteroles to the freckled and bouncy redhead who was seated
next to him. The woman was Sarah Ferguson, daughter of Major
Ronald Ferguson, Prince Charles's polo manager. Such open
friskiness tied in well with Andrew's playboy image, and the
papers immediately began to cover the couple's meetings extensively.

And meet they did, often and publicly. At the time of the
Ascot party, Sarah had been the girlfriend of racing driver Paddy
McNally. It was rumored that, after giving McNally an
ultimatum ("Marry me or else . . ."), Sarah had decisively
dropped him. The palace plainly approved of "Fergie" (as Sarah

was known). It was, after all, the seating arrangements at a royal party that had brought them together. Such things are not random or accidental . . .

Andrew and Fergie's engagement was announced in February 1986, to no one's great surprise. Their wedding took place in Westminster Abbey in July of that year. Although not as grand an affair as the wedding of his elder brother, Andrew's wedding excited the same public enthusiasm. Fergie, of course, could hardly be less like Diana; where Diana's image was shy and demure, Fergie's was effervescent and mischievous. Everyone liked her – she looked as if she would enjoy a game of darts in the local pub. When newspapers reported that Diana and Fergie had dressed up as policewomen in order to gatecrash Andrew's stag night party, no one had any doubt who thought up the idea.

On his marriage, Andrew inherited the title of the Duke of York. The Queen's present to the couple was a lease on the Sunninghill estate, as well as the money to build a family house there.

The tone of the articles about the two royal couples became less and less positive as the decade wore on. The Duchess of York seemed to be permanently on holiday: she beamed from the ski-slopes or golden beaches at least once a week. Rightly or wrongly, the British public suspected that it was their tax revenues that were enabling her to live this enviable life. The "respectable" newspapers began to voice a certain irritation with the British obsession with the younger members of the royal family, and the *Independent*, which had just been established, expressed the broadsheets' boredom with royal stories by covering Beatrice's birth with a single line in the Births, Marriages, and Deaths column in the back pages. Again, there was criticism when, after the birth of Princess Beatrice, the Duchess of York went off to join her husband in Australia, and

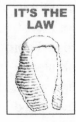
IT'S THE LAW

Montana just legalized the production of caviar.

In the old days in Nevada, a man caught beating his wife was tied to a stake for eight hours a day with a sign that read, "Wife Beater" fastened to his chest.

The Santa Monica, Calif., City Council recently proposed that men be allowed to use women's public restrooms when there's a line of three or more at the mens' room, and vice versa.

In New York City you need a permit to transport carbonated beverages.

You need a license to sell condoms in Washington state.

In South Carolina, wife beaters weren't allowed to hold public office.

A Wisconsin legislator in the 1970s proposed a law providing that no woman over 21 be required to divulge her age. If age information were required by law, women could use an alphabetic code: women in their 20s would use A, women in their 30s B, and so on.

A Maryland law outlaws "female sitters, also known as shills," women paid by owners to sit in their bars and encourage male patrons to buy drinks.

yet again when she took her daughter skiing in Switzerland while she still had a chickenpox rash. Her plans for her new home in Berkshire were derided as vulgar and ostentatious.

What was worse, from the point of view of the royal family, was that it was very obvious that all was not well between Charles and Diana. She was blamed because members of Charles's household were said to have resigned because they found her too demanding. Even in the mid-1980s it was noted that the couple seemed to spend little time together, and that they seemed to barely tolerate each other in public. The days of sunny smiles for the cameras seemed to be past.

By the late 1980s, the tabloids were busy spreading doubts about the strength of both marriages. Prince Charles, they hinted regularly, was having an affair with Camilla Parker-Bowles, an old girlfriend now married. Fergie was also suspected of infidelity with Texan millionaire Steve Wyatt, her financial adviser. Yet no real evidence, apart from whispered confidences from "sources close to Charles" or "a palace insider," were offered. But it seemed clear that the newspapers knew more than they were prepared to print; they regularly hinted that they could not tell the full truth.

Things began to fall apart for the Yorks in January 1992. Maurice Marple, a window cleaner, had been hired by an estate agent to clean a flat in Cadogan Square. While throwing out the

Classic One-Liners
Bernard Shaw: "The British churchgoer prefers a severe preacher because he thinks a few home truths will do his neighbours no harm."

unwanted property left by the previous tenant, Marple happened
upon a thick stack of photos perched on top of a wardrobe. Idly
flicking through them before consigning them to the black
plastic sack, Marple suddenly recognized the face of the
Duchess of York, Sarah Ferguson. Some of the photos showed
the duchess and a handsome tanned man in swimsuits, laughing
and having a good time. Others showed the unidentified man
playing with Princess Beatrice, and riding a horse beside Fergie.
What the other photos showed is not known.

Mr Marple decided that the newspapers would be interested in
his discovery. He took them to the *Daily Mail*, who advised him
to give them to the police. Whether he did this is not clear; all
that is known is that some of the photographs were published in
Paris-Match.

During the next few days, the British tabloids made much of
their restraint in not publishing the pictures. But they dropped
very broad hints that the photos showed the duchess in inappro-
priate positions with a man identified as Steve Wyatt.

In fact, the affair had been known to all Fergie's friends for a
long time. Wyatt was undoubtedly handsome, in a lean, Texan
way, with very white teeth. He and Fergie had met in 1990,
when Prince Andrew was away from home – in the navy – for
all but 42 nights of the year. She was pregnant when she visited
Wyatt's ranch in Texas, but the affair progressed nevertheless.
In a French Riviera restaurant with Fergie and Saddam
Hussein's oil marketing chief (this was soon after Saddam's
invasion of Kuwait), Wyatt embarrassed Lord McAlpine and his
guests by pulling Fergie into his lap with the comment: "Mah
woman and I sit together." Eventually, Fergie was persuaded by
the Queen and her own mother to drop the indiscreet Wyatt. By
January 1992, when the photograph scandal was the talk of
London, the affair with Wyatt was already over.

For Prince Andrew this seems to have been the last straw. On 19 March 1992, two months after the Wyatt photos story, the Yorks announced that they had decided to separate. To a stunned public, this seemed to be a full acknowledgment of the duchess's adultery. Before this new information had had time to sink in, the public was hit with a bigger revelation.

DIANA DRIVEN TO FIVE SUICIDE BIDS BY "UNCARING CHARLES" shrieked the headline of the Sunday Times on 7 June 1992. The story beneath contained some of the most startling revelations from a new book by Andrew Morton, a royal journalist, entitled *Diana: Her True Story*. What made this book different from other similar works – like Lady Colin Campbell's *Diana in Private* – was that it was plainly written with some cooperation from the Princess of Wales. Morton had quite a story to tell. The book revealed that Diana had been doubtful about marrying Charles from the start. Since 1972, Charles had been friendly with Camilla Parker-Bowles; they were so close that they addressed one another as Fred and Gladys. Camilla was married to Andrew Parker-Bowles, a member of the Queen's household, and Diana had known her since 1980. At first, Diana was unsuspicious, even when she learned that Camilla was reputed to "vet" all Charles's girlfriends. She remained unsuspicious when Camilla asked her if she meant to hunt when she was at Highgrove (Prince Charles's new house), and looked relieved when Diana said no. But a few weeks before their wedding, she learned that Charles and Camilla used nicknames when Charles sent Camilla a get-well bouquet inscribed "from Fred to Gladys." And when, on the eve of her wedding, she learned that Charles intended to give Camilla a bracelet inscribed G and F (which, according to an alternative source, stood for "Girl Friday," another of Charles's pet names for Camilla), it dawned on her with an awful sense of

Boobs and Misprints

"Pope escapes."
The Guardian

"A very disagreeable mistake was made by the police-constables stationed at St Austell, a few days ago. A lunatic, an Irishman, had escaped from the county asylum at Bodmin, and the St Austell police seeing an Irishman in the town, and evidently thinking that all natives of the Green Isle are rather cracky, and that this one would do quite as well as the other, marched him off to the lock-up, followed by a lot of boys, although the man had resided in the higher quarter of the town for years. The unlucky prisoner told his captors to go with him to the rate-collector, who would satisfy them that he was not a lunatic, as he had just been paying him a lot of rates, but without effect. After arriving at the police station, however, he was soon liberated.
West Briton

"One of Colorado's oldest citizens and a resident of Walsenburg for about a century died here yesterday. Mrs Quintina was 104 years old at the time of her death, her grandmother said."
Enterprise Times, Brockton, Massachusetts

Joke of the Day
A doctor visited his patient in the
hospital ward after the operation.
"I've got some bad news – we
amputated the wrong leg. Now the
good news – the man in the next bed
wants to buy your slippers.'

certainty that Camilla was her future husband's mistress, and
that he had no intention of breaking off the relationship when he
married. She came close to calling the wedding off the night
before the ceremony.

When, on their honeymoon, photographs of Camilla fell out
of Charles's diary, and when she noticed that he wore cufflinks
with two "Cs" intertwined – which he admitted had been given
to him by a woman he had loved and lost – her worst suspicions
were confirmed.

Understandably, she was shattered. Ever since her parents'
divorce she had been afraid of love, but was willing to suspend
her distrust and learn to become a caring wife and mother. Now
it was obvious that she was simply the third in a triangle, and
that, like so many women who had married princes of the
British royal family, she was going to be expected to close her
eyes to her husband's infidelities.

On the eve of the wedding, Charles allayed her fears when he
sent her a signet ring and an affectionate note. But all the
tension made her eat more than she intended to, then vomit it
all up.

They spent the honeymoon on the royal yacht *Britannia*, and
here again, she began to feel excluded. She wanted to spend

time getting to know her husband – with whom she was by now deeply in love. Charles took along his fishing tackle and a pile of books by his mentor Laurens van der Post, who had written of the bushmen of South Africa, and had been a friend of the psychologist Carl Jung. They hardly ever seemed to be alone. Again, Diana's response to stress was to creep to the kitchen and eat bowl after bowl of ice cream.

What no one realized was that Diana was suffering from the nervous disorder called bulimia nervosa, which involves overeating, usually followed by vomiting. Its sufferers tend to experience extreme mood swings, and may become suicidal.

Clearly, both Charles and Diana had problems. He had thought he was marrying an uncomplicated girl who would enjoy being Princess of Wales and then queen; to learn (as he soon did) that she had emotional problems must have been a shock. For her part, she thought she was marrying a kind of protective father figure who would help her to adjust to her new life. But he seemed to live on another plane, and although he took her for long walks and read her page after page by Jung and van der Post, she felt she was being talked down to.

But the major problem, of course, was her suspicion that her husband was still in love with Camilla Parker-Bowles, and meant to renew their relationship at the first opportunity. They began to have violent rows about Camilla. And once a newly married couple start having violent rows, the marriage has lost its chance of the kind of slow and idyllic growth that can form the basis of a lifelong partnership.

What she now needed was some close support from her husband, a reassurance that all would be well. But Charles was unwilling to offer such reassurance. He seemed to feel that she was suffering from neurotic schoolgirl tantrums, and that what was really needed was that she should pull herself together.

Most of the royal family seemed to feel much the same. On New Year's Day 1982, when she was three months pregnant with Prince William, she threatened suicide, and Charles accused her of being hysterical. When he went off riding on the Sandringham estate, she hurled herself down a long wooden staircase.

It was the Queen Mother, the major architect of the marriage, who found her lying dazed at the bottom, trembling with shock, and who sent for help. A hastily summoned gynaecologist was able to assure everyone that both Diana and the foetus were unharmed.

Far from winning sympathy from her husband, it infuriated him as a piece of melodramatic hysteria. In a sense, the marriage ended then, less than a year after it had begun.

According to Lady Colin Campbell, in *Diana in Private*, Diana also felt that she was an outsider in the royal family. The Queen, says Lady Colin, had absolutely nothing in common with Diana, and "the gulf between them grew worse and worse." Princess Anne simply regarded Diana as "an airhead and a light-weight" and could not understand why Charles had married her. But one day, when Diana dropped into the conversation at the dinner table a question about how they saw the role of the royal family in a united Europe, they regarded her with puzzlement for a few moments, then went back to discussing hunting. Diana's increasing frustration is understandable.

Morton describes how Diana one day threw herself against a glass display cabinet, and how, during one argument with Prince Charles, she seized a penknife and cut herself on the chest and thighs. Charles's reaction was to ignore her.

For Charles it must have seemed that the fairy-tale marriage had turned to a kind of hell. The sweet, shy twenty year old, who was supposed to adore him and be delighted that he had introduced her to a new and wonderful life, had turned out to be a vengeful neurotic who spent half her time in tears and was always complaining. He must have wished that he had taken his courage into his hands all those years before, and married Camilla, who thoroughly understood him.

The arrival of Prince William improved things for a while; Charles loved being a father, and was well suited to the role. Then there was a reaction, and Diana plunged back into depression. She began to see a psychiatrist (Jungian, naturally), but

---

Classic One-Liners
Lord, if I can't be skinny, please let all my friends be fat.

Confession is good for the soul, but bad for your career.

Jesus loves you! It's everybody else that thinks you're an ass.

Money isn't everything, but it sure keeps the kids in touch.

Is reading in the bathroom considered multi-tasking?

Why do bankruptcy lawyers expect to be paid?

continued to lose weight. Diana and Charles moved between their two homes, Kensington Palace and Highgrove, but they had so little social life that their butler described working for them as boring.

On the other hand, Charles continued to hunt with the Parker-Bowleses, and saw Camilla regularly. And Diana "found a shoulder to lean and cry on" in her personal bodyguard, Sergeant Barry Manakee. Morton notes that "the affectionate bond that built up between them did not go unnoticed either by Prince Charles or Manakee's colleagues." Manakee was later transferred to other duties, and was killed in a motorcycle accident. No impropriety has ever been alleged, but it seemed clear that, lacking emotional support from her husband and the royal family, she felt a need to look for it elsewhere.

The romance between Prince Andrew and Fergie provided a welcome diversion. Diana and Fergie became close friends, and Diana, now more confident, guided Fergie through the routine of being a "royal." In public, she was self-possessed and as charming as ever. But she still felt that she was a kind of royal cipher. There was an occasion when she prepared a surprise for the royal family when they were due to spend an evening watching ballet at Covent Garden, and she and leading dancer Wayne Sleep rehearsed a routine in secret at Kensington Palace. The audience gasped when Diana stepped out on to the stage in a silver silk dress, and danced a specially choreographed routine to a song "Uptown Girl," revealing that she had the makings of a first-class ballerina. The audience applauded wildly, and she took eight curtain calls, even curtsying to the royal box. But Charles later told her he thought that it had all been undignified and "showy."

Even by 1987, it was becoming obvious to the press that the royal marriage was under some strain. Diana and Fergie came in for criticism for "frivolity" when both were photographed at a race meeting poking a friend in the backside with their umbrellas. When Diana and a group of friends had a weekend party at the stately home of the parents of a young man named Philip Dunne, a gossip columnist reported that Diana had spent the weekend alone with him. When she was ambushed by a photographer as she emerged from a cinema with a group of friends that included a young man called David Waterhouse, Waterhouse leapt a pedestrian barrier and fled into the night, causing more gossip than if he had stayed put.

In 1987, her confidence fortified by a new doctor who seemed to be helping her to conquer her bulimia, Diana cornered Camilla Parker-Bowles at a birthday party and accused her of sleeping with her husband. Whether Camilla admitted it or not Morton does not record, but he tells us that the explosion "helped Diana to come to terms with her jealousy and anger."

At about this time – in 1988 – a polo player named Captain James Hewitt came into Diana's life when he began to teach Princes William and Harry horsemanship. She visited his home in Devon, and they were soon the subject of suspicion on the part of the royal family. A colour sergeant later told the *News of the World* that he had been part of a surveillance team whose job was to spy on the couple and photograph them making love in the garden. Hewitt's friend Anna Pasternak later wrote a book – with his cooperation – in which he admitted that they had been lovers.

The reason for this oddly brash piece of behavior seems to lie in Morton's comment that Charles and Diana had drifted apart to the extent of marshaling rival battalions of friends in their support. In a book called *Closely Guarded Secret*, Inspector Ken Wharfe, who became Diana's official "minder" in 1987, states that Hewitt was deeply in love with Diana, and wanted her to marry him; Diana, unattracted by the idea of becoming nothing more exciting than an officer's wife, decided to drop him.

Morton also commented that Prince Charles "counted on" Andrew and Camilla Parker-Bowles for social support. Their home, Middlewich House, was only twelve miles from Highgrove House. A Sunday newspaper spoke about the unmarked Ford estate car in which Charles frequently drove to Middlewich House.

When, in January 1992, Prince Andrew and Fergie visited the Queen at Sandringham to confess that their marriage was on the rocks – partly due to the latest press uproar about her relation with Steve Wyatt – the Queen asked them for a two-month "cooling off" period before they announced their separation. This completed, the press was informed that this marriage was over. Yet still Charles and Diana were officially together, even though they lived apart.

When, in 1992, Andrew Morton's Diana: Her True Story was published, after serialization in the Sunday Times, it combined all these scandalous revelations with a glowingly positive assessment of the princess, in which her work for charity and her love for her children featured prominently. In this respect it read like one of the countless glossy coffee table books that portrayed the royal family as practitioners of all the old-fashioned virtues, but Morton, with the help of Diana's friends, had taken this genre and cross-bred it with kiss-and-tell

Joke of the Day
Don't get married. Find a woman you hate and buy her a house. It's a lot easier.

ANIMAL SCIENCE

Pet parrots can eat virtually any common "people-food" except for chocolate and avocados. Both of these are highly toxic to the parrot and can be fatal.

The average adult male ostrich, the world's largest living bird, weighs up to 345 pounds.

The fastest bird is the Spine-tailed swift, clocked at speeds of up to 220 miles per hour.

The hummingbird is the only bird that can hover and fly straight up, down, or backward.

The most frequently seen birds at feeders across North America last winter were the Dark-eyed Junco, House Finch and American goldfinch, along with downy woodpeckers, blue jays, mourning doves, black-capped chickadees, house sparrows, northern cardinals and European starlings.

The turkey was named for what was wrongly thought to be its country of origin.

Hollywood scandal sheets. It sold massively, making Morton a wealthy man.

In the postscript to the paperback edition, Morton begins: "The days of pretending were over forever." The book, apparently, had led the couple to face up to the collapse of their marriage. From now on, they were to live separate lives.

That summer of 1992, Fergie was back in the news. "Fergie's Stolen Kisses" shouted the *Daily Mail* headline. An Italian long-lens paparazzo, Daniel Angeli, had snapped the duchess with her financial adviser John Bryan, a tall, prematurely balding Texan who had been a school friend of Steve Wyatt. They were holidaying together, with the duchess's children, in a villa in the woods outside St Tropez. In one photo, Bryan kisses the duchess's toes. The duchess is topless in the shots. Fergie was already virtually unmentionable within the royal family, and the photographs seemed to make any reconciliation out of the question.

Then, just at the point when Fergie was squirming uncomfortably in the spotlight, it was switched back to Diana again.

On 24 August 1992, the *Sun* published an account of a taped conversation between Princess Diana and a second-hand car dealer, James Gilbey.

"MY LIFE IS TORTURE: DIANAGATE TAPE OF LOVE CALL REVEALS MARRIAGE MISERY" declared the headline. The conversation opens arrestingly:

"GILBEY: And so, darling, what are the other lows today?

"DIANA: So that was it . . . I was very bad at lunch. And I

Classic One-Liners
Multi-millionaire John Jacob Astor III remarked consolingly: 'A man who has a million dollars is as well off as if he were rich.'

nearly started blubbing. I just felt really sad and empty, and I thought: 'Bloody hell, after all I've done for this fucking family.'"

On the 23-minute tape, Gilbey addresses her as "Squidgey" (14 times) and "darling" (53 times), and at one point they blow kisses to one another down the phone. He tells her that he hasn't played with himself for 48 hours, and that a dream he had had of her was "very strange and very lovely too". Diana replies: "I don't want to get pregnant." "Darling, that's not going to happen. All right? . . . You won't get pregnant." After more general conversation, Gilbey tells her: "Just have to wait till Tuesday."

In fact, the tape had been recorded two years earlier, in December 1989, by an eavesdropper on the princess's mobile phone, using a device called a "scanner." It appeared to reveal that Diana had been on intimate terms with Gilbey while she and Charles were still living together. Yet the real interest of the tape lies in the enormous weariness Diana expresses regarding her in-laws. Here was further proof of the misery of the princess and the lack of communication at the heart of the monarchy. A debate about whether Diana and Gilbey did or did not have sex raged in the papers for weeks.

Oddly enough, the tape did Diana no harm with the British public. The suggestion that she had a lover added a dimension to her personality; the comment: "I don't want to get pregnant" substituted the image of a woman capable of sexual passion for the demure schoolgirl persona that had made her seem a permanent virgin.

Prince Charles was reported to have been disgusted by the publicity, while Diana is on record as saying that it was a catharsis.

On 9 December 1992, Buckingham Palace announced "with

regret" that the Prince and Princess of Wales had decided to separate.

Five weeks later, on Sunday 17 January 1993, the *Sunday Mirror* and the *People* published in full a tape of another recorded telephone conversation, this time between Prince Charles and Camilla Parker-Bowles; like the Gilbey–Diana tape, it had been recorded by an eavesdropper. This conversation had, in fact, taken place on 17 December 1989, two weeks before the Gilbey–Diana tape. It was considerably more explicit. When Camilla says: "You're awfully good at feeling your way along," Charles replies: "O, stop! I want to feel my way all along you, all over you, and up and down you and in and out . . . particularly in and out." Camilla replies: "O, that's just what I need at the moment." Charles suggests: "I'll just live inside your trousers or something. It would be much easier." "What, are you going to turn into a pair of knickers? You're going to come back as a pair of knickers." "Or," says Charles, "God forbid, a Tampax. Just my luck! . . . to be chucked down a lavatory and go forever swirling around the top, never going down . . ."

In *Behind Palace Doors*, an even more revelatory book than Morton's, gossip columnist Nigel Dempster reports that when Charles heard about the tape, four days before it was published, he kept repeating: "How can it all have gone wrong so quickly?" He may have been cheered when, after newspaper publication of the tape, a crowd of well-wishers at Sandringham shouted, "Good old Charlie," but a close friend commented: "It was the worst moment of his life. He wanted to be taken seriously, to be given respect as a man. He sincerely believed that he had important things to say. He wanted to be thought profound. And in six minutes of private conversation, a conversation that was nobody's business but his and the woman to whom he was speaking, his reputation was ruined. Maybe it was a delusion that he was something of a sage and a philosopher, but it was a fairly harmless delusion. The downfall of a prince holds a terrible fascination, but he really didn't deserve to be destroyed so publicly."

The year 1992 had been extremely difficult for the Queen, with both her sons' marriages ending in ugly circumstances. In late November a serious fire broke out in Windsor Castle and the emergency services struggled to control it. By the time they succeeded, it had destroyed much of the fabric of the building, including the chapel and historic Brunswick Tower. By tradition it was the government's responsibility to make repairs to royal palaces, and there was much discussion in the newspapers of the burden that the royal family were upon the ordinary taxpayers of Britain, particularly as the Queen herself paid no tax. Seemingly in response to this public grumbling, the Queen announced six days after the fire that she would renounce her tax-free status. In her speech to mark her 40th year as Queen, she described 1992 as an "annus horribilis."

The story was, of course, ongoing. The prince's "downfall" was not as catastrophic as his friend seemed to suspect, and time blurred the memory of the "Camillagate" tape, although it was revived in 1995 by the divorce of Andrew and Camilla Parker-Bowles. And although a *Daily Mirror* poll indicated that 63 per cent of readers believed that Charles was not fit to be king, and that the crown should pass direct to Prince William, there seems to be little doubt that, when the time comes, Prince Charles will become King Charles III.

Princess Diana continued to be controversial up to her death. After announcing that she was giving up public appearances and returning to private life, she continued to appear at many public events. And scandals continued to be associated with her name. Her friend Oliver Hoare complained to the police that a caller was ringing his home in the early hours of the morning, then hanging up without speaking; when the police investigated, they found that the calls were coming from Kensington Palace. And the year-old marriage of England's rugby captain Will Carling came to an end after reports that he was seeing a great deal of Diana.

The *Daily Mirror* poll also found that 42 per cent of readers thought that Britain would be no worse off without a royal family, and that one in six felt that the monarchy would not survive beyond the end of the twentieth century.

Diana's endless capacity to generate scandal was demonstrated again in October 2002, with the trial of her butler, 43-year-old Paul Burrell – whom she had called her "rock" – on a charge of stealing hundreds of items belonging to Diana and Prince William. Paul Burrell, a lorry driver's son, had been member of the Queen's household before he became Princess Diana's butler.

On 31 August 1997, Burrell had flown to Paris, and been handed the clothes in which Diana had died. He had dressed her body in clean clothes for its return to England. That November he was appointed a member of the committee to choose a memorial to Diana. But a month later he was sacked because of disagreements with fellow members.

In January 2000, Burrell was arrested at his Cheshire home, accused of stealing over 300 items belonging to Princess Diana. He was granted bail, and later charged at Bow Street Magistrate's Court on 16 August 2001. The trial itself did not begin until 14 October 2002, but was stopped two days later for legal reasons, and started again on 17 October.

Then, on 1 November 2002, the trial collapsed dramatically when the Queen corroborated Burrell's story that he had told her two years earlier that he had taken certain of Diana's possessions into "safe keeping." But the Queen's intervention was received with widespread skepticism. Was it coincidence that Burrell was about to appear in the witness box on the day the trial was stopped?

Burrell's acquittal was soon followed by rumors that he had been offered immense sums of money by tabloid newspapers for his story.

No one believed that he would be tempted. At a butler's convention in Denver in 2001, Burrell had made the keynote speech, underlining the importance of discretion, and been received with standing applause.

So there was general astonishment when it was revealed that he had accepted £300,000 from the Labourite tabloid the *Daily Mirror*, turning down £1,000,000 from another tabloid – he had chosen the *Mirror* because it had agreed to his insistence that he should not "tell all," but only what he wanted to tell.

A foretaste of the revelations appeared in the *Daily Mail*, in an article by Richard Kay, a journalist Diana had treated as a friend. Kay explained that what was worrying the butler was what was happening to Diana's possessions. Her letters were being shredded, and the Spencer family were taking many of her possessions to their home, Althorp, the Spencer family seat in Northamptonshire. Just before Christmas 1998, Burrell asked if he could see the Queen, and spent three hours pouring out his heart. Diana had not even spoken to her mother, Frances Shand Kydd, for the last six months before the car accident, because her mother had criticized her taste in lovers, with special refer-ence to Muslims (heart surgeon Hasnat Khan, and businessman Gulu Lalvani). Yet now the Spencers were setting themselves up as sole guardians of her memory. Butler felt particularly bitter because when he was sacked from the fund, a "senior figure" (Kay is too discreet to name names) sneered at his working-class origin: "Remember where you're from." Burrell ended that long session with the Queen by telling her that he was taking some of Diana's possessions back home with him "for safe keeping."

When the Serious Crimes Squad arrived at Burrell's home in January 2001, they were searching specifically for the contents of a large mahogany box in which Diana kept intimate papers and possessions – what some tabloids came to refer to as "the crown jewels." The box itself was now at Althorp, empty. The police were armed with a list, supplied by Diana's elder sister, Lady Sarah McCorquodale, of certain things – such as cufflinks and ties – that Burrell was entitled to keep. Anything else, it was implied, was stolen. And so it was that in June that year, Burrell was charged with theft.

Why did he not do the obvious thing, and direct the Serious Crimes Squad to Buckingham Palace, where the Queen would back up his story that he was trying to keep Diana's private possessions out of the hands of the Spencers? The answer seems to lie in Burrell's well-known discretion. The butler felt he had a pact of confidentiality with the royal family. Was he to drag the Queen's name into this sordid squabble about love letters?

The royals were infuriated at the way Burrell was being treated. Prince Charles even had a row with his police bodyguard Stuart Osborne, about Burrell, whom he wanted to help, while Osborne was on the side of the police investigators. Charles felt Burrell was being persecuted because of his loyalty to Diana, and he got so angry with Osborne that he ordered the driver to stop the car and told the bodyguard to get out.

Burrell had had a bad time of it while he was awaiting his trial, and money dried up, so he was on the verge of bankruptcy. That last-minute rescue by the Queen must have come as an immense relief. Without it, Burrell would fairly certainly have faced prison and ruin. The *Daily Mail* had no doubt who was responsible for this; its headline declared:

"THE BITTER SPENCERS, JEALOUS OF HIS INTIMACY WITH DIANA, INSISTED ON PROSECUTION."

Inevitably, the Serious Crimes Squad was also blamed – it was felt that they had plunged into this prosecution, hoping it would bring them as much kudos as the Jeffrey Archer investigation, and allowing themselves to be convinced of Burrell's guilt by the Spencer family. (In fact, Earl Spencer declared after Burrell's acquittal that he was furious with the police for bringing the prosecution on such slender evidence.)

The picture of Diana that emerged in Burrell's *Daily Mirror* revelations showed her as tense, emotionally insecure, and thoroughly neurotic. She had been emotionally fixated on the Pakistani heart surgeon Hasnat Khan, whom she had met at the Royal Brompton Hospital in August 1996, where he was working under the famous heart surgeon Sir Magdi Yacoub. Khan, six feet tall and good looking, was sitting by a patient's bed when Diana came to visit the husband of her acupuncturist Oonagh Toffolo. They soon became lovers, and Burrell used to smuggle Khan into Kensington Palace in the boot of his car. On one occasion she dressed up in sapphire and diamond ear-rings before going into her bedroom and removing all her clothes. Then she came out to go and meet Khan in only a long fur coat. She was on her way to his flat near the Brompton's sister hospital Harefield, in Middlesex, where she would often gain access by climbing through the window.

Khan was a quiet, good-natured man, modest, unassuming, and totally obsessed by his work. He had been twice engaged to marry Muslim girls who had been chosen by his family, but both engagements had fallen through. And it seems clear that he was soon feeling under pressure from Diana's highly emotional nature. After they had spent the night together, she would often telephone him as soon as he arrived at work, once even insisting on speaking to him when he was in the operating theatre. When he was unable to take her calls, she assumed that he was avoiding her, and rang friends in floods of tears. "She was besotted with him," said one friend. This was obviously a recurring pattern – it had happened with Major James Hewitt and Oliver Hoare.

The mild, studious Khan, whose ambition was to become a professor, was soon wishing he had not been drawn into the relationship. Diana was determined to marry him, and to this end she insisted on meeting his family in the small town of Jhelum in Pakistan, where she made a close friend of his grandmother Nanny Appa; she also became a regular visitor at the home of his uncle Omar and wife Jane at Stratford on Avon, and enjoyed feeling a part of the family, insisting on doing the washing up.

She confided to one friend that she was thinking of getting pregnant to make sure Khan married her. Khan found the emotional pressure-cooker atmosphere unbearable, and disliked it even more when rumors of their relationship began to circulate and he became an object of curiosity. He realized that marrying her would simply have the effect of turning him into "Mr Diana" and making him a media celebrity. When Paul Burrell had to deliver letters from Diana into his hands, sitting in the hospital waiting room, the surgeon began to feel persecuted. The less responsive he became, the more obsessive became his frantic lover; finally, he was in full flight, with Diana in pursuit. When he saw her car waiting near his flat, he would hurry away.

When they finally parted in May 1997, they agreed to remain friends. It was after this that she had an affair with an electronics tycoon, Gulu Lalvani. It has been reported that he now accepts

that she was simply using him in an attempt to make Khan
jealous. She did not succeed. Neither did her affair with Dodi
al-Fayed have that effect; besides, Dodi and she were basically
unsuited, for Dodi was too much under his father's shadow to
offer her the kind of qualities she was looking for in a husband.
Burrell dismisses the idea that the two became engaged just
before her death.

The butler's acquittal lit the touch paper of another scandal.
Among the "stolen" articles belonging to Diana, the police were
hoping to find a cassette of an interview with a former palace
footman, George Smith, who claimed he had been the victim of
a homosexual rape by one of Prince Charles's servants; this, he
alleged, had taken place in a kitchen in 1989. (David Davies, a
retired chief superintendent who had been in charge of the royal
protection squad, would later complain about the problems
caused by "promiscuous" gay staff who sometimes brought male
prostitutes into the palace.) Smith reported the rape in 1996, and
there was a seven-month internal inquiry, which ended by
deciding that there was not enough evidence to prosecute the
accused man, one of Prince Charles's closest aides. But it seems
that Diana decided to pursue her own inquiry, and made a tape
recording of Smith's story, which subsequently vanished.
Diana was clearly out to embarrass her former husband
when the opportunity arose. A friend of Smith reports him as
saying that the rapist then stole the tape from Diana's
apartment.

Another item that had now vanished, according to Burrell,
was seven videotapes made by the princess, staring straight into
the camera, laying bare "her innermost feelings about her loneli-
ness and isolation, making stunning new disclosures about how
Prince Charles betrayed her with Camilla Parker-Bowles." The
tapes were found when the Serious Crimes Squad made its raid

on Burrell's home, but were deemed "too sensitive" to be mentioned at the trial.

When the trial of Paul Burrell was abruptly terminated, there was inevitably speculation that there was a cover-up involving the Smith "rape tape," and demands for an inquiry into whether there had been an attempt to pervert the course of justice.

Prince Charles called in a prestigious law firm, Kingsley Napley, to represent his "trusted aide," at an initial cost of £100,000; he also approached a top barrister for advice on what to do if the aide should be named in the press.

When the palace then announced that there would be another "internal inquiry" into the rape allegations, there were groans of disapproval from the press, and more allegations of a cover-up. Why, they wanted to know, an internal inquiry, rather than calling in the police?

One of Prince Charles's top aides, Michael Fawcett, also found himself spotlighted in this storm of allegations and counter-allegations. He was accused of "fencing" Prince Charles's cast-offs, as well as official gifts (of which heads of state inevitably receive a vast quantity), and taking a cut of between 107 and 20 per cent on the sales, the prince receiving the remainder. The Labour MP Ian Davidson, a member of the Commons Public Accounts Committee, said that if the allegations were true, "we would certainly want to look into that. All the money they receive should be used to offset the huge sums that the public purse provides for them." Mr Fawcett, it was later announced, was to go on indefinite leave.

All of which made it clear that, even years after her death, Princess Diana's ability to cause embarrassment to the royal family remains undiminished.

Creative World

- In 1961, the Museum of Modern Art in New York hung Matisse's *Le Bateau* (the boat), upside down for two months without anyone noticing.

- Apparently, Picasso's first word was the Spanish word for pencil.

- Writing as we know it was invented by the Sumerians in 4 BC.

- A Persian man called Rashid-Eddin published the first history book in AD 1311. It was called *The Great Universal History*.

- In AD 1007 a Japanese noble woman named Murasaki Shikibu wrote what is believed to be the first novel. It was called *The Story of Genji*.

- A German man called P. J. Reuter founded Reuters, one of today's biggest international news agencies, in 1858.

- Edgar Degas was absolutely obsessed with ballet dancers. So much so that he made approximately 1,500 paintings, drawings, pastels, and prints of dancers.

Joke of the Day

Two men went duck-hunting with their dogs but without success. "I know what we're doing wrong," said the first one. "What's that then?" said the second. "We're not throwing the dogs high enough!"

- The Austrian newspaper *Wiener Zeitung* is the oldest surviving daily newspaper. It dates back to 1703.

- The best selling book of the world is The Holy Bible.

- During the Ming Dynasty in China, around 500 years ago, 5,000 scholars produced *The Yongle Dadian*, a 10,000 volume encyclopedia, thought to be the world's longest nonfiction work.

- When Aristotle wrote *Meteorologica* in 350 BC it remained a standard textbook on weather for nearly 2,000 years.

- In 1658 the first illustrated book for children was published in Germany.

- Barbara Cartland was one of the world's most prolific writers, publishing a total of 723 novels and on average completing a novel every two weeks.

- James Bond's first appearance in a book was in the novel *Casino Royal* in 1952.

- The Chinese first printed from movable type (similar to the old printing press method), in 1040.

- The Statue of Liberty in New York is made from hammered copper and is the largest one of its type in the world.

- The heads of the four presidents carved into Mount Rushmore in the Black Hills, Dakota are 18 metres (60 feet) tall, making them the largest statue of the world.

- The Zizkov Monument in Prague stands 9 metres (30 feet) tall and is the world's largest horse statue.

- There are rumors surrounding horse statues. It is believed that if the horse has a rider and both front legs in the air, the rider has died in battle. One front leg in the air signifies death from wounds received in battle. However, if the horse has both front legs on the ground, the rider is presumed to have died of natural causes.

- English philosopher John Locke first wrote the words "Life, liberty, and the pursuit of happiness" in the seventeenth century.

- A design made from shapes that fit together perfectly (like a chessboard) is called a tesellation.

- Dramatist and Shakespeare contemporary Ben Johnson was buried standing upright in Westminster Abbey in 1637, to save costs.

- *Murder on the Orient Express* was the first ever novel to be sold through a vending machine. It was sold on the Paris Metro.

- French journalist Jean-Dominique Bauby suffered from the neurological disorder 'Locked-In' (a condition in which a patient is aware and awake, but cannot move or communicate due to complete paralysis of nearly all voluntary muscles in the body). Unable to move any other part of his body, he wrote the novel *The Driving Bell and the Butterfly* by blinking his left eyelid.

- During the three years that it was missing after being stolen from the Louvre in 1912, six replicas of Leonardo da Vinci's *Mona Lisa* were sold as the original, each for a huge price.

- When Auguste Rodin's statue *The Bronze Period* first went on exhibition in 1878, people thought that he must have killed a live human being to put inside the cast because it was so realistic.

- The French government was more than happy to keep Rodin's priceless statues inside heated museums and galleries but they refused to give the artist himself any financial aid for his apartment. He died of frostbite in 1917.

- Although now one of the worlds most-valued painters whose works are almost priceless, Vincent van Gogh sold only painting in his lifetime. Even then, he sold the work titled *Red Vineyard at Arles*, to his brother who owned an art gallery.

- In 1816, as a creative experiment, Frenchman J.R. Ronden attempted to stage a play that didn't contain the letter "a". The Paris audience were not impressed however and their subsequent rioting didn't allow the play to finish.

- Samuel Beckett's *Breath* is the shortest stage play in the world. It consists of 35 seconds of screams and heavy breathing.

- More than 100 million original volumes of writing are stored in the world's libraries.

- The Library of Congress is the largest library in the world. It has approximately 530 miles of bookshelves storing 18 million books.

- An estimated 2 billion people in the world are illiterate.

- Pierre Fauchard was the first dentist to publish a book. In 1728, he wrote *The Surgeon Dentist* that discussed the problem of tooth loss in great detail.

- In 1861, James Maxwell created the world's first color photograph. The image was of a tartan ribbon.

- Samuel Johnson created the first English Dictionary in 1755.

- The first Oxford English Dictionary was begun in 1878. It was finally published in April 1928 containing 400,000 words and phrases in ten volumes.

- *Gulliver's Travels*, published by Jonathan Swift in 1726, was intended by the author to be a satire on the ferociousness of human nature. It is today considered to be a children's story.